GALLIPOLI DIARY 1915

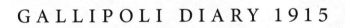

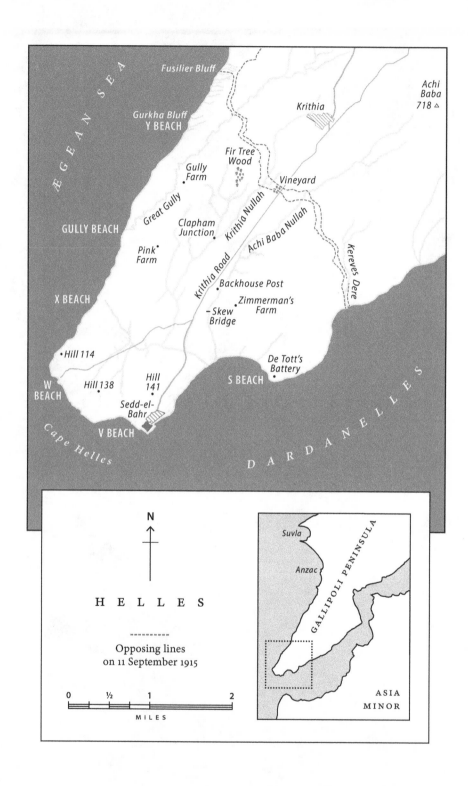

ÆGEAN SEA

Fusilier Bluff

Gurkha Bluff
Y BEACH

Gully
Farm

Great Gully

Clapham
Junction

GULLY BEACH

Pink
Farm

X BEACH

Krithia Road

Backhouse Post

Zimmerman's
Farm

Skew
Bridge

Hill 114

W
BEACH

Hill 138

Hill
141

Sedd-el-
Bahr

V BEACH

Cape Helles

Krithia

Fir Tree
Wood

Vineyard

Krithia Nullah

Achi Baba Nullah

Kereves Dere

Achi
Baba
718 △

De Tott's
Battery

S BEACH

DARDANELLES

N

HELLES

- - - - - - - - - - -

Opposing lines
on 11 September 1915

0   ½   1   2
╠═╦═╦═╦═╦═════════╦═════════════════╣
         MILES

Suvla

Anzac

GALLIPOLI PENINSULA

ASIA
MINOR

ALEC RILEY

Gallipoli Diary 1915

Edited by

Michael Crane & Bernard de Broglio

Little Gully Publishing

L.G.P.

First edition, November 2021

A catalogue record for this book is available from the British Library

ISBN 978-0-6452359-0-6 (hardback)
ISBN 978-0-6452359-1-3 (paperback)
ISBN 978-0-6452359-2-0 (ebook)

Little Gully Publishing
littlegully.com

CONTENTS

MAPS

FOREWORD

THIS BOOK IS THE FAITHFUL TRANSCRIPT of a Gallipoli veteran's memoir that lay disregarded in the Imperial War Museum's archives for more than 60 years.

It came to light in 2019 when the editors collaborated on an article for the Gallipoli Association journal. The subject of the article was a soldier's story called 'The silent nullahs of Gallipoli' that appeared in the 1930s magazine *Twenty Years After: The Battlefields of 1914-18, Then and Now*. The anonymous author we found to be Alec Riley, a former signaller in the 42nd Division. Later, we learned that he had bequeathed three diaries to the Imperial War Museum. These were a revelation, not only for their vivid eyewitness record of the campaign, but also for Riley's narrative style and perspective.

The notebooks, written in a neat hand, tell of Riley's mobilisation, his time in Egypt from September 1914 to 3 May 1915, his service at Gallipoli from 6 May to his medical evacuation on 11 September 1915, and finally his 11-month-long recovery in Netley hospital in England. All three were based on contemporaneous notes kept by Riley. Collectively they offer a unique window into the experiences of a pre-war territorial soldier, before, during and after Gallipoli.

Riley wanted to present his experiences in book form. Sadly, the public's appetite for soldiers' stories had abated by the time Riley had completed his manuscript and he searched in vain for a willing publisher. As such, an eloquent voice from the campaign has gone unnoticed, and a valuable account of trench and nullah lost for years. The editors resolved to get all three of Riley's notebooks into print, starting with the central work, his 'Gallipoli Diary 1915'.

The narrative can be likened in many ways to Joe Murray's famous account, *Gallipoli as I Saw It*. Like Murray, Riley had the opportunity to move freely about the Allied lines. He was attached at different times to all four battalions of the 127th Brigade and two of the 126th Brigade and these diverse postings allowed him to observe and record the unfolding campaign in the round.

In his account, Riley recalls and brings to life the conditions and topography of the southern battlefield and describes, with wry humour and poignancy, everyday life and death, and the horrors of battle at Helles.

Figure 1. Alec Riley in Krithia Nullah, near the Redoubt Line, in 1930. No other named photograph of Riley is known to the editors. (Alec Riley collection)

Long after the war, Riley's focus on the campaign persisted. He revisited Gallipoli independently on at least two occasions. These visits gave him, he wrote, the rare perspective of viewing the battlefield 'from the Turkish and our own points of view, in safety and comparative comfort.'

As he tried to establish himself as a writer, Riley used what he had gathered, opening a decade-long correspondence with Sir Ian Hamilton, the former Commander-in-Chief of the Mediterranean Expeditionary Force. Hamilton treated his work seriously, responding to Riley by writing (and re-writing) an introduction to 'Return to Cape Helles,' a book manuscript for which Riley was unable to find a publisher and is now lost. Despite this, Riley did achieve some journalistic success, most notably the evocative article published in *Twenty Years After* that is probably an extract from his lost manuscript. We have included 'The silent nullahs of Gallipoli' and Hamilton's introduction as appendices.

Another article by Riley, also reproduced in this book, was published by *The Telegraph and Morning Post* on 23 April 1938. Written to mark the 23rd anniversary of the Gallipoli landings, the article drew attention to a 'new' Gallipoli exhibition at the Imperial War Museum featuring photographs and artefacts donated by Riley. The IWM still holds a large number of carefully annotated relics collected by Riley from the battlefield which continue to feature in the museum's Gallipoli displays.

Riley was not only a talented writer. His camera bore witness to both his service at Helles and the scars and relics of war seen on later visits. Some of these photographs he sent to Hamilton. At least two were included in the British official history of the campaign. Twelve accompanied the article in *Twenty Years After*, with a further 29 illustrating two other Gallipoli-related articles in that magazine. Many of the photographs are reproduced in this book. One, taken during a ten-day-long stay on the peninsula in 1930, is particularly poignant. On the 4th of June, Riley had visited the summit of Achi Baba carrying a small Union Flag. He laid it down with stones securing the corners and photographed it, later captioning the picture 'Fifteen years too late.'

What follows is Riley's own account in his own words, with only minor spelling and punctuation corrections. The integrity of his writing has been preserved by the editors who have provided, for context, separate footnotes, maps and appendices.

Michael Crane, Bernard de Broglio

PREFACE

THE PURPOSE OF THIS DIARY is to amuse and interest those of my old companions who may read it. I have done my best to bring to life again some of the incidents, adventures and common tasks, shared during a period unlikely to be forgotten by those who experienced it.

Although I have called these notes a diary, it will be obvious to anyone who reads them that they could not have been written in this form at the times they deal with. It will also be obvious that they could not have been written at all, if detailed notes had not been made at those times.

The original diary contained all I needed, and probably more domestic details than the reader needs, to be able to re-write it in this form.

If it is asked why so many trivialities are mentioned, such as menus, the answer is that menus were one of the chief interests on Gallipoli. There were periods of monotony, many of them, and during these we found the smallest events of great importance and interest.

Additional notes were made while recollections were vivid, and while small details, colours, shapes, could be visualised accurately. The words attributed to various people were usually written down on the spot.

We can all remember isolated or outstanding events and their surroundings, but few can remember any of the times between those events, because they were too monotonous to be worth remembering or recording. I have, therefore, tried to revive some of the monotony as well as some of the excitements of Cape Helles as we knew it. I am aware that each of us saw Gallipoli from his own point of view; also, that no two men had exactly the same experiences, although some of them were shared, so also were hopes and fears, likes and dislikes, and falls from grace.

1

Some of us took advantage of every opportunity to explore as much of Helles as we could. We enjoyed ourselves while we were doing it. Explorers, however, were comparatively rare. Men were too tired to wander about much when the chances came, and sleep was far more important. On the other hand, those of us who did wander about found the changes helpful and memorable when we went back to ordinary work. I have recorded our rambles as fully as possible.

The reader will not forget that our chief interests were three—safety, sleep and food; animal necessities, of course. As we lived like animals, we naturally took an interest in these essentials.

From what appears in certain books dealing with Gallipoli, old school ties serving there suddenly became sloppily sentimental about Troy and the local mythology. Some of these men may really have been able to allow their minds to dwell happily on what most of them found boring in their fourth forms, but how they did it is a mystery. All the officers and men I knew were fully occupied with the present, and lessons in classical geography, tempting at first, soon became rather out of place. The case was different afterwards, when Gallipoli and its surroundings could be considered objectively, and I have added some notes on its associations with antiquity, at the end.

I regret numerous mistakes in transcription, particularly those I have not already discovered; and I apologise to the reader for irritating corrections.

Care has been taken to omit references which could be considered unkind to those concerned. When I came across such references, I found I could only remember most of their occasions vaguely. After so many years, notes of their contexts had little meaning. Where anything of this kind is mentioned, it is simply because we had nothing else to interest us at the time, and when men live in such close contact, a few squabbles are inevitable. However, if any needlessly unkind reference is discovered, I shall be glad if the reader will note it, and let me know, and it will be removed.

* * *

No comments on the higher command have been inserted. I am aware of most of the controversial aspects of the campaign, and of the fact that it is customary to include a few in any books dealing with Gallipoli.

There were times when tactical events were bloody hopeless—using 'bloody' in its literal sense—to all ranks. As for strategy, the only thing most of us knew or cared about the campaign was that Krithia, Achi Baba, and the Turkish lines were in front, and beyond them were Anzac and Suvla on the left and the Dardanelles on the right. It is true that we sometimes wondered what would happen when and if Krithia and Achi Baba were taken—for there seemed to be no point in sitting on the top of Achi Baba, when the Turks would give us the same treatment as our guns had given them. Only a few occasions did I hear the campaign discussed as part of the larger war. What we did know was that at any time an order might come from some far away source, at the end of our line and its extensions, which might affect us, and the battalions we were working with, to our discomfort and disadvantage. The aims of the campaign require no mention here.

* * *

Since the campaign I have explored the Helles area in detail, as fully as I could in ten days. The places dealt with in the diary have, therefore, been seen from the Turkish and our own points of view, in safety and comparative comfort. These explorations have been dealt with in another form, but one thing of interest may be mentioned here: at 1 p.m. on the fourth of June, 1930, I was sitting on the top of Achi Baba, lunching, and looking down on the battlefields of Helles, in peace, perfect peace.

FROM THE GENERAL TO THE PARTICULAR

Extracts from General Sir Ian Hamilton's diary relating to the 42nd East Lancashire Division (TF).[1]

I. 28th March, 1915. Cairo.

'Inspected East Lancashire Division and a Yeomanry Brigade (Westminster Dragoons and Herts). How I envy Maxwell ... They will only be eating their heads off here, with summer coming up and the desert getting as dry as a bone ...'[2]

II. 'Maxwell will have a fit if I ask for them.'

III. 28th April, 1915.

From a cable sent by Lord Kitchener to Lt. Gen. Sir J.G. Maxwell: '... I hope all your troops are being kept ready to embark, and I would suggest you should send the Territorial Division if Hamilton wants them. Peyton's transports etc.'

From Kitchener to Hamilton: '... I feel sure you had better have the Territorial Division, and I have instructed Maxwell to embark them ... You had better tell him to send off the Division to you ...'

IV. 29th April, 1915.

'Anchored off Cape Helles at dark. A reply from Maxwell about the East Lancashires. They are coming.'

* * *

And so, more particularly, we reach the Manchester Brigade of the East Lancashire Division, and more particularly still, the Manchester Brigade section of the Divisional Signal Company; and, finally, to what a single member of that section saw, heard, experienced and recorded.

---

1 Gen. Sir Ian Hamilton, *Gallipoli Diary* (London: Edward Arnold, 1920).

2 Major General Sir John Maxwell, commander of the Force in Egypt. Lord Kitchener had sent the East Lancashire Division (TF) and two Yeomanry regiments to Egypt in September 1914 to bolster this formation.

No. 4 Section (Manchester Brigade) 1/1 East Lancs Div. Sig. Coy, RE and men attached

Captain Williamson (Tim)

Sergeants

Royle (Joe)
Ormesher (Ormy)

Corporals

Hague (Claude)
2/Cpl Riley (Pat)
L/Cpl Williams (Abe)

Pioneers	*Sappers*	*Privates**
C.W. Ridings	Vick	Evans
S. Ridings	Withington	Holmes
Haworth	Barlow	Feddan
Thomas		Palmer
Poole	*Drivers*	Smith
Noble	Dean	Lee
Greenbank	McLoughlin	Wilcox
Pearson	Cooper	Gorman
Hopkinson	Caldwell	Matthews
Dale	Darlington	Carter
Hossack		Bodden
Berry		Johnson

* *Men attached from infantry battalions*

5

CHAPTER 1

Last days in Egypt

Polygon Barracks
Abbassia, Cairo
April 1915

Towards the end of the month, and for some days, we knew that the division was going to move; but where to or when, we did not know. Meeting A.H. on Friday, April 30, he told me that we were going to the Dardanelles,[3] but the exact date was uncertain. That afternoon, however, when active service pay books were issued, we knew that something was likely to happen in the near future.

Saturday, May 1, was a day of general excitement, and of preparation, everywhere and at all times. New batteries were put in the field telephones, and wire was examined for flaws and breaks. New pull-throughs were issued. We were all excited. The usual Sunday orders were cancelled, and a notice was posted on the board that our new address would be:

East Lancs Divisional Signal Coy, RE,
Mediterranean Expeditionary Force.

Sunday, May 2. On the 6 a.m. parade, our active service pay books were made up. Later on, we drew our official clothing. Helmets had been issued when we arrived in Egypt in September 1914, and now we

---

3   In his Egypt diary, Riley refers to A.H. as an ASC officer.

were given British Warms,[4] boots, cardigan, waistcoats, cap-comforters, shirts, braces, socks, pants, tunics, riding-breeches. Besides these we drew hair-brushes, linesmen's belts, and rifle-oil.

I drew, and issued to the brigade section and men attached, iron rations, each consisting of a bag of Spratt's biscuits, a tin of bully, and a grocery ration of tea, sugar and Oxo cubes. This grocery ration was placed in a small oval-ended tin, with a division in the centre and a lid on each end. The whole of the iron ration was carried in a white bag. Although I went round our rooms three times, to make sure that no one had been missed, when I had finished, I was told that one of the attached men was still without his rations, and he had to go without it.

We were so busy and excited about our own affairs that we took little notice of what the rest of the Signal Company was doing. The Lancashire Fusiliers Brigade section had moved off the previous night.

At last, every preparation had been made. I had managed to post a parcel home, containing my watch and some odds and ends collected in Egypt, wrapped in a cardigan. There came a time when we had nothing to do, and most of us spent it hanging about and sitting on our beds talking trivialities and speculating on active service, where it might take us and what it might do for us. We found comfort in numbers.

Our time in Egypt was nearly over. We had enjoyed it; but now that we were leaving it, that last few hours passed slowly and heavily.

One the evening of Sunday, May 2, 1915, No. 4 Section 1/1 East Lancs Div. Sig. Coy RE, left Polygon Barracks for active service.

Having paraded for that purpose, the section was to march down to Boulac Station, and most of it did. What was left was busy collecting an untrained Australian pack-horse and his load; for just as we were ready to move off, he bolted from the ranks and made for his old stable, getting rid of his load and breaking the winding-gear. Ormy, Thomas, Caldwell and I were left to do what we could about it.[5] The train would

---

4 A type of woollen overcoat similar to a greatcoat.

5 Sgt 764 Charles Alfred Ormesher, 6th Manchesters, later CQMS 3721, RE (TF), and CQMS 444578, Royal Engineers. Probably Pte 2391 Richard Thomas, Manchester Regt, later Pnr 11367, RE (TF), and Pioneer 400528, Royal Engineers. Probably Driver 1364 William George Caldwell, RE (TF), later discharged to be commissioned 2nd lieut. in the 7th Lancs Fusiliers, afterwards promoted lieutenant in the Machine Gun Corps. See Appendix IV, biographies of No. 4 Section.

leave Boulac at 11 p.m. We managed to get hold of a lantern, and by its light we followed the tracks of the flight across the sand. Caldwell found the horse in its old stable and brought it back. In an hour we had found most of the pieces and dumped them in a heap on the side of the Suez Road. Caldwell and the horse were sent off to the station with our good wishes for safe arrival, and the rest of us decided that the only thing to be done was to get hold of a gharry for ourselves and the pieces. We telephoned to Shepheard's Hotel and the main guard at Abbassia, ordering a gharry from each, to be certain of one, and then we called at the sergeants' mess.

The main guard people had sent a gharry, and when it arrived, we loaded it with the debris and ourselves; and so we started for active service by being driven to the station in a carriage. Between our barracks and the main guard we passed another gharry. This we supposed to be one sent by Shepheard's people. The driver looked suspicious, as we told him he was wanted by someone else, and told our man to get a move on, before the other driver found us out.

We reached Boulac Station in good time, found the rest of the section, and about 11 p.m., we left Boulac for Alexandria, with a train load of 6th Manchesters and our dog Spot. Tim had given special instructions about Spot—that he was not to come with us;[6] but Spot did come with us, in spite of several evictions, and he reached the quay at Alexandria, and there we saw the last of our old pal. We travelled third class. Later, I heard that Joe, waking up from a sleep in the train, was surprised to find Spot not only on the train but staring him full in the face.[7]

It was early morning, between six and seven o'clock, when we left the train near the quays at Alexandria. My first job was to take our nags to the horse-boat, the *Cuthbert*, and, as one of them trod on my foot, I remembered the *Cuthbert* for some time. Having got rid of the horses, the crew made us welcome to the best breakfast they could give us, or themselves. Oily coffee, thick slabs of bread, and yellowish grease from a large, deep and round tin. We were hungry and the meal needed

---

6 Capt. Charles Harry Williamson, 7th Manchesters (TF), later Royal Flying Corps. See Appendix IV, biographies of No. 4 Section.

7 Probably Sgt 262 Graham Royle, RE (TF), formerly 6th Manchesters, later L/Cpl 238056, Royal Engineers. See Appendix IV, biographies of No. 4 Section.

Figure 2. The *Derfflinger* later renamed HMT *Huntsgreen*.

no improvements. We stayed in the dirty little cabin, talking to our kind hosts, until we thought it was time to get back to the rest of the section. As there was nothing to do, Ormy and I decided to explore a French hospital ship, the *Duguay-Trouin*, moored to a neighbouring quay. It was full of wounded from the Dardanelles. We went on board to see some bloodiness for the first time. One man, with a scalp wound, showed us the bullet holes in his cap. At the bottom of the holds we saw six wounded Turks in a wire-netting cage. They looked in need of a lot of repairing, and had bloody bandages on their heads. The scene reminded us of a picture of the death of Nelson. Having inspected as many more cases as we wanted, we returned to our dump on the quay, had a meal from the dixies, and then took turns in going to a little sailor's café, kept by a Greek, for glasses of coffee and chocolate of a cheapish kind.

The 6th Manchesters were close by, their rifles stacked and each man's kit laid on the ground. I don't know where our kit bags had got to. I never saw mine again after leaving Abbassia.

Wagon loads of khaki clothing, torn, shredded, blood stained, were being taken from some of the transports. This looked nasty and suggestive, and we hoped it would not happen again.

Tim gave me one pound to spend for the section as I thought best, Vick helping me.[8] We took a gharry to the town and spent a pleasant hour or two shopping at Kodak's, a chemist, a hairdresser's, and in the Piccadilly Café, where we mixed coffee and ices behind a cane curtain. Then we spent Tim's money on tins of coffee and milk and cocoa and milk. We thought their contents, in the form of paste, the most useful things we could buy, and distributed the tins as far as they would go round when we got back to the quay, before going on board the *Derfflinger*.

The last of 'Spot'

Hossack was carrying Spot up the gangway when Noel Lee, on the bridge, called out 'You mustn't bring that dog on board.'[9]

It would have been cruel to leave our old friend loose on the quay, so Hossack tied a stone to its neck and threw him into the water; but the stone left the string and sank. While Spot was swimming Hossack got into a boat and rescued him. An Englishwoman on the quay gave Hossack her card and told him that she would look after Spot.

---

8 Probably Sapper 798 Ernest Henry Vick, RE (TF). See Appendix IV, biographies of No. 4 Section.

9 Probably Pnr (later Sapper) 2119 Ernest Frank Hossack, RE (TF), later 444256, Royal Engineers. See Appendix IV, biographies of No. 4 Section. Brig. Gen. Noel Lee, GOC of the Manchester Brigade and a former CO of the 6th Manchesters. See Appendix IV, officer biographies. Riley attributes the story of Spot to Hossack.

CHAPTER 2

On the 'Derfflinger'

We embarked on the NDL *Derfflinger*,[10] popularly known as the 'Dirtflinger.' She carried Brigadier General Noel Lee, the Manchester Brigade headquarters staff, and the 6th Manchesters. It was late in the afternoon of Monday, May 3, when we sailed from Alexandria.

Our quarters were on the iron deck round one of the forward holds. We managed to find a good tea from our rations, and then settled down as comfortably as we could.

The *Derfflinger* had already been to Gallipoli, and a few Australians were on board now. We spent the evening talking to some of them about the Dardanelles, and we were told that rumours of heavy casualties were wrong, and that the Turkish artillery was finished. We were ready to believe them. Good-looking rumours were always welcome.

We tried to sleep on the iron deck, but it was a hard bed and we couldn't make ourselves comfortable. When morning came, we were cold and stiff, and glad to be up and about.

There was plenty of grub in our hold, and we helped ourselves to a tin of mutton for breakfast. Later on, the 6th Manchesters gave us a cheese. We spent the morning making leads for telephone work, and on other odd jobs. Vick managed to repair our winding-gear for the pack-horse.

---

10 Passenger ship operated by Norddeutscher Lloyd (NDL), Bremen. Seized at Port Said, Egypt, August 1914. Later renamed HMT *Huntsgreen*.

If there was one thing we particularly detested, it was winding-gear and Vick disappointed us. Colonel Earle and the Brigadier came down to see us.[11]

On one of the decks there was a giant heap of torn and bloody clothing taken from the Anzac casualties after their landing. The strong sun made it smell so it was sorted out, and most of it was thrown overboard.

We passed land but didn't know what it was. I spent the evening with Ridings.[12] We had managed to get hold of some deck-chairs, and having settled ourselves comfortably, we amused ourselves with speculations about the next few days. Everything in the future outlook had a kind of pleasing uncertainty about it. We were young and full of curiosity. We heard noises; Joe and Ormy had missed their teas. They shared a cabin. Later, I was invited to a salt-water bath with Ormy. We each reclined at a bath-end, raising our legs. That night, I had a berth in the Joe–Ormy cabin. The situation was now well in hand. Our minds were easy, for a tin of paraffin, reported absent from our section stores on our wagon, had been replaced. Its absence was due to improper storage, for the paraffin was found to be mixed with our blankets on the wagon. Tim did his best to have the loss made good, by sending chits to all the QMs on board, but none of them wanted to give paraffin away. Ormy suggested another way, but Tim said he wouldn't have any pinching. In due course, however, we had our tin, and a convenient Australian wagon was one tin deficient.

Wednesday, May 5, started with another salt-water bath. We spent the day with such amusements as a rifle-inspection and making more leads. I had some spare safety-pins, and these I fastened to the ends of leads for sticking through the wire. We passed innumerable islands. Most of them were bare and uninviting, and some were precipitous.

---

11 Lt. Col. F.A. Earle, 42nd (East Lancashire) Division HQ, GSO 2.

12 Probably Sapper 838 Charles William Ridings, RE (TF), formerly Pte 838, 6th Manchesters, later A/2nd Cpl 165863, Royal Engineers. See Appendix IV, biographies of No. 4 Section.

At 3 p.m. Tim re-detailed the detachments. Mine, No. 2, consisted of Berry, Greenbank, Caldwell, Vick, Barlow and Hossack.[13] Joe and I made out our lists of equipment to be carried ashore, and Tim put some wind up us by saying that our landing might be opposed. It was recorded that, on this day, a QMS of the 6th Manchesters issued half a case of biscuits to the signal service.

Meanwhile, the 6th were sharpening their bayonets on grindstones, so we joined in with ours. Then we made our iron-ration bags as brown as we could, by dipping them in a dixie of strong tea.

Men were having their hair cropped as short as possible. Some of them were nearly bald after such extreme haircutting. Others had their initials and regimental numbers left on in hair. I spent some time with Walker and Griffiths, of the 6th.

Food was plentiful. We had gone on robbing our hold until the 6th placed an armed guard in our way. By that time, however, we had made certain of all we wanted, including such things as jam and lime juice, so the guard didn't matter. I spent a very cold night in a deck chair.

In the early morning of Thursday, May 6th, we were near the entrance to the Dardanelles. The sun was beginning to brighten the mist, through which we could see the shapes of warships, transports, and a variety of shipping. The *Derfflinger* steamed slowly along the Gallipoli coast. As we knew nothing about the peninsula in those days, it is difficult to say what we were actually looking at. We seem to have wandered in the direction of Gaba Tepe. There were cliffs behind the shores, and hilly country beyond. The morning mists were still hanging about the higher ground. In the mist we saw red flashes. It was a picturesque and wonderful panorama of land and sea, and war at a distance. We were too much interested and excited to bother about food, until later.

13   Probably Pioneer 1339 John Berry, formerly D Coy, 6th Manchesters, later Sapper 1923, RE (TF). Probably Sapper 257 Arnold Greenbank, RE (TF), later Sapper 194716, Royal Engineers. Probably Sapper 800 Frank Barlow, RE (TF), later Sergeant 444030, RE. See Appendix IV, biographies of No. 4 Section.

The *Derfflinger* was now amongst the general mixture of warships and other vessels. The navy opened fire. Sheets of yellow-flame and clouds of brown smoke came from the big guns. Harsh shattering crashes made our heads ache, but we were fascinated. We watched the shell-bursts on the high ground, and the columns of smoke, earth and dust following the bursts. We had not seen naval shells tear up the earth until this morning. This panorama, with its background of cliffs and hills capped by a red-spotted mist, and its foreground of sea, ships, yellow flames, and brown smoke, and all the noise of the orchestra of guns, was, I repeat, picturesque and exciting. We wondered if the Turks would fire at us, and, if they did, if we should still be fascinated. We should not. We watched the puffs and flashes of bursting shrapnel and noticed that the flashes were mere twinkles. At one time the *Derfflinger* was near the Russian cruiser *Askold*. It had five funnels, and, from these, it was known as 'the packet of Woodbines.' HMS *Majestic* was very busy with her guns. Firing continued throughout the day.

We got ready to go on shore. Telephone and visual equipment was taken from the wagon and placed on the second deck. We collected all the portable grub we could find, and I crammed as much biscuit in my haversack as it would hold. The haversack also held my camera, spare films, spare shirt and socks, body-belt and other odds and ends. My pockets held my diary, pencils and a general miscellany of more odds and ends. Cigarettes and matches had been issued.

The navy's guns went on blasting, but after a time we didn't notice the noise so much; and less, as we steamed slowly back to Cape Helles.

Evening came, and with it our time for going ashore. Lighters came alongside, and about 8 p.m. I left the *Derfflinger* on one of them, taking a drum of wire. The rest of the section followed, on another lighter. S. Ridings and Driver Dean were left on board in charge of some equipment.[14]

14 Probably Pnr 3271 Sidney Ridings, RE (TF), formerly Pte 1193, 6th Manchesters, later Pte 23319, Royal Warwickshire Regt. Probably Driver 1568 William Dean, RE (TF), later 444604, RE. See Appendix IV, biographies of No. 4 Section.

My lighter drew away from the *Derfflinger*. For an hour or so we stayed on deck. The night was cold, and even two shirts and a body-belt were not enough to keep me warm. We went below deck, and I crawled into a narrow gap between two men. There was nothing more to be seen from above, for the ships and land had disappeared into blackness, and I thought the time could be well spent in getting what rest I could. The space under the deck was crowded. We were all lying on the ribs and iron-plating, and we were thankful for human warmth and human stuffiness. We could have stood more stuffiness for the sake of the warmth; and this, with the sound of small waves against the plating, made us sleepy. Then we were disturbed and taken ashore on a small tug.

CHAPTER 3

On Cape Helles

We were landed at a small jetty at the foot of Tekke Burnu, the cliff to the north-west of W Beach, or Lancashire Landing. On the jetty were some of the 6th Manchesters, with lanterns. We had landed in an enemy's country, without his permission, and the event was entirely without romance. I was tired and shivering with cold, in spite of my extra shirt and woollen cuffs. Carrying my drum of wire, I went in search of the rest of No. 4 Section and found it after a time. We made a heap of all our equipment near some stores and arranged for it to be guarded; and then, after a short wait, we were taken to the Manchester Brigade bivouac on the top of Helles Burnu, scrambling up the rough path to get there.

About 1 a.m. on Friday, May 7, I went to bed in a shallow hole, with Ridings and Withington.[15] We huddled together, but we couldn't get warm. I had cold feet in both ways, particularly when the noise started. Rifles cracked, machine guns rattled; guns flashed and crashed, shells flashed as they burst. We realised that we were nearly in it—whatever it was—as we lay there watching the night lit up, listening to the noise, trying to get warm, and hoping that nothing would come near us. Later, we heard that the Turks had tried to clear us off the peninsula that night.[16] Egypt had become just a little monotonous but now we would have given much for some more monotony.

---

15 Probably Spr 1521 Bernard Withington, RE (TF), later Cpl 444115, Royal Engineers. See Appendix IV, biographies of No. 4 Section.

16 It was, in fact, the end of the first day of the Second Battle of Krithia.

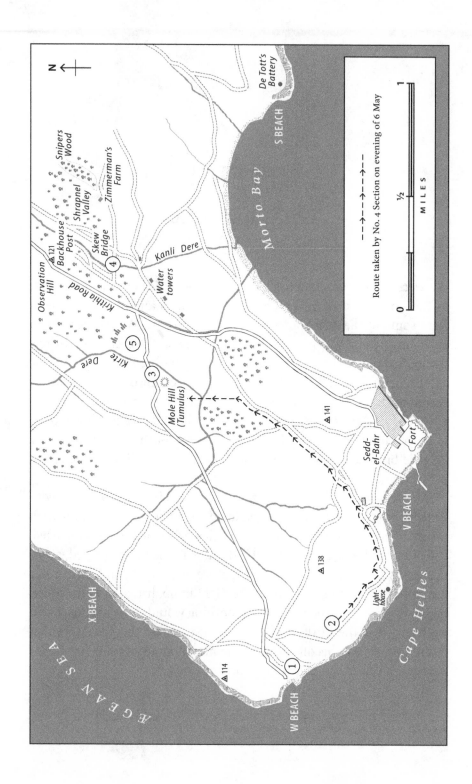

N

AEGEAN SEA

X BEACH

△114

W BEACH

① ②

Cape Helles

Light-house

V BEACH

Fort

Sedd-el-Bahr

△141

△138

Mole Hill (Tumulus)

③

Kirte Dere

⑤

Krithia Road

Observation Hill

△121 Backhouse Post

Shrapnel Valley

Snipers Wood

Zimmerman's Farm

Skew Bridge

④

Kanli Dere

Water towers

Morto Bay

S BEACH

De Tott's Battery

Route taken by No. 4 Section on evening of 6 May

0   ½   1

M I L E S

After a time the noise died down, and when dawn came, we got out of our holes, curious to see what kind of place we had been brought to. We saw that we had spent the night on a gentle slope above the cliff-edge. We wondered what there was beyond the crest of the slope. We knew, soon enough. Then we heard that the Lancashire Fusiliers Brigade of our division had already been in action. The 6th Manchesters had bivouacked on the cliff-top. Near us were dumps of stores, and near the edge of the cliff canvas troughs had been rigged up. The view seawards was remarkable, for we looked down to an immense fleet of warships, transports, and other vessels, large and small. We went down to the beach, and found the fringe of war-litter, and scraps of equipment, particularly near a sandy breastwork.

Then came breakfast. Our tins of coffee and milk paste were very welcome. We took a mugful to Tim, but he wouldn't have it. After breakfast, a rifle-inspection and a full dress parade kept us occupied for a time, and then we were able to explore our immediate surroundings. Some of us walked up to the crest of the slope, and from this we had our first view of the spoon-shaped tip of the Gallipoli Peninsula. Five and a half miles away was Achi Baba, the only outstanding feature of the landscape, and dominating it. The foreground, seen from this crest, appeared to be wooded, rather flat, and of no particular interest. Its appearance, however, gave no indication of the variety of interests we found in it later.

MAP 1

(previous page)

(1) No. 4 Section land here on the evening of 6 May

(2) No. 4 Section bivouac on the night of 6 May and during the day of 7 May

(3) Manchester Brigade HQ and No. 4 Section bivouac from the night of 7 May until 11 May

(4) With the 8th Manchesters signal office, 9–11 May

(5) Artillery battery referred to in Chapter 3

Figure 3. 'Early morning. May 7, 1915. Gallipoli. 6th Manchesters & Bde HQ in foreground.' The photograph is taken from a point south of W Beach, on the cliffs above the sea. (Alec Riley collection)

Shells from the navy were bursting on and near Achi Baba, and batteries of field artillery were firing at targets unknown to us. To our right was a small flying-ground from which occasional aeroplanes took off.[17] A string of wounded French soldiers came along, their dark and quaint uniforms making them look strange to us. Then came a Turk, wounded in the head. We were told that he was a sniper who had specialised in stretcher-bearers. He may have been; but at the time we were prepared to believe anything. Our credulity was remarkable. We settled down comfortably on the ridge, with all the telescopes and binoculars we could get hold of and did what we could to enjoy the situation. In the afternoon a few shells arrived in our district, but nothing serious happened.

The shipping off Cape Helles was the most astonishing spectacle. Again and again we turned to look at it, and we began to realise what a great undertaking the Mediterranean Expeditionary Force must be; and, in spite of a noisy night and cold feet, few of us were without

17 A forward aerodrome, located alongside Hill 138, was used by No. 3 Squadron (later No. 3 Wing), Royal Naval Air Service, and *Escadrille* MF 98 T, a French army air squadron.

curiosity and interest. On the top of Cape Helles itself was the ruined lighthouse, and fort of Sedd-el-Bahr, with the sandy strip of V Beach, and the *River Clyde* near the fort. We explored all these in detail later on. To the east we saw the Dardanelles and the Asiatic shore and hills beyond.

A rough road ran along the cliff-top, and on the landward side of this was our bivouac and that of the 6th Manchesters, with their stacked rifles, boxes and stores of all kinds, heaped and scattered, lines of packs and equipment, and we had a small heap of cable-drums and field telephones.

We threw away everything we thought useless. I threw my spurs behind a dump of biscuit boxes. A Frenchman asked me if I had anything to give away, so I told him where he would find my spurs. The days passed quickly enough, and when we had seen all we could in our immediate surroundings we began to wonder what could happen next, and when evening came, we knew. Orders came that we were to be ready to move, and at 7 p.m. we followed the Manchester Brigade head-quarters along the road overlooking Sedd-el-Bahr and the more distant Dardanelles. From a weather point of view the evening was pleasant, and the air was clean. At that time of the year the peninsula was green, and the evening tints made the landscape attractive. There was also a feeling of excitement as we passed some effects of shell-fire, and a certain comfort in being with our old battalion and the Brigadier; but, at the same time, we knew that we were now on our way to unknown country in more ways than one, and anything might happen.

We turned left and inland, through the green countryside with its olive trees and other vegetation, and at dusk, after a lot of shuffling movements, we found our brigade headquarters, some narrow and shallow trenches at the foot of a tumulus.[18] We were now a mile and a quarter from our first bivouac, and on the lowest part of the tip of the peninsula. We were told to get into the holes in the ground, and to be ready to reel out lines to any battalions. Nobody seemed to know where exactly our battalions were, so there was no reason for anxiety on our

---

18 The tumulus was known as 'the Mole Hill' during the campaign. Riley describes its Homeric connection in his 'description of the Dardanelles and the peninsula,' presented in Appendix VII.

parts. We were content to make ourselves as comfortable as we could in the earthholes, cold and damp as they were. Some field-guns were in action close by, and whenever one of them was fired, we felt the benefit of the harsh bark and the jarring effects. Rifle-fire was continuous, after it had awakened us from our light sleep. It was now quite dark, except for the gun-flashes.

On the morning of Saturday, May 8th, French 75s sounded reveille for us and the Turks,[19] and a few larger guns joined in. The morning was sunny and the countryside beautiful, with its trees and wildflowers. In the warm sun we soon recovered from the cold and noisy night, and our surroundings reminded us of country scenes in England.

We drew field dressings from the Naval Brigade dressing station. Wounded men who were able to walk passed us throughout the day. We were told to be in our trenches by 10.30 a.m. as Turkish shrapnel was expected. We cut branches from the trees to line our homes, and to keep off some of the damp. A few shells dropped near us, and we watched an aeroplane having a narrow escape. As these were the only events of interest, for the time being, we spent most of the morning in sleeping.

Behind a thin line of trees, to our front was a battery of RFA, and while things were quiet, I photographed part of it. To our left front was the higher ground of a ridge running to the north-east. It was 5.30 p.m., and we were getting ready for tea. We had just seen Noel Lee go past, the seat of his breeches held up by safety pins. Tea had to wait, for the near slopes of the ridge, and the top, were being shelled, and our battery was firing. The Lancashire Fusiliers of our division were advancing, and we went to the top of the tumulus to watch them. The white smoke became so thick that we could not see much; but against it and amongst it we could see red flashes of bursting shrapnel, and occasionally we saw men moving about. Our battery ran short of shells, for it was firing six rounds per minute per gun. Men were detailed to carry 18-pounder shells from the ammunition wagons in the rear to the battery. The noise was deafening, particularly when the naval guns started. From the discharges of the nearest guns we felt the wind blowing on our faces and up our sleeves. Ammunition wagons came up at the gallop.

19 French 75mm quick-firing field guns.

When the firing died down our heads ached with noise and excitement. Whatever else it had done, it had made a mess of the ground.

At 7 p.m. we moved out. Joe went with one party to the 7th Manchesters, and Berry, Hossack and I went with Tim. Our party was looking for the 8th Manchesters, but we were soon lost ourselves, and Tim seemed to be fed up. At last we had some luck, we found the headquarters of the 7th Manchesters; but as this was not what we had set out to find, we returned to brigade headquarters, near the tumulus, with nothing accomplished and nothing done. It was nearly dark when we made our way home, and as we passed through some trees on the lower slopes of the rising ground, at the end of Helles, we passed crowds of wounded Anzacs. There would be nearly three hundred of them, walking cases, going from their dressing stations to the hospitals. They were in all stages of dress and undress, and were bandaged, some of them in several places. Some were limping; and others, too weak to walk alone, supported themselves on arms or shoulders stronger than their own. Many were moaning with pain as they nursed their wounded arms, for most of these cases were arm-wounds, and many bandages were bloody. In spite of wounds and pain, or because of them, these men were saying exactly what they thought about the war in general and the Turks in particular, in carefully chosen words. It was generally agreed that the Turks were bastards. Until we heard these men, we had no idea that there was so much illegitimacy in Turkey, and they had a delightful variety of ways of saying the same thing. It did us good to hear it, and we added a few kind words in sympathy. When we had passed the Anzacs we met more wounded from our Lancashire Fusiliers Brigade, and a few from the 6th Manchesters, who had been hit by strays. Heywood had a bullet in his arm, and Gorman had one in the shoulder.[20]

We were glad to be back in our old quarters again for the night, but not for much sleep, as we were shivering with cold and damp. I wore some spare socks as gloves. Our guns started early in the morning, banging and cracking close by.

Our breakfast on Sunday, May 9, was tea and a stew of bully, Oxo cubes, and biscuits, and this, with a warm sun, revived us. Newton,

---

20 Probably Pte 1626 (1686 on MIC and 1914–15 Star Roll) 6th Manchesters, attached No. 4 Section, later L/Sgt 250166 Gorman MM. See Appendix IV, biographies of No. 4 Section.

from the Lancs Fusiliers Brigade signal section, came to see us. We had a topical chat, and he told us that Capt. Humphries had been killed.[21] I didn't know Humphries personally, but remembered him as a quiet lad, travelling daily on one of the Manchester suburban railways.

Later on, Berry and I took a line to the 8th Manchesters. They were a short distance from the old water tower, at the rear and open end of what we called Shrapnel Valley. A stream runs down the valley, whose real name is Kanli Dere, to the sea at Morto Bay. The upper part of the valley was known as Achi Baba Nullah. The water towers were the supports of an aqueduct, but there were no remains of the conduit on their tops. The 8th Manchesters were in trenches made across the valley, which was about 150 yards wide at this point and had no real bounds except a few bushes on our left and a narrow gully on our right, as we faced Achi Baba. In the shallow hole which served as a signal office we found Jennings and another battalion signaller. We made ourselves at home, made the home a little deeper, and raised the earth sides above ground level a few inches higher. The French sector was on our right front, and from it, throughout the day, came stretcher-cases and lighter casualties, making their way slowly towards their hospitals. Shrapnel from the Turks, and occasional strays, wounded a few of the 8th Manchesters. Their adjutant, Captain Collins,[22] came to us and asked what we supposed to be the use of our thin parapet of loose earth, shaking our faith in the theory that earth, however thin, would stop bullets. Collins had the appearance of a toy-shop doll, and a large red bob on his helmet made him look silly, in our opinions. We begged some coffee from some French soldiers close by, made a fire, and cooked bacon and cheese on it and fried biscuits in the fat. Holmes of the 8th was hit on the shoulder, but the bullet did not draw blood;[23] and a spent bullet stuck in the leather pad of another man's braces.

Near the towers, captured rifles had been heaped up, and we saw that many of them were loaded and cocked. We wondered why none of them went off as they were carted away. Rifles cracked all day. Snipers

21 Capt. Arthur Cecil Humphreys, 7th Lancs. Fusiliers. The date of his death is given in Commonwealth War Graves Commission records as 10 May 1915.

22 Capt. C.H.G. Collins, Duke of Cornwall's Light Infantry, attached 8th Manchesters.

23 Possibly Pte 2336 William Done Holmes, 8th Manchesters, later CQMS 202048, 19th Bn Rifle Brigade. See Appendix IV, biographies of No. 4 Section.

were busy and we soon learnt how to distinguish the sound of a Turkish sniper's rifle from one fired on our side. Now and then, when a man was hit, we saw others going to help him, and there was usually a shout for 'stretcher-bearers'; and at irregular intervals we saw the white puff of shrapnel as they burst over the trenches. When snipers were busy and wind was up, Collins became quite excited.

Suddenly, we heard two shots in some bushes on our right. Men were running to the spot to see what had happened, and I ran with them. In the bushes was a body with a sack over its head. It wore a shirt but no trousers and there was a bullet wound in one of the thighs. A fatigue-party was digging a hole, and when it was deep enough, they lifted the body to bury it. They took the sack from the head. The head had a forehead but no face. I felt sick. We were told that a sniper had been rounded up, but I couldn't find out what had really happened.[24] By this time we were ready to find snipers behind all bushes, waiting for us, and were thankful for the company of our companions. Bullets became plentiful, and we were grateful for the real or imaginary safety our shallow holes could give us. That night we lay listening to the whispering or whistling of bullets as they passed a few feet over us, and between us and the clear stars in the deep blue of the night sky. There were fireworks in front, and our guns shook the ground as they were fired. The 5th Manchesters were shelled. We nestled in our hole, two feet below ground-level.

Next morning, Monday, May 10, we soon found that our wire had been cut in several places. I went out for a look round. We found some trenches where the French had lived; and, with Holmes, who had returned for wire so that he and Hossack could mend the line, we looted the trenches thoroughly. We took back tins of mutton, soup-squares and

---

24 According to a post-war account in the war diary of L Battery, RHA, the sniper had been passed by the British advance on 27 April. The Turk, 'who must have been a stout fellow,' had concealed himself in the hollow trunk of an old tree, only yards from the camp established by the gunners. The Turk had a silencer fitted to his rifle and a loophole looking due south. The battery commander began to receive complaints from neighbouring units of his battery taking shots at them. By 8 May, the 42nd (East Lancs) Division were bivouacked south of the battery. After they had suffered several casualties, an altercation arose between an 'indignant' infantry officer and the battery commander. 'To cut a long story short a general "hunt the slipper" was soon in full blast and words will not describe the astonishment of those gunners when the sniper was dragged out of his hollow tree and summarily executed before their eyes.'

Figure 4. Signallers at Helles. (Alec Riley collection)

Figure 5. A 1/5th East Lancs officer's dugout situated close to brigade headquarters in mid-May. Captain H. Hargreaves Bolton (KIA 24 May 1915) is on the right and the officer in the Wolseley helmet on the left is possibly his brother Lieutenant John Bolton who was KIA on 4 June 1915. (Bolton family archive)

a screwdriver and other things. French rifles, cartridges and equipment were littered about. I found a ground-sheet and kept it. Some of us had managed without ground-sheets or blankets since landing, and my cardigan had been left in one of our skips on the *Derfflinger*. It was breakfast time when we got back, and with bacon, mutton, tea, and coffee, we could not complain about the menu.

The 8th Manchesters had many casualties during the day. Most of them were slight; but when a man had been killed by a bullet in his head, we were told to lie low. There seemed to be no end to the trickle of wounded. They were passing us all day. We were warm and comfortable at night; but, as a little gentle rain fell from heaven, we pegged my ground-sheet so that it sheltered me and the man on duty at the telephone. In the early morning, I woke when the rain dripped off the ground-sheet on my face. I wiped it off with my hand, and drained the sheet. When we were up and about, I seemed to be an object of interest to the others, who asked what had happened to my face as it was brown-red in places. My hand was the same. The ground-sheet had blood on it and the rain had washed it off and on to my face.

We heard more rumours of snipers. The rumour business had now started seriously. One of the newest about snipers was that one of them was a German.

Up to now we had managed to get hold of plenty of food, and with a little French I had collected coffee for several meals and a cup of wine for myself. We enjoyed our transactions with our allies, some of whom came over to see us and tell us about their adventures. We found amusement in comparing their clothing and equipment with ours; particularly their baggy blue trousers.

With our duties at the telephone, night and day, we could only manage three hours of sound sleep at night; but it wasn't doing us much harm.

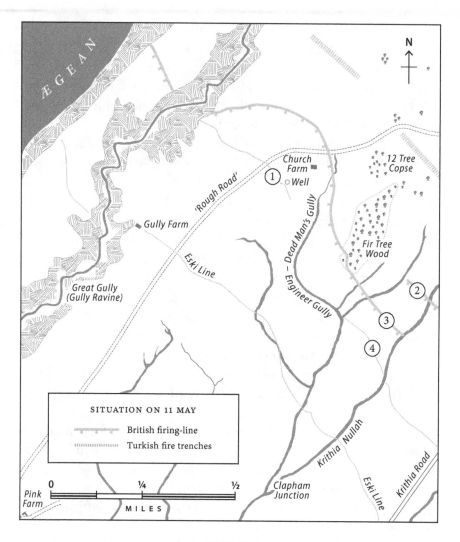

N

Æ G E A N

'Rough Road'

Church Farm
Well
1

12 Tree Copse

Gully Farm

Dead Man's Gully

Eski Line

Fir Tree Wood

Great Gully (Gully Ravine)

Engineer Gully

2

3

4

SITUATION ON 11 MAY

British firing-line

Turkish fire trenches

Krithia Nullah

0   ¼   ½

Pink Farm

MILES

Clapham Junction

Eski Line

Krithia Road

MAP 2

1 Support trench reached by Riley on the night of 11 May

2 Redoubt Line

3 No. 1 Australian Line

4 No. 2 Australian Line

CHAPTER 4

With the 8th Manchesters

At 6 p.m. on Tuesday, May 11, we reeled in our line from the 8th to brigade, and were told to report to the 8th again, and go with them to the trenches.

It was getting dark when we left the headquarters near the water towers. Womersley, the battalion signals officer,[25] was with us, and his signallers. Just before we started, I met Marsden, a big and cheerful man. Like me, he was glad to have a talk, to keep the situation well in hand. The battalion moved in extended lines, and our little party spread itself out, as we came to more open country where we were under fire; and we heard a lot of droning and whistling overhead. Whenever an order came to lie down, we lost no time in obeying it. With my nose near the vegetation I made some observations in local botany, not because I was interested in the humble plant-life, but because there was nothing else to look at.

We moved on in short stages, and slowly, going almost going due north, as we found later. By this time it was nearly dark. Ahead of us we saw rockets, searchlight beams, and white and coloured flares which hung in the air for some time. These firework effects were new to most of us. The searchlights seemed to come from a distant place on our right. When a shower of bullets came over, the question appeared to be not so much 'shall' as 'when shall' I be hit. It seemed a certainty that someone would stop a bullet, and I hoped it would not be in either stomach or head. I had not felt so naked before. Naked and unashamed.

---

25   Lieut. J.W. Womersley, 8th Manchesters. A chartered accountant in civilian life, he was killed in action on 4 June 1915, age 31.

31

We kept close to Womersley, and as it would have been easy for us to lose touch, I kept Berry and Hossack within reach. It was quite dark now, and we were crossing rough ground, full of holes, and we had to get over several small gullies. In daylight the country could be managed easily enough, but it was hard work in the dark, and on unknown land.

At last we found ourselves on the top of a slight rise. In front and below was a trench made at right angles to the ridge on our left. Bullets were arriving inconveniently, so Womersley told us to run and jump in the trench. We did so, and two of us made a clean jump, landing in the middle of an unclean trench-latrine.

When we had got out of it, we found Major Stephenson who told us that Colonel Heys was in the firing-line and wanted us there.[26] We should be taken as soon as a guide could be found. This trench was about three feet deep. There were a few men in it, and they put more wind up us by telling us that they had seen someone killed just where we were standing.

Just as our guide arrived the moon came out. The guide took us to a rough road on the left of the trench. In the moonlight the road was almost white, except where, like islands in a large dark pool, lay the bodies of two men of the 29th Division, face down. Following the road for a short distance to the right, we were soon in the firing-line. I found Colonel Heys and reported that we had arrived with a telephone. The moon had now gone in and the night was very black. Then it started to rain. We were in the Eski Line, at Gully Farm, near the point where the Line almost touched the top of Great Gully.[27]

We found the two signallers who were being relieved—two wet and weary New Zealanders—and took over the line from them.

Colonel Heys was close by. Suddenly, out of the blackness, a man appeared, and Colonel Heys yapped, 'Hullo! Who're you?'

A meek voice answered. 'Headquarters staff, sir.'

Colonel Heys: 'Headquarters staff? What d'you mean?'

The Voice: 'Cook, sir.'

---

26 Major (later Lt. Col.) H.M. Stephenson, 8th Manchesters. Lt. Col. William George Heys, CO, 8th Manchesters. See Appendix IV, officer biographies.

27 By this time the British firing-line had moved a further 400–500 yards on from what later became known as the Eski Line and it is probable that Riley had confused Gully Farm with Church Farm which was just behind the firing-line on 11 May.

All Colonel Heys could say was *'Cook!'* in a tone that expressed his meaning perfectly. That is, until the next meal-time arrived. The situation, including the Colonel, was relieved.

We had the telephone in the low and narrow firing-line. Our clothes were in an improper state, but the rain washed them a little cleaner. The line was sound, but we had very little sleep that was sound.

Early on the morning of Wednesday, May 12, our line was found to be no good at all. Pearson, Dale and Withington came to us.[28] From their tempers they seemed to have enjoyed a bad night. It appeared, also, that they had followed the wrong wire from brigade, and had been mixed up with some mud. They had quite a lot to say. Hossack and I went to have a look at our line. We followed it along the side of a shallow nullah, running down the slope of our ridge, until it ended in open country near Krithia Nullah or one of its off-shoots. Our nullah was about 350 yards in length and we called it Dead Man's Gully.[29] It is obvious, from the use of the two words in Gallipoli references, that the gully and nullah schools of thought had their own ways in the naming of the natural features of the peninsula. They appeared to be interchangeable, but everyone knew what was meant, so it didn't matter. Snipers were busy, so we took care of ourselves in the shallow parts, and when we had examined about 200 yards of line, we decided that we had done enough. Dead Man's Gully had been held by the —— Battalion, part of the 29th Division, and held with a certain amount of trouble.[30] Machine-gun emplacements were scooped out of the north side, and by each of them was a great heap of old cartridge-cases. We found a few dead men, with ground-sheets thrown over them, and we discovered one body so suddenly that the surprise was unpleasant. A shallow stream trickled down the nullah-floor. In one place we found it full of

28 Probably Driver 1121 Edward Pearson, RE (TF), later Driver 440142, Royal Engineers. Probably Pte 3629 Wilfred Dale, RE (TF), previously Pte 2489, Manchester Regt, later 2/Cpl 444567, RE. See Appendix IV, biographies of No. 4 Section.

29 This gully became known as Engineer Gully.

30 Riley probably intended to add the specific battalion later but wasn't able to identify it. The 88th Brigade had held this part of the line from 6 May and it could have been any one of its battalions or possibly one from the 87th Brigade. The New Zealand Brigade also came through on 8 May.

rifles, equipment, helmets, clothing, the contents of haversacks, forks, spoons, bibles, prayer-books, small personal belongings, and thousands of rounds of ammunition. It was a lovely and depressing place, and we were glad to be back to our trench particularly as the passing bullets had made us windy.

In front of the firing-line there was thick scrub where snipers were busy. Hossack had a few shots at it and hit the body of a man of the 29th Division lying in front of the scrub. The bullet must have caught his ammunition, for it set him smouldering, and he smouldered for hours. Rain fell and we were soon muddy. Collins had a recess made for us so that we were clear of the trench, and making life more comfortable.

After a meal we went down Dead Man's Gully again, exploring it more thoroughly, and helping ourselves to two ground-sheets. We found a break in the line at the far end, where we were in open country, and near the 6th Manchesters dressing station. We could hear the pops of a sniper's rifle.

There was heavy rifle-fire at night on both sides. Bullets droned and whistled and shells purred softly as they passed overhead. We were rather cramped in our new quarters in the parados, but even so, it was better than being in the trench.

Breakfast, on Thursday, May 13, was poor. All we could collect was broken biscuit spread with cocoa-paste from Berry's tin. Captain Oldfield called for a talk.[31] He, too, was short of grub. We offered him some of ours but he wouldn't take it. Collins had gone out somewhere or other the night before and had not returned. After a lot of enquiring, a message came saying that he was in hospital. Later on we heard that he had been shot in the shoulder.

Vick came to see us. He adjusted our telephone and told us about his adventures in Krithia Nullah, while he and Abe Williams were laying a line to the 6th Manchesters.[32] As they laid the line, bullets were sweeping the nullah tops. The place was narrow, full of deep pools, mud, and slush. They were up to their knees in it. Abe dropped an earth-pin in

---

31 Capt. Edward George William Oldfield, 8th Manchesters. Killed on 5 June 1915, age 33. Had served in the 2nd Boer War and was later Mentioned in Despatches.

32 Probably Sapper 664 Richard Williams, RE (TF). See Appendix IV, biographies of No. 4 Section.

the pool about six feet deep, and Vick dived in, fully dressed, to salvage it. He was now feeling the effects in his legs. When he left, he took Berry to the 6th Manchesters, leaving Hossack with me.

Gully Farm, a few yards to our rear, was in ruins; but it had a deep well in a kind of yard. The 8th Manchesters had many casualties, mostly to men trying to bring in water from the well.[33] An order was given that no one must go for water in daylight. Our trench floor was watery, so we made holes in tins, and buried the tins up to their tops, so that water could trickle through slowly. It was muddy but we drank it.

Womersley came, and when we told him that there were only two of us to work the telephone relief, he gave us two of his signallers. When they came, they got hold of a pick and a spade and dug our recess until it was large enough for two to lie down at the same time. That night we decided to go to the well and bring back as much water as we could find tins for. Hossack and I found a biscuit tin. We went down the nullah a few yards and turned sharp right to the farm. As Hossack said he knew the exact position of the well, I left him to find it. In the darkness we met some of our men creeping into the trench near the farm. One of them was Marsden, so once more we compared notes on the situation. Meanwhile, Hossack was trying to find the well. We fell over stones and bushes. Then the guns started and flares went up, and we were rather windy. Suddenly, we were horrified to see a speck of light a few yards in front of us, and at once we thought of snipers dug in with enough food and water and ammunition to last them for weeks. This yarn was founded on fact. Hossack had a small automatic pistol which he carried in a pouch. He drew it, and then carefully and cautiously, we crept up to the tiny light, nearer and nearer, until we were up to it. We were very windy that night, for the light came from a glow-worm.

We found the well, lowered the tin on the end of a puttee, filled it and carried it back to our home. In the morning most of the water had trickled out of a small hole in one of the bottom corners, and all we had for our trouble was a patch of mud.

33   The ruins and well Riley described were probably at Church Farm.

That excursion was not the only excitement we had that night, for heavy firing started at midnight, and the noise was deafening. Murphy, the sergeant major of the 8th, came to us and told us to fix bayonets and help to man the parapet.[34] It was no use explaining that our work was to look after the telephone, so we fixed bayonets, helped to man the parapet, and left the telephone to look after itself. When the firing died down, we returned to duty, and found that Tim, at brigade headquarters, wanted to know why we had not answered calls from brigade. It appeared that Noel wanted to know what the noise was about. Tim said quite a lot to me for leaving the telephone and I had a good explanation. Then he asked me where the 8th headquarters was, and when I told him that it was in the firing-line, he repeated 'In the firing-line?' in a surprised and pained tone. However, he got used to the fact, hard as it was. We had obeyed orders, so I left Tim and Murphy to settle the affairs between themselves. Hossack had to take a message to the 6th because their line to brigade was out of order.

On the morning of Friday, May 14, Tim, for some unknown reason, insisted on Hossack patrolling the line to the 6th, which was then working well, and needed no particular attention. To satisfy Tim, we arranged that Hossack should go down the nullah for fifty yards or so, and, when a reasonable time had passed, should tap in and call everybody on the line, particularly brigade. Then, having made as much noise as possible, and told everybody who he was and what he was supposed to be doing, he was to come back to us. This was done, and we were all pleased and satisfied.

We had to be careful not to show ourselves in daylight, and the lie of the land was such that this wasn't easy. A plan was made for shelling the scrub in front, to clear it of snipers, but nothing happened, and snipers and machine-guns were both busy. Food was scarce now, and when we had breakfast, about eleven o'clock, I started on my iron ration. We managed to make some good tea in our home, so things might have been worse. There was a lot of fuss about returns to be sent to brigade headquarters. We managed to get our water-bottles filled. None of

34 A/RSM 3737 Peter Murphy, commissioned to 2nd lieut. on 2 July 1915. Later captain and adjutant 8th Manchesters. Murphy later changed his name to Smith by deed poll. See Appendix IV, officer biographies.

us had washed or shaved for a week; we looked and felt dirty, and we began to feel lousy as well. I give these trivial details because they were noted at the time. They are not of much interest, but they show how we were passing the time, and, no doubt, we thought they were important enough when our interests were limited to trenches and dug-outs.

Next morning, Saturday, May 15, an artillery officer came to see what could be done about shelling the scrub and shifting the snipers. He and Colonel Heys had a look round, and we had our line put through to Y Battery, by brigade. The gunner came to the telephone and explained the situation to the battery, giving them the necessary instructions. I was to look after the battalion end of the line, and when all was ready, word would be given to me by the battery. The Colonel and gunner would observe through periscopes and give me any alterations in range required. The men in the firing-line were told to take care of themselves, and to keep as low in the trenches as possible. Now we were waiting for it. Suddenly the battery signaller shouted 'Fired' to me, and I shouted 'Fired,' as loudly as I could, and the word was passed down the firing-line quickly. The shell burst directly over us so as to catch the scrub. A dozen more shells were fired and the scrub must have been riddled.

Our trench and the reserve-lines were shelled during the day, and several men were hit. We heard that Blakey of the 6th Manchesters had been killed in a fall of trench, and that others had narrow escapes from suffocation. I had no rifle-oil, so I cleaned my rifle with bacon-grease, which made the bolt work easily if it did the barrel no good.

Early on Sunday, May 16, Johnson, the machine-gun officer of the 8th, and another man, were hit.[35] Snipers were busy again, and a few shells were sent to us. Colonel Heys was put through to Y Battery, and, once more the brushwood was riddled. More men were hit; and we were told that Johnson was dead.

The 8th Manchesters were to be relieved, and we were told to be ready to reel in our line at any time. In those days we were very short of cable, and had to be sparing with it. The battalions had no permanent line yet. At night the 8th were relieved by the Essex and Hants battalions

---

35   Second Lieut. Percy Clarkson Johnson was killed on 16 May 1915, age 40. He had served in the 2nd Boer War, retiring as a captain, and had re-enlisted at the outbreak of war.

of the 29th Division,[36] and we were told to reel in. Just before we moved, and while there was still a faint trace of twilight, Johnson was buried. We heard the thud of picks and the scraping of spades, and it sounded a noisy job, and a gloomy one. He was buried on the open ground a few yards from our headquarters, behind the trench. Looking over, we could just make out the shapes of the little party gathered round the grave, and by the light of a flash lamp one of the 8th officers was reading a bit of the burial service in a low voice.

The 8th were leaving the firing-line, and when they had all gone, we handed over the signal office to our reliefs, and started to reel in. We passed the men who were taking over, and one of them, a sergeant, wanted to know who we were and what we were doing and where we were going to. We were both annoyed and said so plainly.

There were four of us, and we were just leaving the trench where it met Dead Man's Gully when the fun started. Shrapnel was bursting everywhere, and the place was lit by the flashes overhead. It burst in front of us, behind us and over us. Then came heavy rifle-fire, and flights of bullets swished over. We found shelter at the trench end in the nullah, and there we crouched, thankful that we were untouched after each shell-burst.

When the firing slackened we started on our night's work. The line was fastened securely to trees and bushes on the nullah-side. Why the hell had it been so well and truly laid? We cursed those who had laid it. Even with four of us on the job, it was hard work reeling that line. We were on the north top of the nullah-side disentangling the line, and had only collected a few yards, when firing started again. Rockets and flares were plentiful, so we got down in the nullah. Frogs were croaking in the stream and there were glow-worms on the bushes. The bodies haunted the place, and we did our best not to see them. The litter in the stream-bed did not please us either. Whenever firing died down a little we started again, but every time we moved something happened. We slipped on mud and stones, and splashed through water. My bundle fell into a muddy hole and I followed it. We got mixed up with trees and bushes. We bumped one another with our rifles. One man's equipment got into another man's way. Now and then we sat down and cursed,

36 1st Bn Essex Regt and the 2nd Bn Hampshire Regt.

and then we did a bit more. We wondered who was where, for bullets come over from back and front. Tempers went from short to worse, and blasting language was the only way to relieve them. Now and then, when flares went up while we were on the top, we stood quite still until the things had finished, for they hung in the air for some time. I put my foot in it when I mistook a pool of mud for a stone.

When dawn came we were still in the nullah, but now we were near the lower end. Tired and bored, we cut the wire, left the nullah and crossed a short open stretch to reach the 6th Manchesters cook house, and here we dropped ourselves, at 4.30 a.m. Tim happened to come along, and seeing us, suggested food and rest. We needed no suggestions in that line, and I was soon asleep, but only for a short time. Snipers were busy. We heard that Aldous had been hit in the eye.[37] After a rest and some light refreshments, we took all the wire we could find to brigade head-quarters. This was in some pine trees at the south end of the high ridge of Krithia Spur, and on the top of it. From this point we overlooked Shrapnel Valley on one side, and the high ground behind the Aegean cliffs on the other side. The pines were growing in shallow limestone earth. Their twigs and cones were god-sends for fires. We had more breakfast, and then I found a convenient hole and slept in it all morning.

Tim suggested that I should stay at brigade headquarters, but I didn't want anything like that if I could help it, and I told him I would rather go out with the battalions. I did not tell him the reason, which was, that we had a much better time with them.

And so ended our first episode. It had been rough at times, but it might have been rougher; and compared with what some of the infantry were going through it was smooth. For the first time since we landed, No. 4 Section was gathered together. When we left Egypt we were well-clothed, healthy, clean and rather fat. We were still rather fat, but already our clothes were getting dirty and torn, and we dressed according to the needs of the hour—much or little. Some had managed to keep clean; others had little or no chance, and I was still unwashed and unshaved.

37 Capt. F.C. Aldous, 6th Manchester Regt, later Lt. Col. in the MGC.

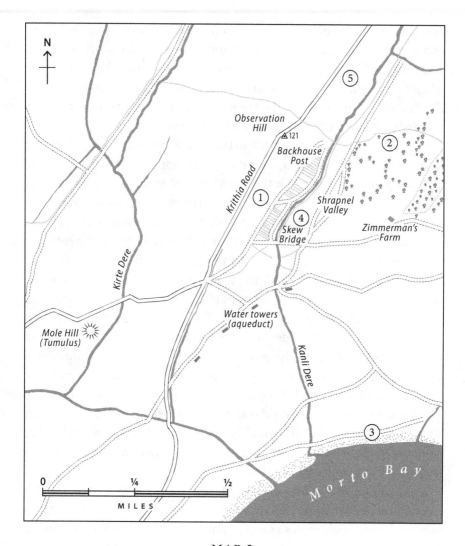

MAP 3

1. Short stay at relocated Manchester Brigade HQ, 16–17 May
2. In the reserve trenches with the 7th Manchesters, 17–20 May
3. Riley's first bathe in the Dardanelles, 19 May
4. Stay at new signal office, 20–22 May
5. Stay at new Manchester Brigade HQ (relocated around 19 May), 22–25 May

CHAPTER 5

With the 7th Manchesters I

On the evening of Monday, May 17, Haworth and I were sent to the 7th Manchesters,[38] in Kanli Dere, but further up than where the 8th had been when we were near the water towers. We had only to go through the pines down the side of the ridge, and we soon found the 7th at the foot of the slope. The hole where we were to live needed improving, so we got hold of a pick and spade and made the place deeper and larger. Stanton, the 7th signal sergeant, came along with his men, and he got in with us.[39] This was my first meeting with Stanton, and we did not know at the time how much we were to share while we were together at various times, both good and bad.

A reveille of shells woke us on Tuesday, May 18. We were tired and dirty, and at first, we couldn't get hold of any rations; but Stanton did his best, and by complicated army methods surpassing all human understanding, we drew them from the companies supplying orderlies, at brigade headquarters. Chadwick was wounded by shrapnel, and Rawson was killed.[40] He was the first fatal casualty in the 7th Manchesters, and although he had been warned to keep down, his head went up once too often. I had taken Rawson's photograph as he was carrying water, in camp at Carnarvon.

38 Probably Pioneer 1102 James Haworth RE (TF), later 2/Cpl 444595, Royal Engineers. See Appendix IV, biographies of No. 4 Section.

39 Sgt 233 John Matthew Stanton, 7th Manchesters. Mentioned in Despatches for his service at Gallipoli.

40 Lieut. G. Chadwick and Pte 1671 Walter Rawson, died 12 May 1915. Both belonged to the 7th Manchesters.

Figure 6. '7th Manchester Battalion's HQ. This was a day or two after the first rain. I lived in the next hole to the right.' (Alec Riley collection)

We took a short walk and reaching a place where we looked over the peninsula to Achi Baba, we discovered some French artillerymen observing for their 75s through a telemeter. They let us have a look, and, as the battery crashed harshly close by, we saw, a few seconds later, their shells bursting with fine accuracy of range along a Turk trench. Turks were moving about while shells burst dangerously near.

We heard that Killick of the 6th was killed.[41] It seemed to be a suggestive name. Stanton heard that his brother had been wounded, and he told me that the bullet had hit him in the stomach, passed through, and the point protruded through his belt at the back.

We had Maconochies for our evening meal—the first I had seen, and a welcome change from bully and biscuits. That evening I had a shave, and it bristled with difficulties, for my Gillette didn't take kindly to beards. When it was over I felt less like a ruffian. My feet were aching, for up to now I had not taken my boots off. The time had come for risking it, so they came off that night, and I wrapped my puttees about my feet for warmth, for the nights were still cold.

---

41   Second Lieut. Richard Killick, died 15 May 1915, age 28. He had previously served in the Madras Volunteer Guards as a lieutenant. Was gazetted into the 6th Manchesters in August 1914.

When we woke on Wednesday, May 19, we found that a plague of ear-wigs had descended on us during the night, and we heard that B—— had been killed, the bullet passing through his neck.

We were about one mile from the shore of Morto Bay, and hearing that two platoons of the 7th were going for a bathe, Stanton and I went with them. We enjoyed our walk across the plain behind the bay through the trees and over the sandy ridge to the beach and then we had our first dip in the Dardanelles. The water was very cold, but that didn't matter, we needed water so badly, and we felt better after it. On our way back we passed many shell-holes. Large pieces of jagged iron were lying about, some of them two or three feet long. These were presents from the navy, and iron golf-balls, innumerable, were also tokens of the navy's esteem.

We had not been home for long when more shrapnel arrived. The balls tore through the pines behind us, on the slope of the ridge, and smacked the ground, and we kept as close to the walls of our home as we could. We heard the rustle of falling twigs and small branches as they were stripped off the trees. Whenever the shells stopped, we sat up and looked round. In the afternoon we had more and heavier shelling, and when this was over, we had tea. The pines provided us with plenty of fuel, and we had a good and varied meal with toasted cheese and jam. We spent the evening washing our socks in the local stream and made drinking cups from some old shell fuse caps we had found. I had a collapsible drinking cup as well. That night I had a blanket for the first time since we landed. We were comfortable until the Turks disturbed us.

On the morning of Thursday, May 20, the Turks disturbed us again. For an hour balls rained through the trees which were now getting splintered and shattered, and our slope was well searched. We crawled against our low walls again. A few high explosives dropped in the open valley, throwing up earth and fumes. We were working our regular duties at the telephone.

A few of the 7th signallers were playing cards in the next hole to ours. Livesey was one of them, and we heard him shout 'Stop throwing at me, you fool!' He clapped his hand to his leg, thinking that someone had thrown a stone at him. It was not a stone but a bullet, and the Turks had thrown it into his calf.

We moved our headquarters to the far side of the valley to a place where the Lancashire Fusiliers had been, and near a shallow stream close to Skew Bridge. Our signal office was in a bit of trench three to four feet deep. In the evening, when the situation was quiet, I went to the stream for a wash and brush-up. There was a man near me also washing himself. Suddenly he gave a jump and a gasp—a bullet had drilled his arm, so I took him to our home, tied him up, and saw him on his way to the dressing station. About the same time a man, standing near our fire, was hit in the thigh.

Fletcher came to us with a drum of wire. Two companies of the 7th were going out digging that night, and we were to take a line out to them and work it. Haworth and I started at 9.45 p.m., laying the line up Achi Baba Nullah. We scratched a nick for it with a mattock, across the road near our office, and then hung it on bushes where we could find any. It was dark by this time, and we didn't know how far we had to go, or where exactly, we were going; so we went on unreeling until we reached a place where, on our left and on the left of the nullah, a communication trench started. The nullah, here, was very shallow, in fact we were nearly in open country. Fortunately, some men came along, and they told us roughly where the place was we were supposed to be making for. As we had not enough wire to reach the diggers, we sent word to the officer in charge, telling him that we were at the end of the communication trench. Then we tried to find somebody to dig us in. The ground was wet and sloppy. Across the stream there was a flat-topped rock. We crawled on to this, and found it fairly dry, but only about fifteen inches under cover. We were laying on it, face downwards, when a shower of bullets came over. We heard them swishing through the grass, a few inches over us, and then smacking the low nullah-side near the trench opening, and we saw them strike sparks when they hit any hard stone. We hugged that rock tight. We loved it. We didn't want to leave it.

Major Staveacre was in charge of the diggers, and orderlies kept us in touch with him, and him with us.[42] It was dark and we had no candles. Staveacre worried about candles. We couldn't get any, or pop around

---

42 Major James Herbert Staveacre. Was in command of the 7th Manchesters when he was killed on 4 June 1915, age 42, later Mentioned in Despatches by Hamilton. He had served in the 2nd Boer War as a sergeant with The Earl of Chester's Yeomanry. See Appendix IV, officer biographies.

the corner to buy some. Nobody knew anything about candles. Odd messages came. We wrote as well as we could on C forms, guessing the direction of the lines for we couldn't tell if we were going straight or not. We took turns at the job, and each managed to get an hour or two of rest.

About 6 a.m. the diggers came in and we reeled our line down the nullah and returned to our home near Skew Bridge.

Friday, May 21, was quiet at first. We had a good breakfast, and Walton came to see us. We had a long talk, telling each other where we had been and what we had seen, for one of the greatest pleasures of Gallipoli was meeting those we knew after a few days when neither knew what the other had been doing, where he was, or even if he was alive. In barracks, where we were all living together, casual meetings meant nothing; but here they meant everything.

We spent a few hours sleeping, or reading some old papers we had got hold of. We were to have moved back to brigade headquarters that night; but just as we had mobilised our kits and were ready, the Turks sent about 20 rounds of shrapnel, two or three at a time. Iron whizzed and whirred, and showers of balls walloped the ground. Several balls dropped in our hole, and we didn't know how they missed us. Pieces of iron dropped on both sides, in front and behind. Our line was cut. We found the break and repaired it; and finding another broken line, we attached our telephone to the home-end and called up. The man who answered us was so officious that we left the line as it was, and for its owners to find and mend the break, instead of doing it ourselves as we intended, and saving them the trouble. The shelling was followed by shouts for stretcher-bearers. One victim was in a bad way. We heard that Capt. Bazley had been hit in the head.[43]

The Manchester Brigade was relieved by the East Lancashires, and our brigade office told us to stay where we were for the night, with the 4th East Lancs Battalion, who took over from the 7th Manchesters. The adjutant wanted company, so I spent some time with him in his

---

43 Capt. Walter Neville Bazley, 6th Manchesters, died of wounds on 23 May 1915, age 42. Served in the 2nd Boer War with the 77th Imperial Yeomanry as an NCO, becoming an honorary lieutenant while on active service.

dug-out.[44] Haworth and I worked the line for the night, in two hour watches, and the night passed quietly. There was nothing particular to do on the morning of Saturday, May 23, so I wrote some letters. The adjutant censored them and did quite a lot of scratching out. In those days I was honest. Later on I found a way out of local censorship.

We spread some branches over our hole, and on them we laid our overcoats to dry in the sun, and to give us a little shade, for the sun was getting hotter now. On the coats we put pine-branches to dry for our fire for dinner. My supply of paper and envelopes was small, so I sent an urgent message home for more, also for pencils, ordinary and copying-ink. A battery of 75s near us shook us whenever they crashed. We called on Nick Robinson, the East Lancs Brigade signals officer, and our friends in that section.[45] James Walsh was always worth calling on. Moore had had a narrow escape. A shell dropped in his dug-out but didn't burst. Hewitt told me that Bazley had died the previous night.

Watters relieved us in the afternoon at 3 p.m. and Haworth and I went back to brigade headquarters, a new one, 500 yards from the old place. We found a good dug-out, and a mail had come in, bringing me a letter, a cake, and some papers. We spent the evening comparing experiences with the rest of the section.

Whit Sunday, May 23, was an easy and lazy day for us. Ormy and I had a wash in the stream. We stood naked in about six inches of water and splashed each other. We were satisfied with this, but some of our section had gone to Morto Bay for a real bathe. Grimshaw came to see us, and told us that Bazley had been buried. Except for very odd shells and a few strays, the day was pretty quiet; and the *Peninsula Press* told us that Italy was on the point of joining in on our side.

Monday, May 24, was a day to be remembered. It was raining when we woke and showery all day. I spent most of the morning in bed. After dinner I took a party to divisional headquarters and drew eight drums of wire and four pairs of cheap pliers with soft cutting edges, from our Company stores. Most of our people there looked rather miserable, and they gave us their reasons when we told them what they looked like.

---

44 Capt. F.M. Livingstone James, East Lancs Regt, attached 4th East Lancs.

45 Lieut. (later Capt.) Geoffrey Nicolas Robinson, 4th East Lancs Regt, later Mentioned in Despatches.

Hossack and I did some business with rum and rifle-rags, and Italy was reported to have had a scrap with Austria. This was our last day before we started to take the war seriously.

Next morning, Tuesday, May 25, the outlook was better. The air was warm and relaxing, and I spent a slack and lazy day. A letter and some spools of film reached me, and with Vick, I bathed in the stream. About 5 p.m. we moved to a new brigade headquarters, about a mile from the one we were leaving, and on the right bank of Krithia Nullah where it is in almost open country. This new headquarters consisted of a few deep holes, roughly squared, with openings from the nullah-side, and a bit of trench inclining towards the nullah. Artillery had been here, for lying about on the top were boxes of fuses, and tins of biscuits, some nearly full. The nullah stream was very shallow. We piled our drums of wire in a square dug-out and leaned our rifles against the side.

It started to rain. Not a shower but a deluge. None of us had any idea of what rain could do before this lot came down. We were standing in the hole with the drums, and in a few seconds, we were soaked. The water rose up to the trigger-guards of our rifles, and some of the drums were soon under water. I had tried to get my ground-sheet over my shoulders, but was wet through long before I could open it out. A young torrent rushed and swirled down the trench, and the nullah stream was fifteen feet wide in a very short time. Men who had walked across before the rain were now cut off, for the torrent was deep and dangerous. Some of us left the hole and crouched against a bank of earth at right angles to the nullah and in open country. We watched the bank turn into mud as it got gradually lower. We were standing in deep mud by the remains of the bank when the Turks opened fire with shrapnel, and they had the range, almost, but not quite, but we were most unhappy about it all. I had only one bright thought, no amount of rain could make me wetter than I was. We enjoyed the sensation of water running down our shirts, breeches, and boots, and we might just as well be properly water-logged as half-damped. The rain lasted for about half an hour. When it stopped, we took our bearings, and helped ourselves to some dry biscuits from the tins. A few shells came over at intervals, most of them dropping over an exposed bit of road on our left. We tried to pull ourselves together. We all needed hot baths, but I had to wait some months for mine. I remember thinking of the times when there was always a hot bath waiting for me when I was muddy, after games on Saturday afternoons.

We had to get hold of our rifles and the drums. No one wanted to go down into the water-hole for them, so we made a fishing-rod from an old rifle-barrel whose woodwork had been used for firewood. To this we fastened a loop of wire at one end and fished up the rifles and drums. All this time water was pouring down the trench, damming itself with the earth it carried, and we had to keep cutting the dams to let the water loose again.

Tim went away somewhere or other when the rain stopped. At 9 p.m. he had come back to us and told me to take a line to the 7th Manchesters. Haworth came with me. I asked him where the 7th were, and the only direction he could give me was that they were over the hill to the rear of our old headquarters on Krithia Spur. This spur divides the two nullahs, Achi Baba and Krithia Nullahs. Our brigade signals would call us up at frequent intervals as we reeled out. We left one end of our wire in the signal office.

It was nearly dark when we started, but we took our bearings as well as we could. We looked at the landscape, and from what we saw we didn't think much of it. As our objective was so uncertain, we decided to make for Shrapnel Valley to begin with, in hopes of coming across the 7th sooner or later. I wore the heel-plate and carried the telephone.[46] Brigade started calling us when we had only gone a few yards down the slope. I let brigade do all the calling, or most of it, and they made such a habit of it that I got fed up and only answered them when I felt inclined.

On the top of one slope we found a trench full of Lancashire Fusiliers, and passed the time of night with them; and we were moving further down when a sap-ful of water, from higher up, opened. The water chased us downhill for some distance before we could get clear. We heard the noise and saw the water reflecting a patch of sky not yet fully darkened. We had dodged the main attack but we were caught by the flank. Meanwhile, we were laying our line in a way that would

46 When connected by a wire to the telephone, the heel-plate served as an earth contact, allowing the operator to use his instrument whilst walking.

have made the best people weep. We didn't care, so long as we were in touch with brigade. Now and then I reported such progress as I could. We spent a lot of time falling over stones and rocks, and in splashing through mud.

At last we reached Shrapnel Valley, and took the line across to the road along the stream, turning left to follow it up the nullah, and fastening the line on such bushes as we could find. We asked everyone we passed if they knew where the 7th Manchesters were. At last we reached the rock where we had spent a night in the lap of luxury. We were told that the 7th were somewhere up the sap on the left, so we went up it. The sap was narrow, and deep in mud and water.[47] It was dark now, and we were carrying full equipment and spare drums of wire. Muddy water, six to ten inches deep, swirled about our legs, and in all this we were laying the line. Then we met an East Lancs battalion coming down the sap.[48] We couldn't move forward, as they blocked the sap and bumped us as they passed. All we could do was to stand still until a few hundreds of them had gone down, and they were in no hurry. We cursed them and they cursed us; but what were two amongst so many? Both of us were very bad-tempered when we were free to squelch on again in our water-logged boots, and lay a bit more line.

Sometime between midnight and one o'clock, on the morning of Wednesday, May 26, we came to the end of a perfect day and started a new one by the side of a well in a little recess to left of the sap, and to our relief we found the 7th headquarters on the neighbouring top. We spread a wet ground-sheet on some lumpy stones round one side of the well, reported our arrival to brigade, and settled down as comfortably as we could. I took the first turn, from one to three o'clock.

If Haworth's appearance, in the light of early morning, was any indication of mine, there was nothing to be said in favour of either of us. We stretched ourselves, had a look at the local tops, and one at the sap to see what it was like by day. We knew what it was like at night. Haworth went to look for food, while I collected the few odds and ends of rations we had brought with us. While he was away Victor Rylands came to the well for water, and we drew it up in his mess-tin on the end

47 Probably the communication trench later known as Sauchiehall Street.
48 The 5th East Lancs.

of a strap and a piece of string tied together. We wished each other good luck and he left me, and I didn't see him again.[49]

We discovered Stanton, and, leaving the well, we made a shallow shelter on the top, large enough for us to lie in, near the CO and adjutant.[50] Bullets were plentiful here, and although our ideas were all about food and sleep, we had sense enough to lie low, for bullets were kicking up the ground or ploughing it, close by. When the firing dropped, we spread our clothes on some shrubs and they dried quickly in the sun. Our boots and socks were stiff and full of mud.

We moved to a new headquarters, 150 yards ahead, and near the sap. To reach it we could either cross open country or go by the sap. As we didn't want any more mud and water we crossed the open country. Our new homes consisted of grave-like holes, head on to Achi Baba, and more or less sheltered by the earth thrown up in making the large trench just in front. Between the holes we placed our belongings. Our part of the place was an improved and deepened latrine near Krithia Road. General Orders for May 26 stated that the East Lancs Division was now the 42nd Division, the Lancs Fusiliers Bde was to be the 125th, the East Lancs Bde the 126th and the Manchester Bde the 127th Brigade.

There was a lot of noise and heavy firing at night.

In the early hours of Thursday, May 27, Stanton found B—— asleep at the telephone, and had him exchanged for Stringer, a good lad, well-liked by us all. Our fire was obstinate and wouldn't burn properly. The telephone was not what it should have been. We were all tired and fed up. Pearson told me that Smyth had been hit in the leg and we heard that the *Majestic* had been torpedoed.[51] Whenever anyone came over the open ground, from the direction of our well, the Turks sent him a few bullets. The sun was strong and we were thankful for our helmets.

49 Capt. Reginald Victor Rylands, 7th Manchesters. A solicitor by profession, he died on 29 May 1915, age 23, after being wounded while advancing the line on 28 May.

50 Lt. Col. H.E. Gresham and Capt. P.H. Creagh DSO, Leicestershire Regt. See Appendix IV, officer biographies. On 27 May Gresham was invalided off the peninsula, handing over command of the 7th Manchesters to Major J.W. Staveacre. All adjutants in territorial battalions at this time were attached regular officers, often coming from other regiments.

51 The pre-Dreadnought battleship HMS *Majestic* was sunk at anchor just off W Beach in the early hours of 27 May by the German submarine *U-21* under the command of *Kapitanleuntnant* Otto Hersing. *U-21* had sunk HMS *Triumph* off the Anzac position two days earlier.

Odd shells passed over us, purring softly, and we saw them burst, usually over the cliffs and beaches. Aeroplanes went up, and we wondered what the peninsula looked like from above. Vick and Mallalieu came along to see what was wrong with our line or telephone.[52] We were glad to have visitors. Vick had a habit of tapping the lines, usually when we were busy with messages. We told him exactly what we thought of him, and the stronger our language was the more he enjoyed it. We had a little joke of our own. We stuck some bullets in the wall of our hole and told our visitors that they had just arrived from the Turks. My turn that night was from 8 to 10 p.m. There was brilliant moonlight, strong enough to read by. Franklin, the RSM of the 7th, came and sat with me, and we talked about the territorials.[53] He said they were rotten, particularly the 7th, his own battalion. I didn't agree with him. But then, he was a regular and I was a territorial, so we couldn't possibly agree on that point; but we were good friends on all others. We talked quietly so as not to disturb the sleepers. We had learned to make as little noise as possible when we took over our duties at night. No one would willingly disturb a sleeper. Sometimes our reliefs needed a lot of shaking and poking to waken them; and then, bleary eyed and sleepy, they settled at the telephone for a few hours, and the men they relieved were asleep in a few minutes.

This place was on higher ground near the centre of the Helles area, and from it, looking south-west, we could see most of the end of the peninsula, excepting the beaches, which were below the cliffs on higher ground near the sea. It was quite a small area, but there were thousands of men on it; all out of sight except those near us. Just in front of us was a wooden cross, made from two bits of flat wood tied together, marking a rough grave. There were plenty of crosses now, isolated, or in little groups. Name, rank, number, and regiment were scraped or roughly printed with indelible pencil on bits of old boxes or packing-cases. Old bootlaces or string was used for tying two pieces in the form of a cross.

52 Sapper 617 John Mallalieu, RE (TF), formerly Pte 617, 6th Manchesters, later Sgt 444594, Royal Engineers. See Appendix IV, biographies of No. 4 Section.

53 RSM (later commissioned) 4234 Harry Franklin, 7th Manchesters. See Appendix IV, officer biographies.

We had heard with delight that some of our bombers had thrown tins of jam to the Turks. These were followed by more tins with burning fuses attached to charges of powder inside a lot of bullets and nails.

We were beginning to hate the sight of Sir Joseph Paxton's face on his rotten old jam-tin labels. We hated Messrs Pink and Tickler too. We cursed them all and ate their jam. Jam-tin bombs were known as 'Tickler's artillery,' but Paxton's and Pink's tins were just as good. Paxton was the only jam-merchant who had the impertinence to put his face on his labels, but the sight of either of them aroused evil thoughts, to be followed by plain and primitive remarks.

Gallipoli in those days was not without humour, and an example was a New Zealander, smoking a dirty little nose-warmer, going up to the trenches with all his kit on a wheel-barrow.

We had musicians with us, and it was always a pleasure to hear the Khartoum Chorus of the 7th Manchesters, with accompaniment on German mouth-organs:

> Two piastres, one buckshee.
> Two piastres, one buckshee.
> We don't care a damn how long we stay,
> So long as we get the Khedive's pay.

* * *

When we landed on the peninsula, we had a new kind of life in a strange country before us, with a freshness, and an interest in the unknown. Now, we had reached the end of this period of discovery. Routine was becoming monotonous, and we were becoming irritable.

We had learnt many things without effort, for new experiences just happened in the natural course of our duties. We had learnt that bullets can turn corners, that lice thrive in Keating's and cleanliness,[54] that our own cooking had failed to give us indigestion, that the sun's heat was becoming greater each day, that large green flies were more numerous, that the smell from the dead was always with us, that we could read the

---

54 Keating's Powder, 'the unrivalled killer of all insects.'

same newspaper several times, and that war is made of blood, smell, lice, filth, shells, noise, weariness and death. It has other ingredients, such as wounds of all sorts and sizes, and even humour at times; and, of course, the arrival of letters from home.

As we had our evening tea and gossip, we saw the red and green lights of the hospital ships, off Helles, come out and wink at us, giving us the glad eye. We wished we could get on board one of them, but we had a long way to go before we managed it.

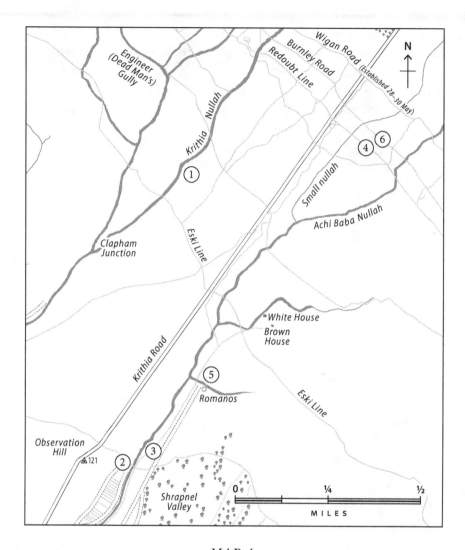

MAP 4

① Move to newly relocated 127th (Manchester) Brigade HQ on 25 May*

*Territorial divisions and infantry brigades were redesignated with a numerical prefix on this day, the East Lancs Division taking precedence (with the lowest number) having been the first complete Territorial division to have served overseas.

② Backhouse Post—7th Manchesters HQ on the night of 25/26 May

③ Move to new headquarters on 26 May

④ Move with 7th Manchesters to take over the left of the brigade's firing-line on the night of 28 May. HQ in the support line

⑤ Visit to Achi Baba stream to bathe and Romanos Well on 30 May

⑥ Move to HQ in second line on the morning of 4 June

CHAPTER 6

With the 7th Manchesters II

Friday, May 28, was quiet except for some sniping. We spent most of it in making leisurely preparations to move to the firing-line with the 7th Manchesters. The sun was hot, making us sweaty and sleepy, but, thanks to Bore, we had plenty of drinking water, and, for shelter, we had fastened a ground-sheet over one end of the dug-out. Vick tormented us by tapping in at times when he wasn't wanted. Evening was beautiful, and we roused ourselves to look at a splendid sunset.

It was dark when the order to move came, and, as usual, it was more exhausting than interesting. We went up the long sap and found our two orderlies waiting at the end. Ralston and I went to the 5th Manchesters signal office, and from there we reeled out a drum of line to the 7th Manchesters' new headquarters. The night was dark, and so was the trench; and the trench was also narrow, crowded with men three deep in places, and all in full equipment. We, too, were carrying all our equipment. We pushed, crawled, scrambled, laying the wire as well as we could on the top of the parados, and knocking down a lot of loose earth as we did it. We were carrying a spare drum of wire and our telephone, and it was hard work getting up and down from the top in the dark, with all the stuff we were carrying, and we stumbled several times. Rifles and machine-guns were rattling, and there was a lot of cursing by us, and by the men we had to push past. At last we reached the 7th and we were pushed about, here and there, until we found a resting-place for the night at the trench end of a latrine passage. Two of us slept in the passage while the other looked after the telephone. Major Staveacre had a busy night, and I had plenty to do until 2 a.m.

On the morning of Saturday, May 29, a man who was wounded, bloody and staggering, brought in a message from Captain Rylands, who was wounded. Rylands and his party had been told to creep out in front of the firing-line.[55] They did so, and dug themselves in, and had lost many of the party in doing it. Several of the 7th had been killed. Riddick,[56] who was in charge of the RE field company men at this part of the line, was annoyed about the Rylands affair, and said so, plainly, when he had a few words with the Manchester Brigade about it. How he was concerned was not clear to me.

We dealt with a message which said that four Turkish boats had been sunk in the Sea of Marmara; and later on another message addressed to OC 5, 6, 7, and 8 battalions.

> Following message begins. AAA. I congratulate you
> and your gallant brigade on their achievement under difficult
> circumstances and am confident that it is only a prelude to
> further good works. AAA. Major-General Douglas. AAA.
> Ends. AAA. GOC 127th Brigade.[57]

This bilge was received with thumbs to noses.

We heard that Hepburn and Standring of the 8th had been killed,[58] and that Rylands and his party were isolated for the time being. In the afternoon, Captain Savatard of the 7th was shot in the head.[59] Sniping went on all day.

---

55 This process, intended to bring the firing-line within assaulting distance (then deemed at 200 yards) of the Turkish line, went on all along the British firing-line in late May. Parties of men were sent out at night, advancing in 100-yard bounds, often under fire, to dig in in pairs. A line of two-man fire trenches resulted which were later joined up to form a new firing-line. Communication trenches were then dug out connecting the old line to the new. In all, the firing-line at this point was advanced three times, moving it forward from the Redoubt Line to Wigan Road, the start line for the Third Battle of Krithia.

56 Capt. (later Lt. Col.) John Galloway Riddick DSO, Royal Engineers.

57 Major General Sir William Douglas, the division's unpopular GOC, known to his troops as 'Little Willie' or 'Peevish Willie.' See Appendix IV, officer biographies.

58 Capt. Archibald James Hepburn, 'killed by a sniper' on 29 May, age 32. Capt. Dudley Hethorn Standring, died 30 May of wounds sustained on the 28th, age 31 and later Mentioned in Despatches. Both 8th Manchesters.

59 Capt. Thomas Warner Savatard, 7th Manchesters, killed 29 May, age 36.

As far as we were concerned the day was quiet. We gave our telephone new batteries, had a look at our line, had a generous issue of cigarettes, had our latrine-office enlarged and improved by the battalion pioneers, and I spent an hour with Poole at the 5th Manchesters headquarters.[60] The 7th headquarters cooks lent us their fire at tea-time in return for a present of wood we gave them. Captain Cunliffe, LFs, attached to the 7th, didn't like us at first, but he thawed in due course.[61]

We all knew that something was going to happen in the near future, and we spent a lot of time in guessing about the form it was likely to take; we snatched at any rumours, however feeble, likely or unlikely, in those days.

The trench was not deep, in this part of the line, and as we walked along it, we had to keep our heads bent. Showers of earth dropped on us when bullets caught the parapet. We were comfortable in our new dug-out. For shelter from the sun we fastened an old ground-sheet overhead, by means of a piece of wire, two bayonets and an old rifle. Firewood was scarce, water was not easy to get hold of at times; we were very dirty, living and looking like navvies. And no one seemed merry and bright, nowadays.

Haworth had the afternoon off. He spent it in making an excursion to our old headquarters, where he stayed for tea. He returned at 6 p.m., and then I was able to go out with Stanton. We were glad to have a stretch, away from the cramped and stuffy trench. We knew a place where we could lie down in the open, taking our ease, but we left it when a shrapnel had dumped a load of balls near us, and returned to an outlook of earth and clay, and to hear from Franklin that Rylands was dead.

My duty at night was from 9 p.m. to midnight, and I wrote down such messages as came by the light of a decrepit candle, shaped like a wriggling centipede. When Stringer was on duty I had to get up to help him, as he was not sufficiently used to the work.

Next day, May 30, being Trinity Sunday, Haworth went to the old headquarters again; and after dinner I went with Stanton for a wash in

60   Pte 1112 Arthur Poole, attached 1/1st Signal Company, RE (TF), formerly Pte 1112, 6th Manchesters. See Appendix IV, biographies of No. 4 Section.

61   Capt. Thomas Henry Withers Cunliffe, 1st Bn Lancs Fusiliers. Died 4 June 1915, age 29.

the Achi Baba Nullah stream. We made the wash into a bath, while we had the chance, and then went on to a spring for a drink of good water.[62] This was our first drink of fresh water. Passing the time of day with two Royal Naval Division men, who were as dirty and shabby as we were, they told us that the *Goeben* had been sunk, and that the *Aquitania* and *Mauretania* were off Lemnos, full of troops. We doubted the news about the *Goeben*. A mail had come in, and Vick brought me letters and papers. There was a lot of noise at night, and the flashes of bursting shells lit the dug-out up. From midnight to 3 a.m. I was at the telephone.

My first duty on Monday, May 31, was to take a tin of tobacco to Poole. He had a lot of papers, and promised to lend us some. Even the prospect of having something to read meant a lot to us. Haworth had scented news of increased pay, but we received it cautiously and calmly. We had breakfast at a rest-cure we knew and having spent a lazy morning examining the line to the 5th Manchesters, we returned at noon. Dick was teasing Ormy by telling him that he had been reduced to lance corporal. Stretch, of the 6th Manchesters, brought us another telephone, a poor one, and the news that Tayleforth was dead.[63] Tim and Vick came up, bringing us another telephone.

There had been an aeroplane over us for some time, and many shells had been fired at it. We watched the tiny puffs of white smoke against the blue of the sky, and they seemed to us to be quite close to their target. It was all very pretty until the pieces came down, whirring and whining pieces of iron smacking the ground. The shell-noses, too, made nasty sounds as they dropped. If there was one thing we particularly detested, it was these aerial noises. Some Very pistols and flares for same had arrived, and we examined them carefully. They were new to us, and, therefore, it was necessary that we should inspect them.

Getting up, on the morning of Tuesday, June 1, was hard. I was sleepy and heavy. Having roused myself, I went to Poole's office, with the 5th Manchesters, and collected some of his newspapers. One of the 5th showed us two broken razors. They had been in his pack when a bullet struck it. Both the handles and the bullet were shattered. After dinner I went down to the stream for a wash, and then for a short rest

---

62   Probably Romanos Well.

63   Sgt 142 William Taylforth, 6th Manchesters, died 31 May 1915, age 32.

on the open ground. These details seem very trivial now, but anyone who knew Helles in 1915 will remember that they were of the greatest interest and importance to every one of us, after being in trenches and dug-outs. When I returned, Vick rang me up from the 6th headquarters at Clapham Junction, and said that he had a letter for me which he had found lying about at brigade. I went down for it, and was told that Fred Wilson had been wounded, and that it was rumoured that Austria had given up. By this time we were suspicious of all rumours. All Stanton's signallers had come up now, and we were a happy family. It is true that we had a few minor squabbles at times, but none of them were serious, and we never quarrelled.

Except for an increasing number of rumours about possible events in the next few days, Wednesday, June 2, was uneventful. I was on duty from 3 to 8 a.m. These night duties were the times to re-read letters from home, and to consider news from the local newspapers ... Major C—— had caused a sensation by hiding one of the parish church vestry books before he left. The vicar had commented about it; but the article gave an epitome of the Major's good works in the parish ... These were the times to write letters, and to explain that brownish mark on the envelope of one of them was Oxo, and not blood; the times to remember white, clean beds, and to wonder if we should lie in one of them again.

Breakfast was cooked by slow-process on the headquarters kitchen-range. When it was over I went down to the 5th where an artillery observation officer had a peep-hole. This was an iron-plated recess in the parapet, with a narrow slit on the front plate, and a little iron door which could be swung over the slit when it was not being used. I had a look through the slit, and saw three or four shells bursting over a Turk trench. It was fairly safe to have a good look around while our guns were firing; but not entirely safe, for the Turks sent us a few bullets. We had another wash, and with Stanton's help, I filled a sand-bag with cones from the pines, and we took back some water to our home.

Thursday, June 3, was a day of great excitement. We spent it preparing to move. Everyone knew that at last the great day was at hand for what we hoped would be an advance. Tim came, bringing some wire with him, and a line was laid to a new 7th Manchesters headquarters. Field company REs were making wooden bridges over the trenches so that the armoured cars could cross. Later in the day the positions of these bridges were marked by small white flags. Dale told me that Firth was wounded and might lose his arm. Aitchison and Bailey had been killed,[64] and Oldham badly wounded by shrapnel. They had all been caught on Krithia Road while taking out some wire. Sergeant Williams had carried on with the work.[65] We heard that Karno had held a special service,[66] and while we appreciated the occasion, we did not like the idea of a special service.

We moved to our new office at night and found it at 11.15 p.m. in an awkward part of the reserve trench.

The morning of Friday, June 4, was bright and sunny. Looking round in the early morning, the landscape had little about it to suggest what was about to happen. Everything was quiet. We had heard that our artillery preparation was to start at 8 a.m., but, at that time, only a few odd shells passed over. Everyone was excited and impatient, and we could not eat much breakfast. However, we did our best with it, for we realised the next meal might be a long way off. Deliberate bombarding was in progress when I went down the communication trench to examine our line, to find everything all right. On my way back I passed Noel Lee, the brigadier, and he said 'Good-morning.' He looked the worse for wear, as far as his clothes were concerned, but he sounded cheerful enough. Shells were becoming more numerous now, and at 11 a.m. the war started. We moved to a new headquarters in the second line.[67]

64 Sapper 880 E. Aitchison and Driver 938 T. Bailey.

65 Sgt (later CQMS) 530 C. Williams. He was later awarded the DCM for his actions.

66 Fred Karno was a famous slapstick comedian at the time. Possibly an irreverent name for the OC, Divisional Signals Company, Capt. Arthur Niven Lawford, RE, later Lt. Col. and CRE 42nd Division. Mentioned in Despatches. See Appendix IV, officer biographies.

67 The trench known as Burnley Road. At the start of the battle, the 7th Manchesters held the extreme right of the division's line, with a front of about 300 yards stretching from Achi Baba Nullah to a point about 180 yards east of the Krithia Road.

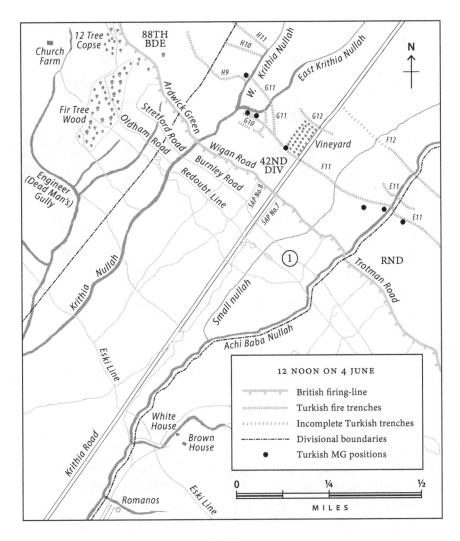

MAP 5

THIRD BATTLE OF KRITHIA

OPPOSING LINES—BEFORE THE BATTLE

① Move to new signal office on 4 June

Figure 7. The 6th Manchesters advance from Ardwick Green on 4 June 1915. (Alec Riley collection)

Shells whizzed and whirred, not far overhead, bursting over the Turks' lines. We peeped over the top, watching the neatly-placed puffs as the shells burst a few feet over the Turks' firing-line. Haworth was at the telephone, and Stanton was at the parapet looking through a periscope. We had this bit of trench to ourselves, and the signal office was a rough seat cut in the parados. By this [time], the Turks had started sending us shells and bullets.

Shrapnel was raining on their lines, but was it doing any good? We wanted to see more and more shells put over, for we didn't want any Turks left to catch our men when they went over, and we were distressed when a few yards of trench escaped, or the range was a short distance out. It seemed as if our guns could never fire enough shells. The excitement of watching it was so great that we suddenly discovered that we were showing far too much body; but the Turks must have been too busy to bother about an odd mark or two.

Then the navy opened fire, dumping heavy-weights on Achi Baba in front, and on Krithia, with its red roofs, minaret and cypresses, just to the front left of Achi Baba. Krithia is a mile from Achi Baba. Columns of dark smoke were rising from the hill, and from the foreground. High explosives were marked by great blasts of white and brown smoke. Lumps of earth were being thrown about, and dust and debris were falling. The hill was like a volcano, and the columns of smoke rising from it were hundreds of feet high, and vertical in the still air above the summit. We wanted to see Krithia's minaret knocked down. The village was being knocked about, and if any poor devils were still in it, they must have had a rough time.

We were breathing smoke and fumes. Rifle and machine-gun firing increased until it became an unbroken noise, and shell-fire became hotter still.

The 6th Manchesters were in a trench to our left front. Just before noon we saw their bayonets come up above ground level, flashing brightly in the sun as the 6th twisted them around, while the men shouted and cheered.[68] We were deafened and dazed by the increasing noise. We seemed to be living in a kind of noisy trance. Our guns lengthened their range. The Turks shrapnelled our lines. We couldn't grasp what was happening, but the 6th Manchesters had charged, climbing on to their parapet and making their way forward as well as they could and leaving their casualties where they fell. We saw two or three of our armoured cars as they crawled slowly over the rough ground. Wounded men came past us, sometimes cheerful enough, always bloody. We saw part of the Royal Naval Division retiring to a line of trench on our right. Major Staveacre rushed into us with a message to brigade asking for reinforcements. Five minutes later, Berry, a 7th pioneer, ran down the short sap shouting 'Staveacre's killed.' He had been shot through the heart while he was helping with a box of ammunition. Messages became urgent. The noise of rifle-fire and bursts and blasts of shells continued, and now bullets were skimming our tops. Still no one knew what was happening.

Then came a quieter period, and in it Dick told us that Dale was hit, and that Noel Lee, at advanced brigade headquarters, had caught a bullet in his jaw while watching the advance. He had been warned

---

68 Riley was about 600 yards from the 6th Manchesters' right flank.

to keep low, but insisted on looking through his binoculars, over the parapet. He would not be helped, and we heard that he had managed to reach a dressing station.[69] Claude was near him when he was hit and gave me full details later.[70]

Wounded cases trickled past us, their stained and bloody khaki often hanging in shreds. We heard that our men were holding their own in the lines they had captured. We saw wounded men who could walk making their way back, slowly, to our lines, and crossing open country. Franklin, the 7th RSM, came to us. We were looking over the ground in front when Franklin said:

'Look at that brave fellow standing up in the open by himself and firing from his shoulder! Ah! He's down. Brave chap!'

We saw him away out in front, near an olive tree. It was Duke Marvin.[71] He had closed the canteen with 'The Two Black Crows' for the last time.[72]

When Noel Lee was wounded, Colonel Heys of the 8th Manchesters had taken over the command of the brigade. Heys was killed almost immediately, as were several of his officers.[73]

It was some time before we heard definite news about the results of the attack, but at last we did hear something. Our men had been told to take two lines of trenches. They had the first one in five minutes, and the second line by 12.30 p.m. They had gone far beyond the second, but

69 Gen. Lee walked back through the Bearer Aid Post No. 1 near Clapham Junction, then onto the main dressing station where he was fitted with a tracheotomy tube. Refusing to be carried by stretcher, he walked on between two stretcher bearers to the main hospital at W Beach, with a chaplain praying alongside him as he walked. On the way he was hit again by three shrapnel bullets which failed to penetrate. He was eventually evacuated to Malta where he died on 22 June 1915.

70 Probably Pioneer (later Cpl) 3614 Ernest Houghton 'Claude' Hague, RE (TF), later 267953, RE. See Appendix IV, biographies of No. 4 Section.

71 Sgt 2177 George Marvin, 7th Manchesters, died on 4 June, age 35. There is a reference to Marvin's death on p. 65 of *With the Manchesters in the East*. 'Franklin says that he and Staveacre could see in the far forefront of the battle Sergeant Marvin engage four Turks simultaneously with his bayonet till shot dead.'

72 The name of an American 'blackface' comedy act.

73 Lt. Col. William George Heys took charge of the 127th Brigade at 12.25 p.m. and continued to command until relieved by Lord Rochdale around 3.30 p.m. See Appendix IV, officer biographies.

their right flank was unsupported and they were enfiladed. The RND had been held up by barbed-wire missed by the bombardment. Both the 6th and 7th Manchesters had lost heavily.

How the rest of the day passed I don't remember, for I made no notes about it.

I looked after the telephone from 8 to 10 p.m. Nothing was happening where we were, and when I went off duty, I lay down in the trench near the signal office.

* * *

June 4 (additional notes)

The line from advanced brigade headquarters to the 6th Manchesters was laid 'on the top,' although the two positions were connected by trenches. Shortly after the attack began, this line was cut in several places by shrapnel. Hossack, with the 6th, was acting as linesman. He repaired several breaks, but they were so numerous that it was hopeless to try to mend them all while the Turks were shelling. Torrys,[74] acting as runner from the 6th to brigade, saw Hossack on the top and called to him to get into the trench. Torrys had a message. He and Hossack went to advanced brigade headquarters. When they arrived, Noel Lee had just been hit in the jaw by a piece of shrapnel. He was propped up on the trench floor and was trying to speak. Torrys handed the message to Claude, and it was read to Noel Lee who looked at it and again did his best to speak.[75]

Claude had been bumped on the head by a large shrapnel ball. In spite of an aching head he looked for the metal, saw the ball roll down, picked it up and kept it.[76]

* * *

74 Probably Pte 2135 J. Torres, 6th Manchesters.
75 Riley attributes this note to E.F. Hossack.
76 This story is attributed to E. (Claude) Hague.

In the grey early morning light, on Saturday, June 5, I was wakened by the fall of some lumps of earth. Thinking something was going to explode I covered my head with my arms and rolled over, for something had bumped on me. When I got up, I found it was a real live body, a RND man, one of many who were jumping over or into our trench, from the front, and the place was full of these men who were rushing along it with fixed bayonets. A few of their companions were lying on top of the parados and firing over us. Some of those who jumped over shouted 'The Turks are on us.' An officer shouted to me 'Get down! D'you know you've nearly been shot in the head?' I got down. I didn't know until he told me. Meanwhile, the RND men had gone further back. We had a look around to see what was going on, and I made sure that my rifle was loaded and cocked. I was wearing my British Warm. A staff officer came to me and said 'What do you make of the situation?'

I answered 'Very little, sir.'

As an afterthought he said 'By the way, are you an officer?'

Having assured him that I wasn't guilty, he said 'Ok!' and went away. I was glad when the affair was over. Being wakened to find myself mixed up with a crowd shooting and shouting 'The Turks are on us' was not my idea of a good time. Later on, we heard it was panic, and no wonder, after June the 4th. We were all very windy, and we sympathised with the infantry who had done all they could to make the show a success, and who had all the dirty work to do.

There was a mixture of firing, and an uncertain atmosphere. Wounded were coming in, bloody, dirty, torn, worn out. A message came through, reading as follows:

> To all battalions. I wish to express profound admiration
> for marvellous gallantry and endurance on the part of the
> Manchester Brigade. The GOC Army Corps ordered present line
> to be held at all costs. He has expressed unbounded admiration
> at your conduct and says he will make it ring not only through
> Lancashire but through the Empire.
> (Signed) Lord Rochdale[77]

77 Lt. Col. Lord Rochdale, OC 6th Lancs Fusiliers, temporarily in command of the 127th Brigade. See Appendix IV, officer biographies.

A quaint conceit. Those who were at Helles on June 4, 1915, and the relations of the men who were killed on it, will not forget that date. It is of no interest to others.

News of casualties came to us. For a start, captains Jackson, Edgar and Kessler were killed;[78] so were Senior, Cory, Pickup.[79] Barrett was wounded, Griffiths wounded, Grimshaw and Walker, wounded. Tear and Newlove were killed.[80] Ogden had been hit in the back, in the nullah, on June 3. Later on Tim told me that all the 6th Manchesters' captains had been killed, but that he was uncertain about Holt.[81] Noel Lee was seriously wounded. Thorburn was killed.[82] We heard that a shell had caught his head but couldn't find out what really happened. These were a few of the officers and men we had known who were killed or wounded. We heard about more, as time went on. There was a feeling that something had been torn away from us. We had never been concerned in anything like June the 4th before, and it left its mark. That evening, we saw a sunset well suited to the times. The western sky was very red, and red was reflected on the pine-trees and olives, on the coarse grass, which was as bloody as it looked, and on our faces.

A Lancashire Fusiliers officer came to our office and pestered us until we got rid of him. I lay down on Stanton's ledge, where some of the 8th Manchesters put me in danger of a bang on the head and gave rise to an argument. I was ashamed of my part in it when I remembered what these men had just been through.

That night there was a devil of a row from shells, bombs and rifle-fire. We were shelled, and the flashes lit up our trench. High explosives were bursting on our right, and my left shoulder ached for some reason or other. I was lucky not be aching far more seriously. We slept as well as we could in our rather cramped quarters, and when the noise of

78 Capt. Stanley Foster Jackson, D Coy, 6th Manchesters, died 4 June 1915, age 27, Capt. Robert Gerald Edgar, 6th Manchesters, died 4 June 1915, age 30, Capt. Edgar Kessler, A Coy, 6th Manchesters, died 4 June 1915, age 28.

79 L/Cpl 758 James Kneale Senior, died 4 June 1915, age 26, L/Sgt 1184 Bernard Charles Cory, died 6 June 1915, age 27, L/Cpl 840 John Burton Pickup, killed on 4 June 1915, age 26. All 6th Manchesters.

80 Sgt Thomas Arthur Teare, died 6 June 1915, age 26, and Cpl 421 George Newlove, died 5 June 1915. Both 6th Manchesters.

81 Capt. Joseph Holt, 6th Manchesters, died 4 June 1915, age 33.

82 Lieut. Edward Francis Thorburn, 6th Manchesters, died 10 June 1915, age 21.

Figure 8. 'Here the camera is looking down upon the upper part of Krithia Nullah over the June 4th battlefield, while Helles Memorial—all but invisible in the reproduction—stands upon the horizon, immediately above the dark bush near the centre of the photograph.' Photograph taken about 1930. (Alec Riley, *Twenty Years After*)

bombing on our right and heavy rifle-firing was not too loud to keep us awake. There were shells in the early morning of Sunday, June 6. By this time we were looking and feeling unwashed again, and I hadn't shaved for a few days. Tim came round before breakfast and we discussed the general situation as we knew it. A wounded man, with his arm bandaged, came to us, and rested for a time. He was worn out and fed up.

Lance Corporal Macartney, one of the 7th Manchester's most useful men, came to see me. He had been taking messages to and from the captured trenches, and said they were full of dead and wounded, giving me some very bloody details.

That fool of a Lancs Fusiliers officer came again—a bigger fool than we had thought he was before. Stanton was irritable; so was I. We managed to weather it, somehow. Suddenly a man ran down the sap. He was shot in the back. We pulled his shirt off, found that the bullet had ripped up a 'V' of soft flesh, put a dressing on it, and got him away. There were several aeroplanes up and we watched some good flying.

We were relieved at night, and moved to some trenches in rear of our new brigade headquarters. We had a rough job in taking the line to our new office. The smell from the dead was very strong at the corner of Burlington Street in the second trench. There was heavy firing at night, and in the darkness, we could see the glowing fuses of the shells as they passed overhead to Helles, and then the bright flashes of the bursts. They gave off a kind of drowsy hum as they went past. We had written some letters on Sunday, and on the morning of Monday, June 7, we took them to the Reverend Kerby, the padre, who had a temporary vicarage at Clapham Junction and left them with him.[83] Clapham Junction was the meeting point of Engineer Gully with Krithia Nullah and it was about a quarter of a mile behind the Eski Line. After passing the time of day with Kerby we went higher up Krithia Nullah to the 6th Manchesters dressing station, where Sergeant Stirling gave me more details about June 4, and told me that Sorton had been killed.[84] Later, I heard that Sorton, to avoid disturbing a man lying in the trench, had jumped on a fire-step to pass him, and a bullet had caught Sorton in the head.

Then we heard what had happened to Ormy and Hossack who were with the 6th on the 4th of June. Colonel Pilkington told them to take their line to a new battalion headquarters in a captured trench (G11, between East and West Krithia nullahs and past the fork reached via West Krithia Nullah).[85] This was at night, about 10 p.m., and they went on reeling out until they came upon Sergeant Clifford of the 8th Manchesters and Hopkinson,[86] who were lying down, shots being plentiful. About them lay many dead. Ormy and Hossack went on until, when they had laid most of a drum of line, they came to the end of a Turk trench where they saw a board with a notice in Turkish. Hossack asked Ormy if he could play it. Suddenly a hand caught Ormy's arm, and a voice whispered 'Where the hell are you going?'

Ormy answered 'We're not going much further.'

---

83   The Rev. E.T. Kerby, Chaplain 4th Class, attached to the 7th Manchesters.

84   Sgt 176 Ernest Sorton, C Company, 6th Manchesters, died on 5th June 1915, age 31.

85   Major (later Lt. Col. and C.M.G.) C.R. Pilkington. Pilkington had assumed command of the 6th Manchesters before the battalion left Egypt when the CO, Lt. Col. Gerald Heywood, was pronounced medically unfit for active service. See Appendix IV, officer biographies.

86   Probably Pioneer 1883 Harry Hopkinson, RE (TF), later Sgt 444595, Royal Engineers. See Appendix IV, biographies of No. 4 Section.

The voice said 'No, by Christ you're not. The Turks are only fifty yards away.'

So they went into the trench, which ran straight. The Turks were holding a semicircular one, facing ours, and the sides of the nullah as well. Our men could see the shapes of the Turks as they crept along the nullah top, trying to enfilade our men from a trench to the right of G11. An officer gave Ormy and Hossack some ammunition to hand out where it was needed. They were shooting at the dark shadowy forms of Turks, as well. They went along the trench asking 'Who wants ammunition?' and Sergeant Orme, the only 6th Manchester man there, who was about 40 yards up the trench near the middle, said 'I bet that's Ormy.'[87] Continuing their distribution, they went to the far end of the trench. When they got back Orme was dead. Holberton, the adjutant, had reached this trench in the early morning of the 5th, and then gone back.[88] At 6.30 a.m. Ormy and Hossack left it, and had to run. Men of all battalions and brigades were now mixed up, and Ormy told me that he had seen a Lancashire Fusiliers' machine-gunner sitting on the top, firing at any Turks he saw. Ormy and Hossack got back to Colonel Pilkington's headquarters, and so ended their adventures of the night of June 4 and 5.

* * *

87 Sgt 218 Joseph Orme, 6th Manchesters, died 6 June 1915.

88 Capt. (later Lt. Col.) Philip Vaughan Holberton, Adjutant, 6th Manchesters. A regular officer, he had served with the 2nd Manchesters in the 2nd Boer War. Appointed Brigade Major for the 126th Brigade in November 1915. He was killed while commanding the 1/5th Lancashire Fusiliers in France on 25 March 1918. Five times Mentioned in Despatches. See Appendix IV, officer biographies.

Figure 9. East Krithia Nullah, close to the end of trench G10 (the short trench parallel to G11), in September 2017. (Michael Crane)

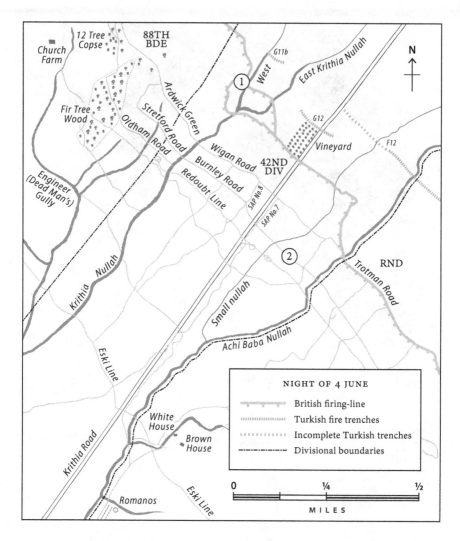

MAP 6

① Approximate position of the Lancs Fusilier machine-gunner mentioned in 'Notes on the night of June 4/5'

② Riley's signal office

Notes on the night of June 4/5

These notes were supplied to me by Ormesher and Hossack. There is a vagueness about parts of their stories, but enough is definite to show that they had spent an exciting night.

Near the East Krithia Nullah end of the trench Captain Holberton was standing near Sergeant Orme, who, in the early morning light, could now use his aperture sight effectively, and particularly on the upper parts of Turks who could be clearly seen as they passed a depression in a trench-parapet on the east side of East Krithia Nullah.

Holberton said, 'For God's sake stop it. You're doing no good killing odd Turks'; and Sergeant Orme had answered 'I'll just have one more shot, sir' when a Turkish bullet caught him in the centre of his forehead, killing him instantly. (At that time our men were firing, regardless of exposure.)

Ormy and Hossack left their telephone at one end of the trench. Hossack returned to the 'phone while Ormy stayed with Sergeant Orme, who said 'There's a good place here,' while Ormy answered 'Not likely. I want to get some cover', and then went to see if Hossack was through, staying with Hossack for two or three minutes.

While he was there a LF came down the trench, carrying a rifle, and saying to Ormy:

'Do you want a rifle with one of those fancy back-sights?'

Ormy said 'Whose is that?'

'It's that Manchester sergeant's. He's just stopped one.'

Recognising it, Ormy returned. Sergeant Orme was dead.

Shooting at a Turk who was jumping into the trench, Ormy just missed an LF's ear. This man was a yard or two in front and to one side; but he got the blast in his neck and said some rude words. The Turk wore a light-coloured uniform.

About midnight the Turks attached the trench—firing and shouting 'Allah! Allah!' as they advanced. Our men saw the flashes of the Turks rifles as they advanced over the ground between East and West Krithia nullahs. The attack seemed to be half-hearted.

During the night our men watched with interest an LF machine-gunner who had planted his gun on one side of —— Krithia Nullah,[89] and sat at it, without cover, giving short bursts of fire whenever he saw any marks, however shadowy. In the dark the flashes showed up clearly. He was responsible, chiefly, for checking the Turks ... At dawn, the men in the trench saw the result of his shooting, as they lay in front. After the attack failed there was little more firing.

Before Ormy and Hossack left for Colonel Pilkington's headquarters on the morning of June 5, Tim spoke to Ormy on the phone, saying:

'You've got to come back to the old 6th headquarters. Don't forget to reel in the wire.'

Ormy: 'We can't come back. It's impossible.'

Tim: 'You must.'

Ormy: 'Well, we'll *try*, but we can't guarantee it.'

The Turks shot at them as they ran down East Krithia Nullah but the LF machine-gunner opened fire. After running about 100 yards, they lay down where the trench-bottom sloped downwards.

Hossack had been observant, for at XX he saw a number of dead Turks sitting in the concave nullah-side. They were covered with flies. At O lay a dead British officer, his hand hanging over the nullah-side. On one finger was a large and notable ring.

When Hossack and Ormy reached the fork, they saw several of our men retiring down the other bank of the nullah.

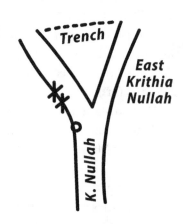

* * *

89 Although Riley does not state which nullah the Lancs Fusilier machine-gunner sat above, it is most likely to have been the West Krithia Nullah.

On the night of June 5, Hossack had taken a line and his telephone, under heavy fire, to a bit of advanced trench held by Mr Hammick and some of the 6th.[90] Throughout the night Hossack alternated between working the telephone and taking a place in the firing-line. Hammick was nervy and kept bothering Hossack as to what was going on. The situation was dangerous, and seeing this, Hossack held an imaginary conversation with brigade for the benefit of Hammick & Co., in a voice loud enough for them to hear. It was clear to all who heard him that reinforcements were coming. There were no reinforcements, and Hossack had not spoken to brigade; for, while he spoke, he had not pressed the lever of the speaking-piece to make contact. What he said cheered and reassured Hammick and his men, and they held on and eventually got away in the morning. Hossack told Pilkington about the incident, and Pilkington approved of it. Claude gave me details about what had happened at brigade headquarters when I saw him later on.

*   *   *

90   Lieut. H.A. Hammick, 6th Manchesters, wounded 14 June 1915.

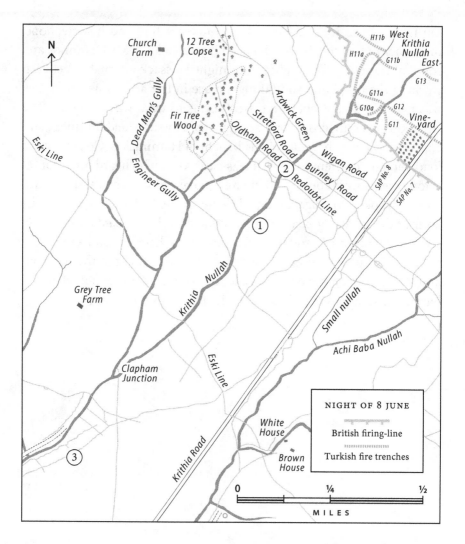

MAP 7

1 Riley's approximate position from the night of 6 June until 9 June

2 6th Manchesters dressing station, visited by Riley on 6 June

3 Rest trenches, 9–14 June

Figure 10. Bathing in Krithia Nullah, near Redoubt Line. Riley may be the subject as he credited the photograph to Charles Ormesher. Figure 11. The same waterfall in Krithia Nullah, photographed in the 1930s. (Alec Riley, *Twenty Years After*)

Near the end of Redoubt Line, in Krithia Nullah, a break in the limestone stratum in the stream-bed had created a small waterfall with a pool below it. This became one of our most popular bathing places and we used to let the water flow down over us. We had others, for any spot where the water was a few inches deep was good enough; and there were some in Achi Baba Nullah. We spent some of our pleasantest times at Helles wallowing in these muddy little pools, and we made up small parties to visit them; for there was no fun in solitary bathing.

On this particular day,[91] while a small group of our people was sluicing in the waterfall-pool, a shrapnel burst overhead, and although the balls splashed the water, no one was hit. The Turks had marked this bit of the nullah, for they sent odd shells with the same range, and bathing in it was always a gamble. We were annoyed whenever our

91 Probably 7 June.

wallowings were disturbed by a scream, a crack, flash and puff and a shower of splashing balls. Ormy and I amused ourselves by standing in the water-fall, inclining our bodies at an angle so that they caught the full flow and keeping the position by holding on to the rock behind the fall.

I stayed some time with Ormy at the 6th headquarters in the nullah-side, near Clapham Junction. Shells were coming over, and it was reasonably safe in Ormy's little dug-out. As we sat there we talked about the battalion and what had happened to it. So many of the men we knew had been killed that there seemed to be very few left. Death on that scale depressed us. When the Turks had finished their ration of shells, I returned to the 7th for an issue of lime juice. There was enough for three of us. I had my share and Haworth had his own and Stanton's as well.

It was about this time that we began to be particular about the exact division of food, and to squabble about inches of shade in the hot, airless trenches and dug-outs. Tempers were showing signs of wear and tear; and that night we had words about a ground-sheet, and how much of the surface we were entitled to. My duty was from 1 to 3 a.m., and when Ralston took over, I lay down on the bed he had left.[92]

Tuesday, June 8, started well. Stanton's pants and socks had disappeared, and the two of us had words about them. The day was slack and only a few messages came through. We had little to do except eat and sleep, like animals. Claude came to see us, and we were glad to have a visitor. We had plenty to talk about, particularly our own position as part of the Manchester Brigade, and how much credit, if any, we could claim. The Poor Bloody Infantry had done so much, and we so little. Claude, however, thought that some small amount was due to us. He told me that he and Mallalieu had tackled Karno about the NCOs' pay, which had not been increased, while the sappers had been given a rise. The NCOs had been forgotten, it seemed; but the mistake would probably be put right.

The 7th Manchesters were relieved at night. Both sides were shelling. Some of those from the Turks were falling too near us to be entertaining, and our eyes and ears were filled with dust thrown up by the bursts.

92 Probably Pte 1422 W.A. Ralston, 7th Manchesters.

Dust fell on us throughout the night, while the flashes lit up the walls of our dug-out. Haworth and I stayed on until the 5th Lancs Fusiliers had completed the relief.[93] I got through my turn quickly enough with the help of a long novel called 'A Man's Code' in a Yankee magazine. It was a silly title, but quite a good story; and I read it by the light of a guttering candle.

A CQMS of the 5th Lancs Fusiliers gave us plenty of rations—bread, cheese, jam and biscuits, and I gave myself a morning's sleep. The men of this battalion gave us some trouble, for they pulled our line down several times. After dinner, on this day, Wednesday, June 9, I walked down to Clapham Junction where I found that Hopkinson was working a station whose call was BY. As our own call was BY, I called up the brigade office and told Joe that two stations had the same call. Joe told me to mind my own business, and back in our dug-out Haworth and I sat back and waited for the fun. When it came, we enjoyed it with ribald jeers. 'Deadhead' was to have relieved us, but he didn't turn up, so we waited until 6 p.m., when Watters, Walsh and Moore came to us. Watters and company decided that something was wrong, as there were two BYs and one of them should have been OM.

However, they relieved us, and we went down to some rest trenches between brigade headquarters and one of our old bivouacs. Going down the nullah we passed a great strip of shell, about two feet long by nine inches broad. It would have given anyone who caught it a nasty gash.

We were glad to be in the open once more, and to see the rest of the section. With them we had little dug-out parties for our meal of tea, bacon and toasted cheese. About this time boxes of dried potato slices arrived. These, when soaked and softened, and then fried, made a welcome addition to our rations.

We compared our various escapes, and saw that the *Manchester Guardian*, for May 18, gave a gloomy outlook on operations in the Dardanelles area. We discussed our chances of going to Imbros with the Manchester Brigade, having heard that it was going there, to

---

93 The 5th Lancs Fusiliers held the portion of the firing-line from the divisional boundary on the left to the Krithia Road on the right, and were themselves relieved by the 4th East Lancs later on the 8th. Records indicate that it was the 9th Manchesters who relieved the 5th and 7th Manchesters on 8 June, taking over the right and centre of the firing-line.

be reorganised. From 11 to 1 a.m., I looked after the line to GN, our divisional headquarters.

For most of Thursday, June 10, a strong wind was blowing dust and grit about, and the sky was dull. Knight, the brigade major,[94] said he would do his best to get our section moved to Imbros with the brigade; but we did not go. I was feeling tired and out of condition, and when Claude told us that we were going to GN, we felt really gutless. We were not interested in divisional headquarters, except to keep as far away from it as we could. However, we had nothing to complain about when we got there, a day or two later.

After dinner I walked over to the 6th Manchesters rest trenches, to see who was still alive. Finding Cross and Griffiths, we discussed casualties. Each of them had lost a brother.

At night, when I was asleep, Torrys woke me. Telephone duties were getting on my nerves so much that when Torrys touched me, I said 'I can't leave the 'phone.'

Poole told me that he was the same. Several times, with the 7th, I woke in the night, thinking I had gone to sleep at the job; and once, Haworth sat up in bed, grabbed the receiver, and sat there holding it to his ear. When I spoke to him he didn't answer—he was asleep.

Torrys told me he wanted Joe, as L.C.M. was threatening to put him under arrest.[95] There had been an issue of rum. There had also been words and blows about a candle. We told Torrys to shut up and go away.

After a night of grit in my teeth, I was up early on Friday, June 11. I found Joe in the nullah, looking very miserable after some of Stirling's pills. A strong wind was blowing the dust about, and it was rather like a khamsin, in Egypt, without the heat.

After breakfast, Ridings and I went to GN for letters, and found everyone there looking fed up; particularly with Karno. Rumours were plentiful. One of them was that the division was moving, not including the Signal Company. We, also, were tired and fed up, and would have given a lot to go home; another rumour was that we might do so. We

---

94 Major H.L. Knight, CMG, DSO. See Appendix IV, officer biographies.
95 Possibly an abbreviation for Lance Corporal Mallalieu.

rested all afternoon and felt better when we got up. The 6th had not gone to Imbros yet. We heard that St. Leger Davies had been killed.[96]

On the morning of Saturday, June 12, Tim told us that the sea had been too rough for the brigade to embark. There was a sore feeling—the brigade was licking its wounds. They would heal, but old territorials would always see the scars. As time went on the losses became more real to the survivors, and not only in our old battalion; for we had got to know and like many officers and other ranks in other battalions and brigades in our division. We remembered a song, popular at company dinners and smokers in Manchester; and now, so many who had listened to it knew what 'The Trumpeter' was sounding.[97] They were lying dead, between the lines and about Krithia Nullah.

That evening, while we were sitting in our dug-outs, our lines were shelled. High explosives came over, dropping at first near the road, and then near the stream. Earth and iron dropped, after the bursts. There was a lot of dust, and clouds of smoke rose from the shell-holes. While everything was dropping, I crouched against the side of my home until the thumps and rattling ceased. After one burst a lump of earth dropped on me. I saw it coming and gave it my shoulder, breaking it up, and bits of earth filled my mouth and ears. The same explosion had done more damage in another dug-out near mine. Greenbank, Hossack and Noble were in it when the shell burst amongst the dug-out.[98] Greenbank and Hossack were partially buried, and the shaken earth had buried Noble up to his chest. Greenbank and Hossack got out of it quickly enough. Driver Norris ran over from the 6th lines bringing a spade, and Noble was soon released, but he was shaken. The crater was 12 feet deep and 20 feet in diameter. Lord Rochdale, the brigadier, sent across for the senior man in our group.[99] That was me. I went over to him, and he asked what I meant by letting the others stand round and draw fire. Tim was with him, so I said that we were looking for our telephones

96 Capt. Oswyn St. Leger Davies, 6th Manchesters, wounded on 27 May. He recovered and as Lt. Col. later commanded the 8th Lancs Fusiliers. Killed in France on 5 April 1918.

97 The title of a song with lyrics by J. Francis Barron and music by J. Airlie Dix.

98 Probably Pnr 1392 George Richard Noble, RE (TF), formerly Pte 1392, Manchester Regt, later Sapper 3618, RE (TF), and L/Cpl 438775, RE. See Appendix IV, biographies of No. 4 Section.

99 Lt. Col. Lord Rochdale, OC 6th Lancs. Fusiliers, and temporarily in command of the 127th Brigade.

which might have been buried, and which I knew were quite safe. What I was really doing was looking round for a chance to take a photograph. Hossack took one as soon as the smoke cleared, and someone at brigade headquarters said we hadn't been long in getting a press photographer on the spot. I don't think Rochdale knew what I was talking about, as I referred to the telephones as Ds. Tim did, of course. Anyhow, Rochdale did not say any more about it.

Parties were told off to go to GN to draw 10/– for each man. My party was the first. GN had moved, and I couldn't find it. Haworth and the others found it, and Karno told them they should have been there at 9 a.m., so no one had his 10/–. We didn't know why there should have been this sudden desire to hand out some money. We finished the evening discussing the rumours about going home. We couldn't find where they originated, but they had even reached General Douglas, who promised those responsible something to remember, if they were found out; but they were not.

Our morning's work, on Sunday, June 13, was to collect and count blankets left in a trench by the 8th Manchesters. I was in charge of it, and, like the others, I was annoyed that a brigade section should be turned into a fatigue-party; and, amongst ourselves, we did not hesitate to say so. However, we collected 80 blankets, and dumped them at the nullah end of the trench. Having done so, I reported the blankets to Nick Robinson, who refused all responsibility for them. Tim went to GN after breakfast, and I took another party to collect ground-sheets, keeping a square one for myself. Tim had told Joe that we were to go to GN after dinner, and at 2 p.m. I went with Ormy's party. When we arrived Lawford showed us our dug-outs. He was affable and received us in a friendly spirit. I was feeling rotten, but some tea revived me. After tea, the Turks shelled the hill to our left with high explosives; and soon after, our second party arrived. John wanted to know why there wasn't a dug-out ready for him, so he was given a few reasons, to our general amusement. That night there was a rum-shortage, except in the dug-out shared by J—— and Challinor, and we thought they were corrupt.[100]

---

100 Spr (later Sgt 426906) 1247 James William Challinor, formerly 1/4th East Lancs Regt.

GN was having parades, but Nuttall, our CSM,[101] told us to lie low and say nothing, when 6 a.m. came, on Monday, June 14. After breakfast, we found that the cleaning of harness and cycle-lamps was on the programme, and as I had no interest in either harness or lamps, I arranged to be detailed to go hunting for visual equipment with Ormy. It had been left with the 6th Manchesters. The two of us got away before anyone thought of something else for us to do. We wandered off, towards Helles and W Beach, meeting Harrison of the RAMC. After a talk with him we went on to the beach where we discovered a dry canteen and bought two shillings worth of biscuits. They were dry and tasteless, but they were round, and softer than Spratt's. After a talk with one of the Worcesters, we met a RND man. They did not recognise one another but after talking about Manchester for some time, he and Ormy found that they had been at school together. I met A.H., of the ASC, and he wasn't encouraging about the going home rumours.[102] Ormy and I amused ourselves, that afternoon, watching some consignments of newly arrived troops.[103] Sergeants were bellowing about details of equipment and other trivialities. A few days on Helles would soon cure them.

We met Peate on his wagon, and as the afternoon was warm, we were glad to ride back to GN; and in return we helped unload some bales of straw, getting covered and filled with dust from them.

Our holiday was over now, for Tim sent two messages after tea, and two parties of four each were to go out to the Lancashire Fusiliers and East Lancashire Brigade signal offices. I went to the East Lancs with Thomas, Hopkinson and Poole. Having reported ourselves to Nick he sent us on to the station BK, from which we were to take a wire out to BKA in the firing-line.

101   CSM 240 Roland Harry Nuttall, Royal Engineers.

102   A.H. was an ASC officer who had warned Riley in Egypt on 30 April 1915 that the Division was bound for the Dardanelles.

103   Troops of the 52nd Lowland Division.

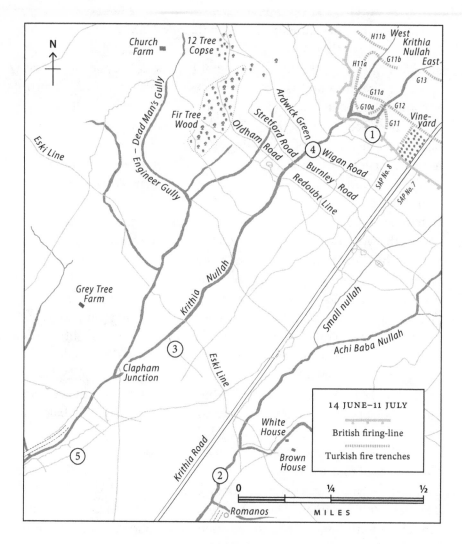

MAP 8

① Riley's firing-line position from 14–23 June

② Bathing pool in Achi Baba Nullah visited on 20 June

③ Signal office RC, 23–27 June

④ Signal office, 27 June–11 July. Poole killed here on 5 July

⑤ Rest trenches 11–19 July

CHAPTER 7

With the East Lancs Brigade

Jim Walsh and Bleasdale, of the East Lancs section, reeled out for us, and helped us along generally, and as we were feeling stale, we were glad of their help, particularly as they knew the way to reach BK with least trouble. We had been able to go as far as that station in the twilight, but it was dark when we left BK for the firing-line. Our wire came to an end about ten yards short of the line, at a spot where we were near a traverse in the communication trench, and here our helpers left us. It was dark now. Suddenly, bombs and whiz-bangs came from the Turks, and flares went up. We crouched behind the traverse without bothering to attach our telephone to the wire. Bombs were flashing as they burst, and rifles and machine-guns rattled a few feet in front. The noise made our heads ache. Poole was with me. I don't know where Thomas had got to, nor did I bother about him. He would turn up in due course. The noise died down after a time, and I reported our arrival to Captain Polden. I asked him for two men, naming them, and he sent them to us. As usual, there was comfort in numbers, and we were soon more cheerful.

We spent the morning of Tuesday, June 15, in preparing to settle down as comfortably as we could. We were given two Maconochies. Major Nowell came.[104] He had quite a lot to say about things he knew nothing about, and I gave him a few suitable answers, in due course,

104 Major (Lt. Col. from 5 July 1915) Richard Bottomley Nowell. In temporary command of the 9th Manchesters, then holding the division's left sub-section firing-line, from the divisional boundary on the left to a point 100 yards short of the Krithia Road. See Appendix IV, officer biographies.

getting our own back by methods known to all brigade signallers. The daily, lying rumours said that the division would go home on Sunday.

An Australian was killed in the firing-line that afternoon and his body, covered with a blanket, was taken down on a stretcher.[105] Wilton was sent to help us, Wilding having gone to his battalion. We explored the firing-line, and through periscopes we had a look at the surroundings. We saw a dummy trench in front of the line. Eight bodies were lying on the earth thrown up along it. They lay quite naturally, as if they were just going to fire. Dead were lying on the open country on all sides.

When the day cooled, we dug a seat in the trench-side. The ground here was sandy and soft to lie upon, and we slept on the trench floor near the traverse. The sun went down, and a damp wind blew over from the front bringing with it the smell from innumerable decaying bodies. The smell was so strong that it was all we could do to keep still in it. We went on breathing the stench.[106]

My turn was from 9.30 to 11.30 p.m. Respirators, made of muslin and tow, had been issued to the East Lancs.[107] The tow had to be damped and tied about nose and mouth with the muslin. Wilton lent me his respirator for the night. The smell was always strongest when the damp wind blew over; and now lice were breeding quickly, large green flies tormented us, and our trench floor was full of maggots from the dead.

I spent part of Wednesday, June 16, making a tea-strainer out of an old iron-ration tea and sugar tin. We pierced a lot of little holes in it with a corkscrew, and two larger holes near the top, one on each side, so that we could put a pencil or bit of stick through, and hang the strainer in a mess-tin of boiling water. The 9th had given us a good ration of cheese.[108]

105   Probably Gunner 3513 Stanley Pearson, Australian Field Artillery, 1st Brigade HQ, who died on 15 June 1915 and is now buried at Skew Bridge Cemetery (SP A.35). Pte Charles Watkins of the 6th Lancs Fusiliers describes this incident in detail in his book, *Lost Endeavour*. Watkins recalls that two Australians demanded, despite his protests, to have a try at sniping. It proved an ill-judged request resulting in Pearson being killed and his companion badly wounded.

106   This was the same trench my great uncle, Pte 1210 Jack Crane, of C Company, 9th Manchesters, left with 100 of his comrades to attack G10 and G11 on the evening of 7 June 1915. Jack and 20 of his company were killed in the action and their bodies were still lying in front of the firing-line at this time. (Michael Crane)

107   Tow was a term used to describe a type of cotton waste.

108   The 9th Manchesters.

Lice were active. We itched and scratched until we were tired with scratching. We turned our clothes inside out and ran the burning ends of cigarettes up the seams. The crack of a frizzled louse was one of the sweetest sounds we knew.

Rain came at 9 p.m., so Poole and I draped ourselves with ground-sheets and sat on our shelf, playing chess with Poole's pocket set. In a few minutes we were so sleepy that we lay down for a sleep until we were disturbed by a bombardment at 2.30 a.m. Something was catching it, but what it was we neither knew nor cared; for by this time we were taking whatever came along, caring little or nothing, one way or the other. I had got hold of some creosote and, having diluted it, soaked my handkerchiefs in it and kept it within smelling distance. It was a change from the scent of corpses, anyhow. Broadbent had been to see us, and gave us some favourable views about the rumour. Everyone wanted to believe what we knew couldn't happen.

Colonel Heys of the 8th Manchesters had been buried in this part of the firing-line, and a neat wooden cross marked his grave against the parados. On Wednesday, the body had been dug up to be taken away, and two men passed us, carrying the swollen remains in a blanket with a belt strapped round the middle. Both men were tall and thin, worn out and hopeless looking. The sagging weight nearly doubled them up, and as they shuffled slowly past us, they looked as if it was all they could do to carry themselves, let alone a heavy corpse. We hoped they would not dump it anywhere near us. So passed Colonel Heys.[109] We had seen a lot of him in Egypt and in our earlier days on Gallipoli, and his passing depressed us. The smell seemed to become fainter, and then it was stronger than ever. We had filled some old flare-cases with creosote and held them to our noses. An interfering officer had come and gone, and another officer had been taken down in a blanket.

The night was cold and damp, and we were restless. Wilton managed to sleep through it. His nose must have been a useful one, compared with ours.

Maggots crawled out of the sandy soil at night, and each morning, when we woke, there were hundreds of them under us and on the

109 Colonel Heys was reburied in Lancashire Landing Cemetery ... over three miles behind the firing-line!

ground-sheets. We lived in a headquarters of maggots; pale, wriggling, stinking blasted things. As we sat on our ledge, we watched the sandy trench floor heaving with them, and the sight fascinated us. We couldn't keep our eyes off it.

On the morning of Thursday, June 17, Major Hickey came round looking for General Hunter-Weston and Brigadier General Frith; they could not be found for a long time.[110] For dinner we had a good stew of bully, biscuits, Oxo cubes and dried potato slices. After that we declared war on maggots. We had found a lot of Turk cartridges, and pulling the bullets out with our pliers, we made a heap of the tiny black squares of explosive. Then we rounded up as many maggots as we could find, mixed them with the powder, filled old flare cases with the mixture, planted the charged cases on the parapet, and fired them with a match. They fizzled like primitive fireworks. That afternoon, while on the prowl in some trenches where the Lancs Fusiliers had been, and looking for literature, I met two men who, in the days before we thought of war, had rowed against my crew at Agecroft Regatta. We compared regattas with trenches. Most unfavourably for trenches. As we had several mutual acquaintances, our meeting was pleasant.

The Turks put up a Red Crescent on our left front, and it was supposed to be a blind for some kind of German dirty work. As it was the only bit of excitement available, we sat in our trench watching maggots and killing as many as we could.

We were annoyed when we heard that REs were to be lent to the 29th Division. This was a rumour; but the bombs, shells and noise, that night, were not rumours. They came at a time when hopes were low, to dirty, lousy, sleepy men, fed up with Gallipoli and war. Our curiosity about war had been satisfied long ago, now.

Fat green flies tormented us all day and every day. When we opened a tin of jam the flies were inside as soon as our knives; and when we spread a touch of jam on bread or biscuit, we had to keep it moving until we could eat it, and then the flies came to our mouths. We drew our rations of bread, biscuits and bacon for the next day.

110   Major C.J. Hickie, Brigade Major, 126th Brigade, Lt. Gen. Aylmer Hunter-Weston, commander VIII Army Corps, and Brig. Gen. H.C. Frith, commander 125th Brigade, respectively. See Appendix IV, officer biographies.

Friday, June 18, started quietly. Poole was feeling bad, and we supposed that the cause was the local smell. He didn't want dinner at mid-day so we had tea instead. A scorching sun, smell, maggots, green flies, lice and headaches had taken away our appetites; but we played chess, and then we were lucky enough to get hold of an old *Daily Graphic* and a *Union Jack*. Mr Sexton Blake, assisted by Pedro and Tinker, was devoured greedily,[111] and even a *Boys' Friend* was not despised. We could read anything, however trashy. In fact, such trash was about all we could find brains for. We were becoming mentally dulled, living for the day and the hour, for food and sleep, and for very little else. It seemed impossible that a day would come when we should leave this place of torment. Sometimes we got hold of copies of *Truth*, and from them we enjoyed all the scandals of the home front.

Our men were digging a tunnel in a new sap when I was doing some exploring. They had made a vertical pit, and from this the tunnel passed under the parapet. The sides were propped up. A man who had been hit in the head was carried away, moaning. He had been laid in a blanket as usual. I drew two respirators from the 9th Manchesters, for Poole and myself, and some tobacco. Two tins of it, and three boxes of matches. The 9th Manchesters were generous.[112] Poole benefited from the tobacco issue. He went down to the nullah for a wash, and he needed it badly.

We heard that an attack was due in the evening, and it materialised at 7.30 p.m.[113] First we were shelled. Then came the usual noisy crackle. Shells burst round us, and rifles and machine-guns made a hell of a

---

111 A fictional Victorian detective, his bloodhound and his street-wise orphan assistant.

112 The 9th Manchesters were particularly fortunate in their battalion quartermaster, Major Michael H. Connery. A former regular of 40 years' service, Connery was known in the division as 'the King of QMs' and was renowned for keeping his battalion well supplied. Although twice wounded and despite being in his early sixties he remained with the battalion until it was evacuated. He was awarded the MC and was also Mentioned in Despatches.

113 The attack had been aimed at trenches H11a and H11b and had been carried out by B and C companies, 9th Manchesters (supported by troops of the 10th Manchesters). When the assaulting troops reached the enemy's firing-line, they found it packed with Turkish troops getting ready to launch an attack of their own. Many of the attackers jumped into the trenches and were never seen again, others were killed by Turkish shrapnel as they lay on the enemy's parapet. When the survivors finally retired the Turks followed, capturing a portion of the British firing-line and some sections of communication trenches behind it. Attempts by the 126th Brigade to organise a counterattack failed. In the end it fell to troops of the 4th Worcesters and 5th Royal Scots to retake the lost trenches, which was achieved but at a heavy cost. It was the 9th Manchesters' bloodiest day of the campaign with around 35 men killed and a similar number wounded.

row. We tried to find out what was going on. Earth was flying about and dropping in all directions, and some of it was dropping on us. At one time so much was coming down that we stopped our work until it had finished. Our line to the East Lancs Brigade office was clear enough. Through our periscopes we could see great billows of smoke rolling over the ground in front of the firing-line, and we could make out the shapes of a few of our men when the smoke thinned a little. In the firing-line our men were bobbing up for shots, and bobbing down as soon as they had fired. There was a strong smell of fumes; a change from that of corpses. Major Allen came to the telephone, and with Major Nowell's help explained the situation to brigade:

'Our men got into a trench and had to retire. The Turks followed them and then tried to push still nearer our firing-line. Probable result—casualties on both sides.'

Highly probable.

We heard that the Turks had put up a white flag during the morning. Our people had answered with another one. After a time the Turks shot ours down, but, luckily, none of our men had exposed themselves. The Turks' white flag was supposed to have covered sandbagging or some such work. From three to five hundred Turks were reported to have surrendered.

Next morning, Saturday, June 19, we heard that the attack had failed. The Turks had driven our men back and had captured several yards of trench on the other side of the nullah. For breakfast we had a generous ration of ham. Heavy firing in the morning slackened towards noon. We had chess after breakfast, and then came a visit to the nullah for a wash—my first for a week. In the nullah I met Cooper, Clapham, Bleasdale, Lewis and Jim Walsh, all from the East Lancs Brigade signal section.[114] We had a real heart-to-heart, man-to-man talk. Most of it concerned certain officers we knew, their declines and falls in popular esteem. Two wounded men were brought down. Both had head wounds, and there was little hope for either. One of them was Wilton's pal.

In spite of their success the Turks had lost heavily, the night before, and there was some rejoicing about it.

114 Probably Driver 1155 Reginald Cooper, RE (TF), later Driver 444069, RE. See Appendix IV, biographies of No. 4 Section.

I cleaned my rifle, darned my socks, listened to a bit of brisk bombing, got hold of two copies of *Tit-Bits* from the Lancs Fusiliers, and brought the day to a perfect end by making up my diary in brilliant moonlight.

There was a strange atmosphere about Sunday, June 20. When Poole and I had played our game of chess, which he won, as usual, he went to call on Haworth and Noble, our nearest section neighbours. Later on, Noble returned the call, and he and I decided to spend the afternoon bathing in our old pool in Achi Baba Nullah. We were going down the famous No. 7 Sap, and had only gone a short way, when the Turks shelled it. Round after round of shrapnel burst in the sap or on the tops. We crouched, sheltering in places clean and unclean. Continuous crashings and patterings of balls made us windy. A shell ploughed up the trench-floor. The words we used were magnificent, if not original. I lost sight of Noble. He told me, later, that he had gone in a Lancs Fusiliers' trench, and when one of them asked if he was hit all he could say was 'Am I beggary! Am I beggary!' The word was similar to beggary, anyhow. Although this shrapnel had followed us down, we heard later that it was really a present for the Royal Scots Fusiliers who were moving in the open. It was, of course, satisfactory to know that the Turks were not bothering about two signallers who were going for a wash, but they had succeeded in mixing us up, in a sap full of smoke and dropping lead. When it had finished, we went on to the pool, had our bathe, and returned home to receive visitors—Thomas and Hopkinson. They would not stay long, however, as Thomas said he could smell something. There was no doubt about it. We had been smelling it for days. Then Haworth called. He and Claude were full of faith in things in general. Poole and I thought this was a good sign, for Claude was a cautious oracle, rarely making a mistake when he uttered wisdom. When a few shells had burst near our house that night, however, we were not sure; and the REs had found a mine-wire in a T trench near our part of the line. The telephone was working hard at 10.30 p.m., Major Nowell was talking through it for quite a long time. During the night some barbed-wire was brought up. There was brilliant moonlight again while I was on duty.

About 5 a.m. on the morning of Sunday, June 21, heavy firing started on our right. Clouds of smoke rolled down towards Helles and hung over it like a thick mist about 200 feet high. Shells were bursting along the Dardanelles shore. The Turks were searching for our batteries with shrapnel. A battery to our left rear was firing briskly. We watched the bright flashes, showing up against a dark background. The Turks had their range nicely. Noise and smoke increased. The ground quivered with the bursts of high explosives. So did we. Shells whizzed over us. Then we heard muffled roars, and saw columns of smoke, and flying earth and iron. The noise became louder still, and deafening to us. Before one explosion and its debris had settled, another was happening a few yards away. Heavy firing started in the French sector on our right.[115] Then came a rumour that the French had captured two trenches. We hoped they had.

Bombing was thick at night; and a bit of metal had caught Wilton on the face, cutting it slightly.

Tuesday, June 22, brought a little variety, for two aeroplanes were up, over our area. Later on we heard that one of them was a Taube, and the other British. The Taube was being chased.[116] I met Sergeant Harrop, an old Abu Zabal acquaintance.[117] I told him where we were, and he came round to see us. When the Turks had captured one of our trenches, a night or two before, they had cleared off with most of Harrop's private possessions, including all his money and tobacco.[118] The three Hs, Haworth, Hossack and Hopkinson, called for a talk and a general review of the situation as we understood it.

115   Known by the French as The Third Action of Kereves Dere.

116   The first successful air combat at Gallipoli. Flight Lieut. C.H. Collett DSO, piloting a Voisin biplane, encountered an Albatros B.I of the Ottoman air service over the peninsula. The observer, Major R.E.T. Hogg, knocked out its engine with rifle fire. The Ottoman aeroplane went into a steep dive, flattening out at 65 feet over the Allied trenches and alighting on the slopes of Achi Baba near Ali Bey Farm. French 75s were spotted onto the machine, but the Albatros was later salved and repaired.

117   Sgt 1126 James Cox Harrop, C Company, 9th Manchesters. Commissioned 2nd Lieut., 30 May 1917, later promoted to Captain, to command a trench mortar battery. See Appendix IV, officer biographies. Abu Zabal was a large Marconi signal station in Egypt, about 14 miles north-east of Cairo. It was guarded by troops of the East Lancashire Division for the duration of its time in Egypt.

118   C Company, 9th Manchesters, formed the consolidation party for the attack. These men were ordered to stack their packs in trench H11 (captured on 4 June). When the Turks counterattacked, they seized the portion of H11 containing the packs, most of which were carried away by the enemy.

In the afternoon, the Royal Scots Fusiliers arrived. We had read an account of their train disaster at Gretna, in a *Sunday Chronicle*.[119] They were quaint lads with broad Scots accents, and were confident about the future now that they were on the peninsula. Most newcomers were. They would be less confident in a week, or even less than a week. We heard that the Manchester Brigade had returned and would take over on the following day. The rumour about returning to Blighty was now off. We sliced some potatoes and fried them for tea. Whatever else happened, we saw to it that our menus were as varied as we could make them.

On Wednesday, June 23, we found that the Manchester Brigade really had returned from Imbros, and we were told that it had not enjoyed itself very much. In fact, it had a rotten time. The 5th Manchesters said they were glad to be back. We were certainly glad to see them. The Scots made us tired. Barton, the Lancs Fusiliers postman, gave me some field postcards, and a green B envelope. These were not only green but franked as well.

We were told to come in during the course of the morning. While we were at QEL, the East Lancs Brigade headquarters, a shell dropped so close to it that we lost no time in getting further back, before any more arrived. We went to divisional headquarters where Tim gave us two hours for dinner and orders to report to Newton at QLF, the Lancs Fusiliers Brigade headquarters.[120] Poole came with me. In due course we found Newton, and he sent us to a station known as RC in a trench on the right of Krithia Nullah, just past Clapham Junction. There had been a certain amount of official tomfoolery about rations for men of brigade sections when they reached battalions. In most cases the battalion signallers supplied us with extras to plain rations immediately we arrived, although, officially, these were not supposed to be available until we had consumed—a most excellent word—those we took with us, which did not include extras. After a day we became attached to one of the companies for rations. We had reason to believe that RC would not

---

119 On 22 May 1915, a train carrying two companies of 1/7th Royal Scots ran into a local train. In what became known as the Quintinshill train disaster, 210 officers and men were killed and another 224 injured.

120 For location of Divisional HQ, see Map 11.

come up to scratch, and I pointed this out to Newton. He looked tired and worried, but he agreed, and we had nothing to grumble about. It was merely a technical point, but it was important from our end of the line.

We found RC by following the wire, suspended on old rifle-barrels stuck upright in the ground. Their stocks had become firewood. The wire led us up, from Krithia Nullah, to a steep and narrow trench inclining up the nullah-side, where the earth was chalky loam. RC was on the top, quite near the nullah. It was a luxurious place. We had ground-sheets overhead, a seat, candles, plenty of food, and drinking and washing water were at hand in the nullah. I went gleaning in a deserted trench, and returned with a tin of jam, firewood, a blanket and a pack of cards minus the ace of spades. Poole had got hold of a *Weekly Times* at GN, and I had four letters to read.

What more could we possibly want?

Fletcher was with us. We heard that we had been promised a furlough by the King, or Kitchener, or someone else. We didn't care who promised it if we could only have it. Fletcher stayed on with us. I spent my night-watch, from midnight to three in the morning, writing letters. I could not sleep much when I was relieved. We had the usual nightly splutter of firing, but it did not disturb us.

No rations came for breakfast on Thursday, June 24, but we had plenty to be going on with. Fletcher was relieved during the morning. Then the heat arrived, getting hotter as time passed, and stronger as well. We felt as if we were being suffocated, gasping for a slight breeze. The dug-out was full of flies, fat green devils. We were both bad-tempered and we cursed the heat and the flies. Egyptian flies were infants compared with these green ones.

Ormy, Thomas and Barlow came to us. They were laying a new line. Ormy told me that Sergeant Clegg of the 6th Manchesters had been killed.[121] We wondered what the Diggle Rifle Club would do without him. He had been the secretary. In those days we found it hard to realise that the club, like other pre-war organisations, might not exist now. Our visitors were feeling the heat. We were all too hot and fed up to talk much, and there wasn't much to talk about either.

---

121   Sgt 93 John Clegg, 6th Manchesters, died 4 June 1915.

We drank gallons of water, and always wanted more. When we had it to our lips, we knew that it wasn't water we wanted, really. We didn't know what we wanted—except one thing; to get away from that hell-hole. But we went on drinking water.

Tim came to see us on Friday, June 25. He hadn't much to say to us, or for himself. Ormy, Thomas and Barlow followed him. Thomas looked at us and blinked. He had nothing to say. No one had. Poole and I talked very little. We had exhausted all our topics, except food and rest. We had even finished thinking about the time when the war would be over. Only the present mattered and that not much. Ormy was feeling the strain. So was Tim, although he was as neat as ever. I envied him his fly-whisk.

Ormy was well-dressed this morning. He was wearing a cowboy handkerchief, and his helmet was curious. He had cut the neck-shade off and had only the narrow front-shade left attached to the dome. Ormy told me that the night before, he, Claude, Mallalieu and Joe had had words with Tim. Rum had been mixed up in the case and there had been some good fun. I had no difficulty in imagining the scene, for Ormy gave me full and graphic details. It concerned the excursion to Imbros. Division had said that half of No. 4 Section, which was ours including Tim, and half of No. 2 Section could go. This was unpopular with all concerned. Later, it was decided that No. 2 only should go, so ours stayed behind. We blamed Tim, but we were wrong. Tim's reputation was secure, but for a time some of us had one up against him, and we were wrong.

A man in the 4th East Lancs told me that Major Hickey had gone to England and had said that he would 'see the headquarters people in Lancashire before long.'[122] Whatever this was supposed to mean, we hoped he would, if anything in our interests was likely to follow. In childlike faith I rang Claude up on the strength of it. Claude was as hopeful as ever, and his optimism did us good.

Next morning, Saturday, June 26, we had an increase of heat. It came from the air, the earthy walls around us, and from the ground-sheets above us, and it made us gasp. The brigade was returning to the

---

122 Major Hickie was admitted to hospital on 24 June suffering from the effects of a wound received on 4 June 1915. See Appendix IV, officer biographies.

trenches, and in spite of a lying slogan the men were downhearted, for they thought they had finished. Turk aeroplanes flew over our lines. We heard they had dropped leaflets, advising us to give up, but I did not see one of them. Letters and papers came, and Abe Williams gave us a Maconochie. We called on the 7th and 6th, to see Noble, and Hopkinson who was always cheerful, being very young. Noble had a way of his own. This time however neither of them were feeling up to much. We heard that Chanak was on fire. We hoped it was; and every other fort anywhere near Gallipoli as well.

We started Sunday, June 27, with a wash in the nullah. Tim came round. He looked bored, and he bored us. Our line was poor so the 8th had to transmit most of our messages. We had a few plain words with Tim about rations. We had been brooding over this matter, so now our minds were relieved. Haworth informed me that we had got some of our own back, and as I recorded the fact it must have had importance at the time. Nash and Nuttall came to take over from us. Both of them had been slightly wounded and had been to Cairo and back. Poole and I moved up to the 7th Manchesters.

CHAPTER 8

With the 7th Manchesters III

Macartney gave us tea with milk in it, some syrup, and other luxuries; and then, wandering down to Krithia Nullah, I found Murphy, the RSM of the 8th Manchesters, hanging out in the nullah-side.[123] He gave me a good meal of stew, and then some tea with plenty of whisky in it. As we sat and talked, he entertained me with his opinions on Kitchener's Army, or the bit of it we had on this part of the peninsula, comparing it very unfavourably with territorials. Murphy and I were always good friends, and the points of view of RSMs were always worth hearing. It was nearly dark when I left Murphy. I made my home for the night near the 7th headquarters kitchen, and night-thoughts were about the bombardment due on the next morning.

About midnight, the noise of an aeroplane overhead wakened me. Franklin came and sat with me, and as it was rather hard work resting in that hovel, I was glad to have his company.[124] As we talked, we heard the frogs croaking in the nullah-stream, and the splashes of the tortoises as they dropped in the water from the nullah-sides. How we hated the everlasting croaking of the frogs! I can hear them now, as I write.[125]

123 C/Sgt (A/RSM) 3757 Peter Murphy, commissioned 2nd lieut. on 2 July 1915, later captain. See Appendix IV, officer biographies.

124 RSM 4234 Harry Franklin, 7th Manchesters, later commissioned 2nd lieutenant. See Appendix IV, officer biographies.

125 According to the divisional history, the frogs' unusual croaking (making the sound 'Bivouac! Bivouac!') was at first mistaken for the call of a local species of duck. Others attributed it to Gurkhas signalling between themselves whilst pursuing some unfortunate Turk. The tortoises were probably turtles, which still abound in the nullahs.

The four battalions of the Manchester Brigade were arranged as follows: the 5th Manchesters, supported by the 6th, were on the left of the nullah, and the 7th, supported by the 8th, were on the right.

The bombardment started at 9.30 a.m. on Monday, June 28, and both sides were letting it rip. The 29th Division made a great attack on the gullies and ravines on the Aegean side of the peninsula, and on our left front. The Ghurkhas were helping. The country was rough and difficult, the gullies were deep, rough and steep-sided.[126]

The guns roared. Smoke billowed over the ground. We saw the bright flashes of shrapnel as they burst in the smoke. High explosives threw up the earth, debris and smoke. Gorse and grass caught fire, burning with brightened red flames. A large shell burst just behind us, to remind us that we were not forgotten. To our left rear we saw the observation sausage as it cleared the level of the cliff-top.[127] Then came the noise of guns and rifle-fire combined. We could see the 29th advancing on a slight rise to our left front. At times a long line of men in extended order, at others, a handful, holding their rifles with bayonets fixed in the most useful position. We saw more men, but were not certain who they were. Our men were approaching the Turks' lines. Here and there men stumbled, or sank down and lay still. For an instant the smoke thinned, and we saw our men reach the chalky parapet of the Turkish trench. They stood along the top, and then they disappeared, except for lonely figures apparently lost in the smoke. We borrowed Clifford's glasses to have a letter look. Some Anzacs were with our men.[128] All this time shrapnel had been bursting over the 29th and high explosives were tearing up the ground. Our heavy shells had torn up trenches and their surroundings, and the whole area was shattered. Later on, Franklin told me that the 29th had captured five Turkish lines, besides odds and ends of ground of varied value; and Captain Creagh, the 7th Manchesters adjutant, told me that a Turk battery had been captured.[129]

---

126 Later known as The Action of Gully Ravine.

127 Kite balloon of HMS *Manica*, spotting for HMS *Talbot* and attendant destroyers.

128 Probably gunners of an Australian field artillery battery.

129 Capt. Peter Hubert Creagh, DSO, Leicestershire Regt, attached as adjutant to 7th Manchesters. See Appendix IV, officer biographies.

A message came through, saying that No. 4 Section must work all our own lines. As we had only two men with each battalion, this would mean longer on duty and less time off. However, it never materialised.

This battle had three parts, morning, afternoon, and evening.

In the afternoon our side attacked again, and once more we saw our men charging through smoke, debris and shrapnel. Our trenches were shelled. The noise was deafening, and we used our buzzers for messages.[130]

In the evening we couldn't get our people on the far side of the nullah on the telephone. I had a look at the line and found it cut by a shell-burst close by. I had just mended it and got through when there come another great burst of shell and rifle-fire. Our men had made another attack. We heard that this one had failed. A shower of bullets made me feel glad to get home. It was strange how much security we felt in our own homes and with men we knew. A lot of old tins and other rubbish had been thrown on our parapet. We could hear the bullets pelting and riddling them.

That evening, at sunset, we saw a remarkable picture. Pine trees on the western skyline stood out, black and grotesque, against bright red light. The whole of the nearer landscape was red. Grass and scrub smouldered or blazed on the red and black folds of the ground, and several men wounded in the attacks were burnt by these fires. High explosives were still throwing up smoke and debris, shrapnel was still bursting and the smoke was tinged red. Everything was red. A bloody sunset, closing a day of bloodiness; and on the ground lay bloody corpses.

By this time we were used to seeing the curious things that shells could do with smoke. Sometimes they left a mixture of brown and white fumes and streamers. Sometimes the smoke shot up vertically, at others it shot outwards horizontally. Some of them gave off dirty looking black-grey smoke.

Bullets could make a variety of queer sounds. They could buzz, ping, swish, make a noise like a tuning fork. They could also turn corners, for bullets are very clever.

Periscopes were like magnets. They could attract bullets, and many a broken mirror dropped in pieces down the chute.

130 The buzzer on the field telephone was used to transmit messages by Morse code.

Figure 12. 'Gallipoli. In the firing-line.' (Alec Riley collection)

Before breakfast next morning, Tuesday, June 29, brigade told us that they could get no reply from the 6th Manchesters on the far side of the nullah. I went over to see what was wrong and found the signals dug-out full of sleepers. They were snoring like hogs, including the operator who had the earpiece on. I woke Abe Williams who was in charge, and we decided to tell our brigade people that the line was cut, and I had found the break and mended it. From the way they spoke to me it was obvious that they didn't believe me, but as they couldn't disprove it, they had to let it go. Then we had to deal with the operator. We did what we could to frighten him and arranged that Abe should give him a future series of frights during the day.

We heard that Hayes had been wounded by a bomb. One of his arms had several pieces in it. We spent most of the day sweating, and enduring lice and green flies. These prevented us from resting comfortably. Lice were using the knee portions of our breeches for breeding-grounds, so we cut off the tight parts above the knees, leaving the rest as baggy shorts. The PBI rolled their trouser-legs up or cut them off above the knees. We took our trousers or breeches off, turned them inside out, and louse-hunted, or chatted, up the seams with knives, matches, cigarette-ends. We turned our shirts inside out and hunted up every seam. It was interesting to see men, nearly naked, doing what they could to clear their garments of chats. Our skins were sore with scratching. We might feel fresh after a wash or bathe, but we had to wear the same old creeping clothes after it.

Asiatic Annie, a Turk battery on the far side of the Dardanelles, was busy all day. Most of the shells fell on the right. We could hear the distant pop of the gun, the faint whirr, and then we saw the brown smoke following the crash of the shell. The target did not seem to be anything in particular. All the Turks did was to pump shells at Helles. Our guns were firing as well. Our line was bombed, and the bursts were close enough to make us careful.

The 7th and 8th Manchesters changed places, and we stayed on with the 8th. They had a wire to the firing-line which was given TN as a call. This had to be worked. That evening the Turks shelled the trenches they had lost the day before.

Poole and I washed ourselves in an ancient and leaking biscuit-tin, with jagged edges, half filled with muddy water we had collected from a miserable gutter at the end of the sap.

At 9 p.m. the Turks attacked. The navy joined in, and once more the air was full of smoke, flashes and shrieks. Some of the flashes were like sheet-lightening. Rifle-fire came in heavy bursts, and, once more, the scrub was set on fire. The noise was deafening, and, as usual, we were slightly dazed. We heard that all attacks had failed, but it was a noisy and exciting evening.

Next morning, Wednesday, June 30, the French shelled and attacked the Turk lines opposite their sector.

We were lucky with grub that morning, for we had drawn a large piece of lean ham and half a tin of syrup. As time went on we became more pig-like in our habits. We wiped our knives and forks on our breeches. Usually, there was nothing else to clean them with. We were living in a trench at this headquarters and we slept in hollows scooped out of the walls on the floor-level. In some of these it was possible to lie full-length, in others it was not. We spent our rather cramped days and nights between our beds and our seat in the wall, when we were not able to get away for a short time. And we were fortunate, compared with the infantry. We got hold of some literature. Two magazines, a *Daily Mail*, *Times*, *Truth*, and a *Daily Despatch*.

By this time disease was making headway at Helles. As I wrote before, we had all been fat and healthy when we landed; and now we could see our companions getting thinner, weary-looking, and going about their work with little energy. Faces were looking grey and drawn. The infantry looked worse—those of them who had survived.

The face of Helles had changed. It had been quite pleasant to look at in the early days, when it had the green of spring and plenty of wild-flowers. Now it was turning brown, and it had a blasted look about it.

Our artillery included L Battery and its VC.[131] They had come to the peninsula from France. They told us that they wished they were back in France. No one seemed to like Gallipoli. We hoped our guns would always have plenty of shells, and we felt half-starved if there wasn't a big bombardment before an attack.

We lived in hell's heat, hoping for a cooling breeze.

That night we saw a wonderful show of lightening. I had never seen anything like it. Bright and clear, it lit up the whole place. Murphy said it was better than Belle Vue.[132] Overhead, also, we saw the glowing fuses of passing shells.

Franklin's thigh stopped a bullet on Thursday, July 1. We heard this with regret, for Franklin was a friend of ours. A slight breeze was helpful. I didn't want any grub and spent my time off-duty resting and reading. The day was quiet, apart from a few odd shells and little bit of rifle-fire. About this time the 7th and 8th changed places again, and Stanton was with us once more. In the evening a message came through saying that the Turks had landed fresh troops.

Claude came up for tea on Friday, July 2. We entertained him with two tins of M and V,[133] syrup, jam, marmalade, bread and tea. It was a change for Claude, to get away from brigade headquarters, and we were

---

131   Three members of L Battery RHA were awarded the VC, one posthumously, for their gallantry at Néry during the Retreat from Mons in 1914. The battery was reconstituted and sent to Gallipoli as part of 15th Bde RHA. The two VCs did not accompany the battery but Gunner 53537 Herbert George Darbyshire and probably Driver 68372 Frederick Alick Osborne served at Helles. For their part in keeping the guns supplied at Néry, Darbyshire and Osborne were recommended for the VC, awarded the *Médaille militaire* by France and promoted bombardier. Darbyshire was wounded when a 5-inch howitzer on the Asian shore shelled the battery on 12 July 1915. According to L Battery's war diary, Darbyshire died the next day. He is buried at Lancashire Landing Cemetery.

132   Belle Vue Gardens was a popular amusement park in Gorton, Manchester.

133   Meat and vegetable stew.

glad to have him with us. As usual, he was hopeful, and he brought me two letters. Poole was feeling ill and food did not interest him. We heard that Noel Lee had died from his wound, also, that Sergeant Flemming of the 6th was dead.[134] There was more lightning and heavy rain at night, and when I took my turn of duty from 10 p.m. to midnight, I sat in the rain wrapped in a blanket and a ground-sheet.

It looked like rain again on the morning of Saturday, July 3, but only a few drops fell on us. The day was quiet. Enver Pasha was rumoured to have visited the Turkish lines.[135] We wondered if his visitation would make any difference to us. Greenbank sent a message to signals SR and BS (6th and 7th Manchesters) that 'The OC has been pleased to authorise the following advances in Engineer Pay, dating from May 30, 1915. 6d to 1/– 2nd Cpl. Riley and L/Cpl. Williams,' which lifted mine from 2/8 to 3/2.[136] Our line was cut. Mending it, and collecting letters from the 8th, filled in some time. Poole had a rest while I went for the mail. Thomas called for talk and refreshments. Later on Vick came up. He told us that P.B. had said that he was going to teach his men respect for their officers. We thought and said that this was more than he could do. When we heard the rumours that the French had captured 50,000 Germans near Metz, we didn't believe it. The day ended with a show of flying, and shells at the aeroplanes were well aimed. For tea we had coffee and some chops Stanton had got hold of.

On Sunday, July 4, there was a big explosion behind the French sector on our right. We heard it was Turpenite, and that this was a new explosive the French were trying; but our explanations were often vague and inaccurate. We also heard that an ammunition dump had been blown up. Whatever it was, we heard plenty of noise and saw plenty of smoke. Then we heard that a French transport had been sunk. Later, this became a cargo boat.[137] Ormy and Feddan called,[138] and Pearson

134 Sgt 316 (216 on some records) A.J. Fleming, 6th Manchesters, died of wounds in Alexandria on 18 June 1915.

135 Enver Pasha was the Ottoman Minister for War.

136 Two shillings and eight pence, to three shillings and two pence per day (the equivalent of 11 or 17 pence in today's money).

137 The report was correct. The French transport ship *Carthage* of 5,600 tonnes was torpedoed by the German submarine *U-21* on 4 July off Cape Helles.

138 Probably Pte 1881 Frederick A. Fedden, 6th Manchesters, later Pte 3300, RE (TF), and finally Pte 444520, Royal Engineers. See Appendix IV, biographies of No. 4 Section.

followed them. Stanton and I had a long and serious argument. I don't remember the topic or the result, but I had five drowned flies in my tea.

At 3.45 a.m. on Monday, July 5, and during my term of office, the Turks attacked our lines to the left of Krithia Nullah. A message came, saying that they had attacked J12 and H12 trenches. At J12 they had been beaten off. The result at H12 was not then known. Both sides were shelling, and then the Turks started on our reserve trenches, and we were in one of them. They found us at 7.45 a.m. Business was brisk that early Monday morning. At first, we didn't take much notice, but when whiz-bangs started to arrive, regularly and frequently, we took a lot of notice and as much cover as we could. As usual, earth was flying about, and balls, singly, or in the clusters stuck in their smoking grease, were dropping against the parados and on the trench-floor.

After a time we thought we'd risk breakfast. We had the telephone on a seat in the parapet to the left of a traverse. The kitchen was a tiny fireplace to the right of the traverse, made against the parapet in a small hollow a few feet from the ground. The 7th headquarters kitchen was in a dug-out a few yards away.

I was at the telephone, so Poole went round the traverse to boil some eggs, and toast some cheese for me, as I didn't like eggs. Stanton, Ralston and Hargreaves were with Poole. A shell blew the mess-kitchen to blazes. I saw it full of smoke and litter. Shells were blowing chunks of parapet away. A whiz-bang burst near our kitchen and I heard Poole say 'If the Turks aren't careful, they'll crack these eggs,' and everybody laughed. When the eggs were boiled, Poole got them out of the mess-tin, saying to Stanton 'Look sharp Serj! They're hot.' Stanton put them on a blanket. Another whiz-bang arrived. There was a cloud of dust, shattered earth, dropping lead and iron. Some of the balls dropped at my feet. I had huddled up against the wall, as close as I could get. This one had burst over our fire-place. Almost at once I heard 'stretcher-bearers!' from round the traverse. I was a bit dazed, but I knew something had happened. Clifford, the 8th signal sergeant, who happened to be with us at the time, looked round the traverse and said 'Men hit. Round there.'

I said 'Is it Poole?'

'Yes.'

I left the telephone and went round. Poole was lying on his back on the ground, with a ball through one of his eyes. He was dead.[139] Long after, Stanton told me that he caught Poole as he fell, and with his own back to the parapet, supported him for a time. Before he died Poole opened his remaining eye and tried to speak. Balls from the same whiz-bang had caught Ralston. He had two in his back. Ralston fell down and tried to crawl along. Stanton put his foot on Ralston to hold him there, for whiz-bangs were so well-placed that he might have caught another if he had managed to get up. Our fire-place had been blown out.

We had dragged Poole into a hollow under the parapet and covered his head with his tunic, when another shell blew a great lump of earth on him, half burying him as it crumbled. Hargreaves ran down the trench and across to the 6th for Dr Norris, who came along immediately.[140] But this was only a matter of form in Poole's case. Then we had to think of the living, of Ralston and his wounds. His shirt had been pulled off, and as he was led away to a dressing station, I saw that his face was as grey as a dead-man's, and his eyes looked startled. I said good-bye to him and wished him good luck. Captain Creagh, the 7th adjutant, came along when he heard about Poole and told us he was sorry to hear it.

I had to get back to the telephone. None of us wanted breakfast. The first thing to be done was to write out a message to brigade signals, reporting Poole's death. Another message from CO to brigade was brought to me. I called up, but as no reply came and I was getting my own signals, the line was obviously cut. Everyone seemed to be busy, so I left the signal office to look after itself and set out to find the break. I followed the line, pulling it here and there, along the trench where it was laid, and found the break where a shell had burst on the parados. Just then there was a chance of several more breaks, for whiz-bangs were bursting over the parapet and bullets were flicking loose earth about. The parapet was low, and I crouched as close as I could get to it. There was no one in sight and I felt lonely, and more so as I knew that my old partner would not be waiting for me again.

A short piece of bared wire was sticking out of the loosened earth

---

139 Pte 1112 A. Poole, 6th Manchesters, died 5 July 1915, age 25. See Appendix IV, biographies of No. 4 Section.

140 Capt. A.H. Norris, RAMC, Medical Officer for the 6th Manchesters.

of the gap, and scratching in the opposite side I found another piece, pulled both sides until there was enough loose wire to fasten them, made the join and ran back to the telephone to see if I was through. As there was no reply and my own signals were clear, I went back to the break, unfastened the join, scratched again, found another spare end and tied that to our line. This time we were through. After telling Mall and Claude what had happened, I sent the messages.

We dragged Poole's body clear of the fallen earth, and then it was my job to empty his pockets and take care of all his personal belongings. Two pioneers of the 7th told me what to do with them when they arrived with a stretcher.

We took Poole down to Krithia Nullah, and buried him in a small level bank against the nullah-side, about twenty yards further up. Joe, Ormy, Claude, Haworth, Noble, Williams, Hopkinson and Pearson were there, all who could be spared. Tim did not come for some reason or other, and we wanted him. The Rev. Kerby's service was short. The heat was great and we had to hold our helmets up to shade our necks. A wooden cross marked the grave for a time, and now Poole has a grave and headstone in Twelve Tree Copse Cemetery, not very far from the nullah.

Ormy and Claude came back with me. We parcelled Poole's watch, papers and photographs, and later on I took them to Kerby in the nullah. He explained to me that he could not send them himself; they must go officially, through brigade and divisional headquarters, and we sent them the following morning.

After the funeral I was in no state to take on a duty for a time, and crawled into a shelter, but I could not sleep or rest comfortably, and turned and tossed about until evening when it was cooler and I felt better. Stanton had very kindly seen to the working of the telephone all day. When I left the shelter I went to see Stanton and Haworth who were in the nullah. By this time I wanted some food. Hopkinson had made what we called an Achi Baba pudding. This consisted of bread soaked in water, and half a tin of jam mixed with it, making a thick paste; and the whole lot was boiled in a mess-tin.

When we had eaten all we wanted we sat on the nullah-side, talking and listening to the tortoises splashing in the stream and the croakings of the frogs. We hated these noises, for nights were often made hideous with them. There were evenings in the nullah when they were the dominant sounds. We could hear the low voices of men in neighbouring dug-outs in the nullah-sides, and the occasional pop of a rifle, but louder than these were the splashes and croaks. The *Peninsula Press* for the day said that the Turks were using new recruits against us. It was sound propaganda, and may, of course, have been true.

I felt better next morning, Tuesday, July 6, after a good sleep. We wrapped up Poole's things in his cardigan and sent them to brigade. The day was quiet. I stayed on the telephone all morning, and then took a walk to BS where Noble said a few things to me about Tim, who, it seemed, was quite near us when Poole was buried.

Robinson, a man attached to our department, was looking after us now, and doing our cooking. Nothing was too much trouble for him, and he took his turn on the telephone, and extra turns as well sometimes. Then he would carry all our water. We never asked him to do anything. It was always done before we thought of it. He made a large Achi Baba pudding for dinner. It was too rich for me; but Robinson got rid of my share as well as his own, and he said he felt bad when he had eaten it. At this time we had more jam on hand than we wanted. We had five unopened tins, and two more with only a little taken out of each. There was plenty of rum about that night, and plenty of rumours as well. There seemed to be a connection between rum and rumours.

Having finished my turn, at 2 p.m. on Wednesday, July 7, and after some more Achi Baba pudding, I paid an afternoon call to Pearson, hearing more scandalous talk, and, also, that K—— had been too busy to enquire about King and Lewis, who had both been wounded, when L—— rang up. We didn't take any of these scandals very seriously, and they varied the monotony; as such we enjoyed them, trivial as they were.

While I was at the MV signal office, there was a big explosion just behind it. We didn't know what it was, and as nothing had touched us, we didn't care. We had no new rumours, but brigade sent up two parcels, for Noble and me. Mine contained a large slab of Peter's Chocolate and a pound of Mackintosh's Toffee, so there was chewing at the 7th headquarters later on, in the nullah.

Our station calls were changed:

MC (Brigade headquarters) . became ZLG (familiarly 'Zedel-ji')
WG (5th Manchesters) . . . . became MRE
SR (6th Manchesters) . . . . became MRE
BS (7th Manchesters) . . . . became MRG
AG (8th Manchesters) . . . . became MRH

Our division, now the 42nd, was YDB.

The 125th Bde . . . . became ZLE
The 126th Bde . . . . became ZLF
The 127th Bde . . . . became ZLG, as just mentioned.

On Thursday, July 8, the battalions changed places. We spent the evening chewing sweets and arguing, Stanton, Hargreaves and I, on war prospects, Stanton losing, and the debate ended with a friendly tea-party. Looking down to Cape Helles, at night, was a popular pastime; for the red and green lights of the hospital ships were still winking invitingly. We wished we could click for a berth on one of them, just a gadget-wound would have done, but we had no luck. We heard of men awarding themselves with wounds, but we found it hard to believe, and we could never run these stories to earth. All we could do was to watch the twinkling colours, hoping, yet without hope, that the day would come when we should be on board a hospital ship.

From the high ground where we were now living we could look down on the place where brigade headquarters was fixed near the side of Krithia Nullah. We saw shells bursting near it and if we happened to be talking to the brigade operator over the telephone, we gave them warning when shells passed over us:

'There's a shell just gone over. Look out!'

Brigade headquarters was shaken up often enough, and earth and dust fell on it. When anything had happened we enquired about damage, and full details were given to us. When messages were scarce, we spent a lot of time and portable electricity in conversations with brigade operators and signal masters. Anything would do, so long as we could find something to talk about.

One day, when Walker was doing some cooking for brigade head-quarters in the nullah, he happened to be stooping over a dixie on the fire when a shell burst behind him and a bit of it caught him on the back-side, without puncturing him. He jumped up, both surprised and shocked, at being caught bending, and he didn't hesitate to say so. After that, Walker warned anyone who happened to be about to be careful, as he had been hit on the back-side.

Taking a look round at 2.15 a.m. on Friday, July 9, I saw the light of a big fire on our left, and a smaller on our left-front. It seemed to be burning scrub. Between 4 and 4.40 a.m. I couldn't get an answer from ZLG, our brigade. Noble told M—— that he had been calling ZLG for an even longer time. M—— reported to Joe who sent for Noble and me to make reports. We arranged that ZLG should call up the battalions every quarter of an hour, and if no answer was received, a linesman would be sent out.

I had written to Poole's parents, and showed my letter to Claude and Haworth, as they were particular friends of Poole; but as both had already written, we decided that another from me was not necessary, and I destroyed it.

The evening was warm when Noble and I set out for ZLG, and I was not wearing my tunic. When the air cooled at sunset, I was chilled, and feeling generally out of sorts, so Noble lent me his tunic to wear on my way home. Vick had given me a Maconochie to take back. When I reached the 7th, I found that Stanton was feeling ill, too. A stiff rum gave me warmth and sleep.

When we woke on Saturday, July 10, there was a cool breeze; a complete change, after the heat we had endured. I left my tunic off but wore my overcoat as I sat at the telephone. While we lounged in the nullah, that evening, the Turks shelled our headquarters, the commu-nication trench, 'Stanton's Hollow' (that NCO's favourite resting-place), and they shattered the officers' latrine. An interesting Saturday evening.

On Sunday, July 11, Tim, Phillips and Thomas came to see us. The 6th Lancs Fusiliers relieved us in the evening, and Deadhead took over from me. We went back to the old bivouac where Noble had been mixed up in a shell-hole. There I split a Maconochie with Albert, had a talk with Newton, and wrote some letters. Hopkinson did some unofficial censoring.

CHAPTER 9

Stock-taking

About this time we came to the end of what may be called the second period of our time on the peninsula. No definite changes marked these periods, but they were noticeable. In the first weeks we were fresh and in good condition, then we settled down to routine, and now we were feeling the effects on health. Life, for those who still had it, was becoming very monotonous.

I have already mentioned the green, flowery and pleasantly wooded appearance of the peninsula when we landed. Then it reminded us of some parts of Cheshire. Now it was becoming shrivelled and brown, blasted by shell-fire, withered, trodden by armies, no longer pretty; it looked like a midden and smelt like an opened cemetery. Achi Baba had been a green hill, now it was brown and bald. We tried to imagine what the place would be like when the armies had gone. Achi Baba would be green again, the trenches would fall in and flatten, communication trenches, through which thousands of men had passed, would be long and shallow depressions, and frogs and tortoises the only inhabitants of gully and nullah. Sedd-el-Bahr would be rebuilt. Pink Farm and Krithia too. Turkish children would sell scraps of metal to ghoulish tourists. We should not like to be on the peninsula while tourists were there. They would defile it. How curious it would be if we could walk right up to Krithia and Achi Baba, without hearing a rifle shot echoing ... so we imagined. Then we woke up. A shot had echoed. We wondered what our area and lines looked like from the top of Achi Baba, as we surveyed him from many points, and what Krithia was really like, inside.

When we landed, I could carry all my possessions in a haversack. Now, I was carrying an infantry pack, two water-bottles, one on each side, and a third—officer's pattern—in a haversack. I had two haversacks, two mess-tins, infantry and cavalry, and three spare razors, for slicing meat and bacon. When I ran short of shaving-soap, I helped myself to a stick from a dug-out, the only theft I regretted. My camera case had worn out, so I made a new one from a khaki-drill trouser-leg I had found and the tape from an emergency ration bag. When envelopes were scarce, we used official OHMS, or folded message-forms, A, round the letters and stitched the edges. We had abolished the custom of having our letters censored. By giving our words that our letters contained nothing improper, it was easy to have several empty envelopes signed by officers we knew. I had five or six on hand usually; and we could and did oblige one another on demand. Adjutants were our chief sources of signatures. We rarely bothered our own officers.

* * *

We had already cut the knees from our breeches, and now we had cut off our shirt-sleeves above the elbows. This we regretted when the sun scorched our arms. Our clothes were dirty and ragged. We were scavengers, rooting in all kinds of rubbish-heaps for little bits of things we thought might be useful. We were in sympathy with all tramps and outcasts. We wondered if our mothers would know us. The best people would most certainly not.

A time came when we took to our Arcadian life. Ormy was our pattern. We wore helmets, shirts, socks and boots. We girded our loins with linesman's belts, or the part just above them. Our waists were more slender now, and perhaps more graceful than they were when we had waxed fat in Egypt. The sight of half-a-dozen of us gracefully reclining on the sward in the shade of an olive-tree would have tempted any watch committee. Some of us made a point of going about as improperly dressed as possible, and we did it for some days. Ormy went as far as to wear two helmets, one jammed on top of the other.

On Tuesday, July 20, Joe showed us a note from Tim relating to our dress and habits:

Men have been seen knocking about the brigade headquarters very inappropriately dressed, in fact very nearly nude, and this practice must cease.

There were two olive-trees whose shade was popular with us. We slept under one of them until its branches were trimmed by shrapnel. The other was further back, and in the open. We sat under it, listening to Joe and Mall as they told us all about the Turks. We were surprised to hear how illegitimate some Turkish ancestries were. When we were under that tree we were never allowed to lie or sit still for long at once. The sun was hot and the shade limited; and as the patches of shadow moved, we had to move with them. Those little gatherings under the olive-tree were very pleasant.

* * *

Some parcels had arrived for Poole after his death. We followed the rule that if anyone went west, parcels should be opened and divided, everyone sharing as far as possible. As we opened those for Poole we couldn't help thinking of the news on its way to the senders. Perhaps they had it already.

We enjoyed our bivouac evenings, after the cramped trenches and dug-outs. We paid calls, and we received company, dispensing such hospitality as we could afford. Some days we were rich; others poor, and glad to be invited to share a parcel someone had received from home. We made one-pence and half-pence bars of plain chocolate into drinks. We started serious cookery. I have already dealt with Achi Baba puddings. Besides these we had Krithia cakes. The recipe is as follows: powder army biscuit as fine as possible, grinding it with an old shell-case on a mess-tin lid, and damp powder to a thick paste. Collect dripping from meat and bacon rations (stored, in a bit of dirty newspaper, in an earthy recess in the side of the burrow), melt the dripping, mould the paste into little flat cakes, drop them in hot fat in a mess-tin lid, infantry pattern, fry until they are hot and spongy, and serve while hot.

Cleaning mess-tins was always a bore, so we left them until the fat had hardened and the next meal was ready, and then we took them down to the dirty little gutter in the nullah, cleaned the grease out with

mud or a wet sod, rinsed them in dirty water—no doubt full of germs—
and dried them on a bit of newspaper, a towel or on our shirt-laps.

There were several wells at Helles. They were round, and surrounded
by parapets a few inches high, of stone. We used them for washing
purposes. Sometimes we climbed down, inside, to the water; but usually
we lowered a weighted biscuit-tin or a canvas bucket, and then douched
each other, ladling the water with a mess-tin. We enjoyed this so much
that a wash of this kind often lasted a quarter of an hour, or even longer.

* * *

Sometimes our work was varied; more often it was very monotonous
routine. The hours of duty depended on the number of signallers at
battalion headquarters. They may have been two, three, four, or occasionally more, hours. In its simplest form our work was to lay wires,
repair them when broken, send and receive messages. Sometimes the
messages were full of interest, and sometimes there was excitement
in getting them through. Repairing breaks was even more exciting at
times. This was linesman's work, but we couldn't wait for a linesman
every time there was a break. At times these men had to turn out at
short notice, when brigade had called up a battalion without getting an
answer, although the line sounded all right. When we went out looking
for breaks we made as much of a holiday out of it as we could. Earth-pins
were scarce, so we made our own, using old bayonets, and new ones if
necessary, bits of shell-cases, pieces of tin from biscuit boxes, buried,
with a piece of bared wire fastened to them and to the telephone. After
a time the buzz of a telephone got on our nerves. It had the effect of a
strong acid on metal. We used the telephone for entertainment now and
then. For example:

Brigade rings up Abe's station.
ZLG: 'Hello! Is Lance Corporal Williams there?'
Abe: 'Yes.'
ZLG: 'Sergeant Ormesher wants to speak to you. Here you are.'
Abe grunts. 'Well?'
Ormy: 'Is that Abe?'
Abe: 'Yes'
Ormy: 'Can you swim?'

(We all knew what Abe said. It can be found in the Service for those Unnecessarily Disturbed.)

Another example: we had a signal for 'all stations' on our brigade lines. When things were quiet somebody would get hold of as many of our four battalion stations as possible and, having got the operators' attention, would shout:

'And they all cried with one accord—'

To which everyone on the lines answered, in unison, 'Wight ho!'

This was supposed to be Tim, indicating agreement. I think Ormy started the custom.

Tim's revolver amused us. It was cheap and Belgian, but it was the only one he could get hold of at the time. He had been wounded slightly by a splinter of shell. He was reported as a casualty but didn't go to hospital. He told me it was nothing.

Tim was a good brigade signal officer. I knew others as good, but none better, personally. His toilet was one of the wonders of Cape Helles. He never lost his neatness. How he did it we didn't know, but Claude told me that it took Tim a long time every morning. Of course, he had not to go pigging it. We grumbled at some of his tactical errors, but we knew a good man. And we knew that he had a good section. So did he, for he never interfered with us, so long as the stations were properly worked.

* * *

Papers from home amused us, particularly when they showed pictures of 'soldiers' happy faces.' One of these pictures showed three grinning guardsmen who had been close-cropped before going on active service. We had been close-cropped, but we had not seen anything in it worth making a fuss about. When that catch-phrase '… who has done his bit' reached us, we were hopelessly outclassed. We couldn't compete with it. We hadn't enough profanity to deal with it. As for 'King and Country,' that made us sick.

We had adventures in barbering. Noble was useful with horse-clippers and could remove surplus hair from the heads of his companions very efficiently. Any old dug-out would do for a barber's shop. One sight to be remembered was Vick shaving Hossack's beard with a safety razor. Hossack's face held a pleased expression.

Hossack was worth looking at when he paraded for a turn with a battalion. In addition to official equipment his belt carried a useful-looking hatchet, and dangling from the belt was a red cap which he had taken from a dead Turk. He had got hold of a periscope, and this he carried with a piece of string fastened as a sling, on his back.

I had dumped my bandolier behind some bushes, to save weight; but I soon thought it advisable to get hold of another one and had no difficulty in doing so.

The arrivals of mail were popular events. About this time some bags of mail were brought to brigade headquarters and dumped just outside my dug-out. At the time I was standing up, changing my shirt. I had just pulled it over my head and dropped it over one of the mail-bags when a shrapnel dropped a lot of balls. Some of them went through the bags and one of my shirt-sleeves had five small holes through it.

* * *

There were wonderful collections of odds and ends in and near the nullahs, trenches and dug-outs, and particularly on and in the parapets. We could pull out bits of equipment, clothing, old rifles, rusty bayonets, old mess-tins, and everything else men had left or thrown away. Parapets were also middens. Over them were tins, broken boxes, barbed wire, twisted and rusty; and immeasurable packets, clips and single rounds of SAA were lying about, mixed up with the parapet, or trodden into the trench floors. Here and there were broken periscopes, with shattered mirrors and splintered wood-work. Someone had used his respirator for a bandage. This bloody rag lay in a nullah.

Unburied dead lay between the two front lines. Many of the bodies had swollen in the heat until they filled out all the spare clothing. They looked unnatural and horrible, and some of them had been lying there so long that they looked like part of the ground. Clothing, equipment and bodies were returning to earth. I saw many so far decayed that they could hardly be distinguished from their rough surroundings.

* * *

Cemeteries and lonely graves were dotted about Helles, particularly in the gully and nullahs, and near the beaches. The groups of graves varied in size; so did the wooden crosses. Some of them were very primitive in the early days, before 'regulation crosses' arrived. At Clapham Junction, on the right side of a shallow nullah on the left, I found some scooped out places where there were old envelopes with 'Body here' or 'Bodies here' scribbled on them. The envelopes were stuck in split-ended sticks which were planted in the covering earth. At Clapham Junction a large wooden cross was placed at the point where a small nullah ran to the left of the main one. This cross stood out from the cluster of small ones around it, and it was known to all who passed Clapham Junction. It was a great land-mark. I made no note of its commemorative purpose. In the nullahs, the groups of graves became larger and more numerous, as time passed. Each grave had its cross, however primitive. Sometimes they were made from twigs, crossed, and tied together. Or, there were more elaborate ones made from flat pieces of wood, as previously described. Most graves were identifiable. We were more concerned with life and how to keep it than with death and how to remember it; but the graves of Gallipoli will be remembered by those who saw them or made them for their simplicity and often picturesque settings, as well as for their real purposes.

* * *

Figure 13. Signal 'office' at Helles. (Alec Riley collection)

The signal office is in a small dug-out recess in the second line. The tops are edged with sand-bags. On the floor, and in the middle of the dug-out, is a wooden box, used as a table, and growing more decrepit as it is used for firewood. On the floor is a mess-tin lid, holding the greasy remains of a meal. The mess-tin itself holds an inch of cold, milkless tea, waiting to be thrown away with scraps of bread and biscuits. Near it is a chipped enamelled mug, a dirty-looking thing, also holding cold tea.

Here and there bayonets have been stuck in the wall, and on their shafts are hung water-bottles, haversacks and clothing. A dirty towel dangles from one of the haversacks. The soap has fallen, and lies on the floor, gritty and dirty. Knives and forks, also, stick in floor and walls. Bits of old newspapers litter the place. Small earth cupboards contain unconsumed portions of rations, and candle-ends and their grease. Rifles lean in the corners.

The telephone hangs from a bayonet, and over a seat cut in the wall. On the seat is a pad of pink forms and some carbon paper. A roll of old messages waits to be sent to brigade. A dirty little stump of pencil is likely to roll off the seat, to get lost in the dust of the floor. Wires lead from the telephone to the open country above, and are suspended on bits of wood or old rifle-barrels, or lie in nicks cut in a trench-side, as they go down to the main line in the nullah. The earth-pin is a bayonet.

There is a primitive fire-place in one of the walls. Near it are pine-cones, twigs and chips from the packing-case.

Two men are living in this hole. One of them is on duty, sitting by the telephone. The time is between twelve and one in the morning and he is half-way through his period of duty. All is quiet, and he almost forgets where he is, until a rifle-shot reminds him as it echoes over the lines. The noise has a long, drawn out throb which continues for some seconds. Then all is quiet again. The only light comes from a single guttering candle. The man on duty looks round in the dim light, and at his companion asleep on the floor. His face would be white if it wasn't so dirty. The poor devil looks weary, worn-out. He looks quaint in his cap-comforter. It will soon be time to wake him. His ration of sleep will be finished; for these men can only have sleep by rations, or none at all. Loose earth rattles down on the telephone and fouls the contacts. The man on duty presses the key to hear if the thing will buzz. It buzzes, and the brigade operator wants to know what's wrong, and is disappointed when he is told, and says so plainly.

The man on duty wonders what is going on in England. In his own home. He sees, in imagination, the postman delivering the letters he has written ... it is breakfast-time there. How he wishes he was having it at home! His own bedroom would be empty, the door closed. The lamp in the road would be sending a patch of light on the wall ... he is dozing ... a rifle-shot rouses him, and he looks round at walls of earth and clay and remembers that there are odds against going home. Even if he stays where he is, the war won't stop, and there are plenty of others to fill his gap in the ranks; but if X—— was killed, life would be duller. However, he is still alive, and can write another letter. Too much thinking is bad.

It is time to wake the sleeper. Nothing happens when he is shaken and prodded. At last he moves, stretches himself, and asks what time it is. Three o'clock, and nothing doing. He gets up slowly and takes over the duty. The other man lies down, and as his eyes close he hears his relief settling himself on the seat for the worst watch of the night.

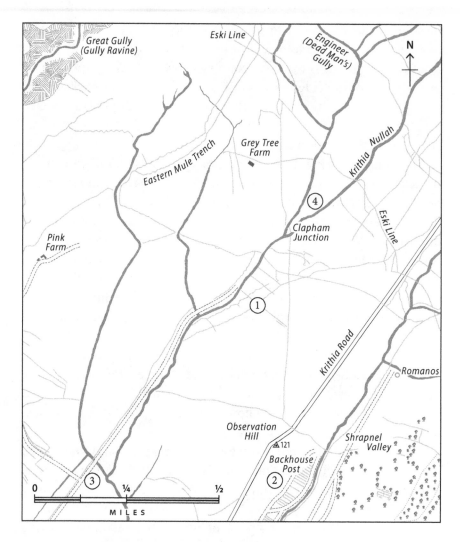

MAP 9

(1) Signal office, 11–19 July

(2) 127th (Manchester) Brigade HQ from 19 July. Riley stayed here 19–21 July

(3) 126th (East Lancs) Brigade HQ. Riley stayed here on the night of 21 July

(4) 5th Manchesters signal office, 22–29 July

CHAPTER 10

With the 5th Manchesters

A heavy bombardment on the left front woke me on Monday, July 12.[141] We were all up and about very early. Then another bombardment on the right started, in preparation for an attack by the French, who attacked and made good. A few strays and some odd rounds of shrapnel came our way. I drew my rations from the 7th Manchesters, making a profit in tea on the transaction, and cooked them at brigade. I had a morning of sleep, with my respirator-muslin over my mouth to keep the flies off. A mail arrived after dinner, bringing two parcels for me. I had received a surplus of mittens, so gave some to Claude and Haworth. We set to work on the box of Bourneville chocolate biscuits, clearing half of it at one sitting.

Something was happening in front. When we looked round to see what was going on, we saw some wonderful smoke effects on Achi Baba, where, once more, high explosives were sending up black, brown, yellow and white columns of smoke and fumes. The hill looked like a volcano.

Another bombardment started at 5 p.m. We saw four large and simultaneous explosions on Achi Baba, near the top. The hill was hidden in smoke. Krithia, also, a collection of ruins behind a thin belt of trees, was being shelled. Streamers of smoke, and high columns of it, rising from Achi Baba, made a curious picture, and we tried to photograph the effect. Krithia must have been hellish, from what it was receiving. It still kept a few red roofs, and the minaret was still standing.

141 The preliminary bombardment for the Action of Achi Baba.

To our left we could see the smoke from the navy's guns rising in clouds over the high ground behind the cliffs. The sausage was up.[142] The observers in it must have had wonderful views of the smoky panorama. We watched the show until we were tired of it, and then went back to our hovels for our evening brew of tea and a talk. I was sitting in one of the holes with Pearson. We were facing each other, and had just put our faces together to light one cigarette from another, and leant back to draw, when a bullet passed between us, just where our heads had been a few seconds before, and smacked the side of the hole. We said nothing, but we looked it. This day, Alex Sanderson, of the 5th Manchesters, was blown up at Clapham Junction. We heard that the shell had burrowed under his dug-out before exploding.[143]

On the morning of Tuesday, July 13, we heard heavy rifle-fire on the left, and apparently coming from the Achi Baba-flank direction. George Harrison was hit in the thigh but didn't go into hospital. We tried to take some photographs. Apart from the arrival of a few odd rounds of shrapnel, we had a quiet day. I shaved in the muddy little nullah-stream, and Noble cut my hair with horse-clippers, giving me as close a crop as he could, and close-crops were the only hair-cuts of any use to us there.

An Indian-paper edition of *Our Mutual Friend* had been sent to me from home. I had written, asking for it, at the time when literature was scarce and I had a sudden desire to read anything that had nothing to do with war. When it came, however, I found I was in no humour for Dickens; but I had something, now, that I could carry about and read when I felt inclined.

Claude told me that German South West Africa had surrendered unconditionally; but, as his source of information was doubtful, we were the same, and, anyhow, we were still on the peninsula.

At 4 p.m. Achi Baba's bald head was bombarded again, from the right, and once more we watched the smoking hill receiving all that was sent him without changing his shape.

In the evening I visited Ormy and Hopkinson. As we sat in their dug-out we discussed a way to win the war. The discussion developed

---

142 Kite balloon of HMS *Hector*, spotting for the guns of HMS *Prince George* and attendant destroyers.

143 CQMS 261 Alexander Sanderson, 5th Manchesters, died 12 July 1915.

into a detailed and intimate description of the Q—— family, in Manchester, who may have had good reasons of their own for doing what they did. The evening ended when Joe called, telling us to keep our respirators handy as the Turks were going to use gas. I stuffed two sets of waste into my muslin, damped it, and hung it on the dug-out side, within easy reach. Nothing happened.

On Wednesday, July 14, breakfast was poor, and we grumbled accordingly. When we had finished grumbling, I took a small party to the little pine-wood on our left. There were deserted trenches in the limey, strong earth where the pines grew. Between us we collected a good supply of pine-cones and branches for our cook-house fire. We were enjoying this little excursion when an 18-pounder gun, hidden in the trees, was fired, startling us, and causing some cursing. It was firing over us. We made the wood-collecting job last until we were tired of it. On our way back we met Stanton, who told me that our old friend Gresty had been killed by shrapnel the previous afternoon.[144] The shell had, apparently, done no damage—and then Gresty had been found.

Our active service pay books had been made up; mine, to 3/2 per day. When we reached our bivouacs Joe came round for signatures in receipt of our £5 mobilisation bounties. Truly the army moved in a mysterious way, its wonders to perform; but how dull the army would be without mysteries. They never ceased to amaze us.

After dinner some of us went to Gully Beach for a bathe. We enjoyed the bathe. What we did not enjoy was dressing ourselves again in the same lousy clothes. While we bathed, one of our monitors was firing 15-inch shells, and the Turkish guns were firing at the monitor. Their range was good, but they didn't score, and the shells, dropping in the sea near the monitor, sent up great splashes.

There were two monitors at this time, low in the water, and each of them had two 15-inch guns. We enjoyed watching them give a show, as we sat on the cliff-top looking down on the sea. We saw the guns parallel with the deck. Slowly, the snout of a gun would rise, until it had reached an angle high enough for his shell to clear the cliffs. Then, suddenly, the ship would be smothered in clouds of brown and yellow smoke, and, a second or two later, our eardrums rattled with the crash.

144 Pte 1313 F. Gresty, 7th Manchesters, died 13 July 1915.

We heard the shell purr over us and saw it make a nasty splash where it dropped and burst somewhere near Achi Baba.

We had plenty of fun and horse-play when we bathed. Humour usually took the form it does when boys go to the baths. We were all fond of water, and bathed whenever we could. There were dead horses, and much of the unsanitary, in the sea.

When we returned to the bivouac we found that the Turks had shelled it. An empty case had rolled into Barlow's dug-out. We heard that Gill, of the 6th, had been hit in the eye.

Feeling tired and lazy, I lay low for most of Thursday, July 15. It was a quiet day, with only such events as an issue of lime juice, and another of rum—six tablespoons per man. Challinor said that he had 'seen it in writing' that we were to go to Alexandria next week. We considered this, and decided that there was rum in the rumour. Joe was after Challinor about grub. At least he said he was. We wondered.

Late that night, or early in the morning of Friday, July 16, we heard mysterious sounds. They woke us; and when we had roused ourselves sufficiently to sit up and take notice, we saw a gun-flash reflected on the clouds over Asia way. We heard the soft purr of a shell in flight, a crash when it fell, but no explosion. More flashes in Asia, more crashes or thuds in Europe. Some shells hit open ground, others crashed through trees. There were no explosions. Before we were tired of listening, we had counted forty, and every one of them was a dud. We went back to bed. After breakfast Ormy and I went to one of the wells for a sluice, and after dinner we had another bathe at Gully Beach. It was a hot afternoon, and we wallowed in the sea for most of the afternoon, acting the goat as usual.

On Saturday, July 17, we were told that some of us would have to go out to battalions in the afternoon. We prepared ourselves by having another wash at the well. At 3 p.m., Haworth and I started for the 10th Manchesters, of the East Lancs Brigade. We had nearly reached the headquarters of the battalion when Lomax stopped us and told us that the move was cancelled, and that we could go back to our bivouac. On our way up the nullah we had very dry throats, and we had called, and had one, at every drinking place we knew. In most cases we had several. We were so dry that we drank at places the water was labelled 'Unfit for drinking.' We did not care. We wanted water and drank until we couldn't drink any more, and then drank more. Neither of us were feeling up to much, and we walked slowly, crawling along, from one drinking place to the next, making a long stop at each, and particularly at a place where the right nullah-side started to rise. Here we waded through thick mud to a little hollow scooped in the bank, where clear water trickled down to a shallow basin in the mud, where two inches of water collected when the basin was full. Some thoughtful wight had left 'jam-tins, 1, troops, for the use of.' The tin was there for weeks. It was part of the nullah equipment. Whenever we ladled water from the basin the rest was muddied, but that didn't matter. We drank it thick or clear. We drank in turns. When we had both finished, it took us some time to pull ourselves together. Haworth looked ancient. I felt it.

As soon as Lomax had told us to go back to the bivouac in the nullah, we decided to have a preliminary rest in the Redoubt Line. Here, two of the Lancs Fusiliers, seeing that we were not looking bright, took pity on us, and gave us some tea from their short rations. We were both very grateful. They gave us some rumours as well. The 5th Manchesters had, it appeared, gone up to the trenches, and had been sent down again. We only missed one drinking-place on our way back to the bivouac, where we had more tea and a Maconochie. We both felt as if we had had enough, and most of No. 4 Section was feeling the same.

Next morning, Sunday, July 18, Tim told Joe, who told the corporals, who told the other ranks, that the same pairs would go out again. Haworth and I were to report to Newton at the Lancs Fusiliers Brigade headquarters, a little way up the nullah.[145] We reported to Newton, and found the move cancelled again. Humphries was with this headquarters at the time. We spent some time with him. He was a problem, and we didn't know what to make of him. He was now very thin and had a gone-in look about him. It was not pleasant to see a man we knew going down the nick. A few shells dropped in the nullah so we took cover. One of them fell close to Noble. We returned to the bivouac where, at night, rumours were thick.

On Monday, July 19, I cleaned my rifle. I mention this because it needed a pull-through very badly indeed. Mine was not the only dirty

---

145 Second Lieut. R.S. Newton, 6th Lancs Fusiliers, OC No. 2 Signal Section, Fusilier (125th) Brigade.

rifle, either. Brigade headquarters was moved further back, to a bivouac near the 6th Manchesters lines. We were all tired after the move. Joe had booked dug-outs for the NCOs. There were six of us. He had, however, missed John; but John never failed to find a night's shelter somehow, somewhere. When John came along and discovered the situation, we enjoyed his oratory, and the ruddy tint of his remarks. Ormy didn't score by the way he treated the situation. It was humorous and could quite well have been left at that. This headquarters was in a shallow nullah, a few feet wide and from three to six feet deep. In due course we went to bed. The night air was damp. We had not been lying there for long when a strong smell of bodies reached us. We made several attempts but could not locate them all the time we were there.

Mallalieu and Claude had been signal masters at brigade headquarters for so long now that they needed a rest, and other NCOs took on the duty for a day at a time.

Tuesday, July 20, was my day. I did not enjoy it at all. I wasn't used to this work, and the heat was great while the shade was nil. I tried to write a letter but could find little to write about. I tried to read but could not settle down to it. A certain amount of work came along, and swarms of flies. Major Knight, the brigade major, didn't like new people, and new people didn't want the job, anyhow. No one was pleased.

There was a big red glare over the French lines at night. Some of us got up to speculate about it. Whatever it was, the fire was a good one. We heard it was petrol.

About this time, one dark night, J—— saw a distant but mysterious light. In righteous zeal, and with an eye to further enquiries, he aimed a stick at it, so as to have the direction marked by daylight.

When we bathed on the morning of Wednesday, July 21, we found that a strong current was running, and so did not risk going out very far. Vick gave me a Maconochie, and Ridings gave us his symptoms. He was feeling several, all at the same time, and we listened intelligently.

After tea we went to the East Lancs dump to draw some telephones and a commutator, and other things needed for our work, and then Berry and I went on to the East Lancs Brigade headquarters, in the nullah, where we spent the night in some very poor and shallow hovels.

* * *

Day after day, we watched the PBI going up and down the nullah, to and from the trenches. Some of them looked like old, tottering men, bowed, stooping, and most of their faces were colourless, except that they were grey or dirty. Now and then we heard some odd remark, but there was very little talking, and less laughing. There was so little to laugh about, now. Even when a smile was raised, it was very soon cancelled.

New arrivals were bright enough. They were surprised when we showed them Achi Baba and wanted to know what we had been doing since April. They knew all about it in a few days.

The greater part of Helles was under rifle-fire, strays, of course, in the further corners; and the whole of Helles was under shell-fire, except for a few stretches of shore, under the cliffs. There were no resting-places out of range of the Turkish fire, and there was no rest from lice, flies, maggots, smells, and very little from heat. It is true that the Turks could not fire on every square foot of Helles at the same time. Small scratches were becoming septic; enteric, dysentery, or some form of them, had caught thousands of men already.

* * *

Next morning, Thursday, July 22, the nullah was shelled while we were having breakfast. Berry and I went out to the 5th Manchesters, whose headquarters were in the sharp angle of ground between the main nullah and a shallowing one branching to the left. The angle was fairly flat on the top, and about twelve feet higher than the nullah level at this point of Clapham Junction. There was a small ridge along the angle, about 150 yards from the sharp point, and we had our headquarters at the tip of this ridge. The 5th Manchesters were in a reserve trench, a few yards in front of us.[146] We had room enough for three.

Clapham Junction had many dumps. There was one of old clothing and equipment taken from dead and wounded. At first, we did not like using or even handling anything taken from the dead. Now, we did not care what we used. Necessity had taught us not to care where the things we needed came from. We could either have them or go without them, and we soon got over our prejudices. We were often on the prowl for useful and liftable articles for private or professional uses.

146 A section of the Eski Line between Krithia Nullah and Engineer Gully.

There was a large ammunition dump at Clapham Junction. There were dug-outs for horses on the right, the water carts of local units were kept close by. We had not far to go for water—any cart would do.

Berry and I spent most of the day enlarging our dug-out and making it more comfortable. As it had been a latrine, we had to do a lot of digging, and it was hard work. The highest wall was on the side towards the Turks, so we arranged the signal office department against it, and sat with our backs to the front. A curving trench, three or four feet deep, led to or from the dug-out. We did not like the place at all. But we had some steak for tea, improving the outlook. Z—— arrived at dusk. I knew him of old and was not pleased to see him; but we had to make the best of him. He brought me some socks and a new mess-tin.

Innumerable and unopened tins of bully were lying about. We used them for building fireplaces. Old shell-cases, lying flat, at an angle to each other, made good fireplaces also. For fuel, we had cones and twigs, gorse and heather stalks, scorched dry in the hot sun.

Next morning, Friday, July 23, Berry was not bright, so I let him lie low while I interviewed the quartermaster in his store at the end of a narrow sap on the left of the small nullah. He would only give us tea, biscuits and jam for breakfast. (My diary calls him a swine.)

A draft of Kitchener's men came to the 5th Manchesters in the morning. They were the first Ks we had seen, except for a few we had passed in the train when we went to Southampton, in September, 1914, and they were drilling in civvies. We watched them carefully and curiously.

Shells were bursting behind the Eski Line, near Krithia Nullah, on our left, and our guns were bombarding Achi Baba. The Turks sent a few to our brigade headquarters as well. I went down to the brigade head-quarters later on, and found letters, a *Times* and a *Public Opinion* waiting for me; and a parcel as well, containing a Jaeger Balaclava, socks, gloves, chocolates, paper and pencils. Before leaving I interviewed Cooper, who gave me some good steak to take back with me. The line between the 8th Manchesters and brigade was broken, according to a report from Hossack, so I called at the 8th, and Hossack and I inspected the line. We found a break and repaired it, but not having a telephone with us, we couldn't tell whether we were through or not; and we were about to risk it, and go back, when I found another break. Having repaired this one we found, in due course, that the line was all right.

In the afternoon the Turks attacked on the left, but a message reported that they had been driven off with loss. Both sides seemed to be very nervous. I noticed that the Clapham Junction area was thick with scrap-iron, barbed-wire, spent bullets, shell and rifle ammunition. Shrapnel balls and bullets lay thick round some parts of our lines. Fire must have been highly concentrated at some earlier period.

On duty that night I had a private gorge of chocolate. There was bright moonlight, and in it I wrote letters and shaved, at 1.30 a.m. on Saturday, July 24. The dug-out was eight feet square. I have mentioned the high wall on the front side; the opposite side was low, and as I sat on the ground looking down the wider part of the nullah towards the Junction, and beyond, I could see flashes of Turkish high explosives as they searched our country.

When the moonlight failed, we lit our candles. They melted in the heat of the daytime, and we had to reshape them at night, pulling the wick through the soft grease until it was somewhere near the middle. Now and then, when we were hard up, we collected the guttered grease, rolled it into a sausage, and used it again.

From signs and rumours, the near future was full of promise. There would be much noise and all that went with it. Messages led us to suppose that the Turks would attack us shortly. In the meantime, they sent us eight rounds rapid. Ridings told me that they were duds. 'Rapid' and 'rounds' were known as 'wapid' and 'wounds' (rhyming with 'sounds'). As to the expected Turkish offensive, the whole show was offensive, to us.

A bursting shell wakened me in the early hours of Sunday, July 25. Z—— was on duty. Clapham Junction and the nullah were being shelled. In the brilliant moonlight I saw two men coming up the short trench to our dug-out. I could hear '— — ·— · ·' '— — ·— · ·' Brigade was calling. I knew what was wrong. Barlow, one of our linesmen, was now in the dug-out. Z—— had been caught asleep or awake by so few seconds that they did not matter. This was the end of his fooling. He had gone to sleep on duty, time after time, and we had dealt with him unofficially. In his favour, we knew he was entirely the wrong man for our work, and it was not his fault that he was doing it. Haworth had reported it to Joe, and there was trouble. Having compared notes with Claude, I went to brigade headquarters in the morning and had a talk with Joe.

Figure 14. Remains of an ammunition dump near Pink Farm in May 2017. (Michael Crane)

Later on, I went to Gully Beach for a bathe with Ormy and company. We had fooled about, as usual, and were about to leave the water and return to our clothes, which were dumped on the rocks or stones, when the Turks dropped a shrapnel on the edge of the Gully Spur. Sixteen men were knocked out. We made for the shore, and our clothes, as quickly as we could. While we were dressing, the stretchers were carried past us to a marquee. About half of the victims were stretcher-cases, and the others had gadget-wounds. In the marquee the stretcher-cases were placed on one side, and the slightly wounded on the other. As we were always more or less exposed, there were times when we forgot about it, and the Turks had not unlimited ammunition; but we were always ready to take a hint, and I made myself as scarce as I could when iron and lead were about. In the course of business, there were times when we could not do much about it, but we were not looking for accidents.

On our way back we met Forrester, Winn, Watson and Ellis, who were working a visual station near Pink Farm, and having quite a good time, except that the job was monotonous. There was a large ammunition dump near their station.[147] They showed us a hole bored in the ground at an angle of 45 degrees by a shell from Annie. The ground, at the surface, was split in line with the hole. Close by we saw a nasty looking snake, green, yellow and spotted, with a two inch diameter belly. He wriggled in the scrub.

Through our telescopes we saw the smoke of Kum Kale, which had been set on fire by shells from the navy.

Returning to the 5th Manchesters, I collected some steak and rice from Noble, and a Maconochie from Abe Williams. When I was back Tim came along to see me about the case of Z——. Tim's intentions were clear. I said what I could to ease the situation, and told Tim that Z—— had been bad all day and was not well enough to keep awake at night. Tim reported the case to the CO of the 5th Manchesters.[148]

We made an apricot-jam pudding for supper. We made it in a piece of respirator-muslin. Matthews called to see us. Occasionally, when we were using our bully-tins fire-place, one of the tins would burst with a sharp bang. Our primitive cookery was not without excitement.

From two to two-thirty on the morning of Monday, July 26, we couldn't get ZLG, our brigade, when we called. Then we heard Thomas on the line. The line had been cut, and Thomas had found the break and mended it. I was afraid it was another Z—— case and was relieved to hear that it was a real break. Z—— was like a damp-cloud. I went to brigade, and then for a bathe. Ormy and Noble were carrying out a series of aquatic experiments, and the rest of us were doing what we could to dish their submarine exploits. Poor Ridings was shocked at some of Ormy's infamies.

While we were having tea, at the 5th headquarters, the RSM came for Z—— and me.[149] We went to the CO's dug-out. I told Colonel Darlington that Z—— had been ill for some time. Z—— was far more

147 These deep ammunition dugouts can still be found in the wood immediately to the west of Pink Farm Cemetery.

148 Major Ernest Fletcher, while Lieut. Col. Henry Darlington was in temporary command of the 127th Brigade (7 July to 1 August). See Appendix IV, officer biographies.

149 Probably WO Class 1 5834 John Morrison, DCM and Mentioned in Despatches.

awkward than ill, really. He got away with it very easily. Twenty-eight days fatigues and sent back to his company. He had been well off with us, and we had warned him time after time; but he showed no signs of improvement, or interest in keeping a good job. I was glad to get rid of him, he caused too much worry and anxiety. I hoped there would be no more cases like his. Z—— was resentful. He blamed me, not realising that I had done all I could for him when he was in a dangerous position. I overheard two of our old soldiers sympathising with Z——. I was supposed to be asleep when these secrets were being broadcast. Neither of them had anything whatever to do with the case, and the value of these opinions was nil; but we were all gossips and scandal mongers in those days. Most of us had sick minds in sick bodies, and what Messrs N—— and K—— said about me was no worse than what most of us had said about others. Z——, however, had no sympathy from anyone else. He had been a nuisance in every signal office he had been sent to. No one would report him, however, as we knew what he would have to endure in the firing-line, and we could not send a man back to the hell of alarms, excursions and danger. N—— and K—— said what they had to say, to Berry, who also expressed himself freely, and not about his own business. Berry, again, was no worse than the rest of us. We had little to think about, and plenty of time to think a little, and a bit of scandal was a godsend to those of us who were not immediately concerned.

On Tuesday, July 27, Z—— turned up for breakfast, but he was sent off to his company. He reappeared, however, once or twice later on. It was a relief to have his case settled.

A letter from home told me that it had 'poured with rain' there. We should have welcomed a little rain, so long as it was not too much; for the sun was very hot. It seemed to be hotter than ever and my head was aching.

A battery had been brought up. Gun-pits were being dug about fifty yards from us, on the Clapham Junction side of our ridge. The diggers worked hard and quickly all day, the reliefs taking over in a few seconds.

Berry and Matthews went to clean themselves. On his way back Berry did useful work, bringing plenty of grub with him. A few shells came over but nothing serious happened. Price, of the 5th, came and sat with me while I kept my evening watch. He told me that there were now only four of the original Eccles and Patricroft Company of the 5th

Manchesters on the peninsula. This was typical of most of the infantry companies in our division. We had heard that we were supposed to be having a holiday saunter to Constantinople, few casualties, fine weather, and a good time. Who was the liar? Price told me about his West African trading days, and his opinions of missionaries, and then gave me an entertaining account of the way he and the vicar of P—— had crossed each other. I finished my turn with a night shave.

Next morning, Wednesday, July 28, we found a pleasant surprise waiting for us when we looked round. During the night the battery had brought its guns up and placed them in position in the pits. Their muzzles pointed directly over our dug-out.

We heard rumours of more inoculation, and, as usual, the suspicious ones announced their intentions of not having any.

We managed to have a bathe in the afternoon at Gully Beach. It was our custom to undress in some old dug-outs near the cliff, and then to walk along a stone jetty and dive from it. An officer was posted on the jetty to stop men from diving. This time he was asleep, so we crept past him, and I photographed him as he squatted there.

There was a coast road along the shore under the cliffs. Processions of men passed along it. Those who were going away from Great Gully looked as pleased as anyone at Helles could look; those who were going to Great Gully did not look pleased.

When I reached our office the fun started. The guns made it. Their shells just cleared our top-wall. They were close enough to give us the benefit of their blasts. Dust and earth were shaken down, falling on us, down our necks and breeches, and we found dust in our socks. We did not wear our tunics or puttees, unless occasions demanded them. Helmets or cap-comforters, shirts, breeches which were shorts nowadays, socks and boots, made our ordinary dress. The guns gave us flame, smoke, noise and loose earth, and every discharge shook us. We damned and blasted the bloody artillery until we were tired of doing it. Our heads ached, but we had to stick it. I padded the ear-piece of the telephone with a handkerchief, but it didn't make much difference. I held pads of handkerchief against my ears. Blasts of wind flew at us. When the battery closed down at night we were truly thankful. We had aching heads, but we slept well at night.

At 8.50 a.m. on Thursday, July 29, the guns started again, but we didn't notice them quite so much. In this office I kept my watch hanging on the tip of a root sticking out from the back wall. We moved up with the 5th during the afternoon, taking over from some Ks who did not impress us favourably. I had left my watch on its root and went back for it. The old dug-out was empty, but the watch was not there. I went on to brigade for letters. Joe Etrain was with us now. He looked after us well. His steaks were masterpieces. We amused ourselves by opening Turk cartridges, and extracting their neat little quarter-inch shells from the tip-cavities of the bullet points.

Friday, July 30, started with a scorching sun. We had a tired feeling. Our position was on the left of Krithia Nullah on Clunes Vennel. The signal office was in a trench, and the telephone was placed on a seat cut in the parapet. It had room enough for two. The battalion signallers, or attached men, had a home a few yards from ours. Ten yards from the office, a shallow trench met ours at right angles. We had a ground-sheet fastened over our seat. This kept the sun off and the heat in. The heat became hotter. The day's feature was our first issue of dried fruits, and Joe Etrain made a bread and currant pudding for dinner.

In the afternoon, a message arrived, saying that 'a decisive victory had been gained over the Turks on the Euphrates, and to celebrate it our troops in the firing-line would fire a *feu-de-joie* at 5 p.m., and the troops in the other lines would cheer.' There was great excitement, and we checked our watches with brigade time. At 5 p.m., we heard a crackle right across the peninsula, and a few high-explosives were sent to the Turks as well. We heard no cheering.

Joe Etrain and I took several water-bottles to Krithia Nullah for filling. We found a long queue at the carts so we left the bottles with Holmes who filled them for us, and we collected them later. A mail had arrived, bringing me letters and papers. Someone sent me some fizz-tablets which livened up lime juice and put a sparkle in it.

On the morning of Saturday, July 31, I went to Clapham Junction again for water. It was our custom to take all the empty water-bottles from our little groups when we went down to Clapham, and it took some time to fill them from the carts. The water was, of course, chlorinated. I had to wait in the queue a long time, and in the strong sun and heat, I didn't like it at all. Our telephone was out of order. Someone had to take it to brigade. This caused an argument. It would take some time to have the telephone repaired and therefore a long wait; and as there was nothing else to go to brigade for, no one wanted to go at all. After some words Berry took it. I had asked for a watch, and Berry brought back the only one we could have. That is, the only one brigade could, or would, spare. Our new watch was one of character. It had a gunmetal case, and no glass. Before long the large finger broke off, leaving a stump. We had to do something about it, so we stuck a thin grass stalk on the stump, and placed the watch in a small round Players' tobacco-tin, with a hole cut in the lid. We padded the tin with message-forms. When the CO asked for signal time I showed him the watch. He said quite a lot when he saw it, but the watch kept good time. Stanton came to see us. We heard a big noise on our left, and were told that a Turkish redoubt was being shelled. A message came through about the throwing of messages into the Turks' trenches. Five were thrown over from the 5th Manchesters. In the evening I went to see Noble and Stanton. It was windy and we saw lightning. We heard heavy but distant firing on our right. The 7th Manchesters were in the trenches behind ours.

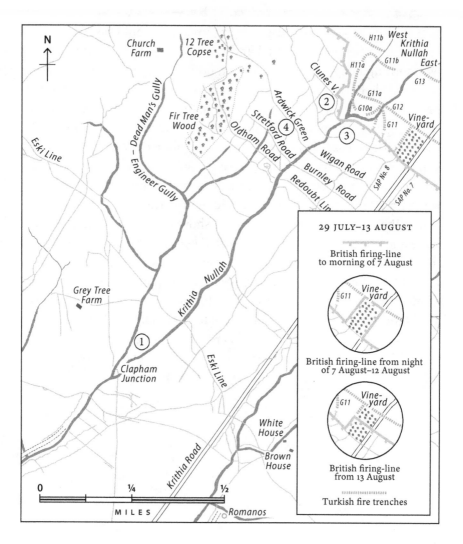

MAP 10

(1) 5th Manchesters signal office on 29 July

(2) 5th Manchesters signal office on 29 July–1 August and again 5–10 August
Also, 7th Manchesters' from 1–5 August and again 10–13 August

(3) Duplicate firing-line

(4) 7th Manchesters HQ after reliefs carried out on 5 August

CHAPTER 11

August

Sunday, August 1, was a busy day for our guns. A message warned our men to keep low. Firing was continuous throughout the day. The 5th and 7th Manchesters changed places, and X—— went to help Noble and Hargreaves. I was glad to get rid of him and his grumbling, and to be with the 7th once more. One of the 5th Manchesters brought us some Turk bombs. They were like iron cricket-balls. The charge was yellow. There was a ring on the iron case, and the fuse was tucked under an overhanging bit of metal fastened to a screw.

On Monday, August 2, I went wood-hunting with Livesey of the 7th. We explored a pine-wood on our left. This would be Fir Tree Wood or very close to it. We were now amongst the pines we had seen looking so black and ghastly against the sunset. We explored the wood in detail, and filled a sandbag with cones and twigs for our fires in the cook-house and trench, for we brewed tea at frequent intervals. There were deserted trenches amongst the trees. This place was an easy mark for snipers, who were marking a bend in one of the trenches at a point where it followed a rise of the ground. Here, a notice-board warned us to be careful. We were. I collected a razor, for slicing meat and bacon. Our guns were bombarding the Turk lines, and they were doing it all day. The noise was monotonous, and by this time we were not taking much notice of it, unless it sounded louder than usual. At times we hardly heard it at all. When anything dropped near us we heard that, and took notice, and cover, if there was any. Apart from our guns, some distant firing on our left front, and a few odd rounds passing over us on their

137

way somewhere-wards, the day was quiet. The distant firing seemed to be on the coast. From what I heard on the telephone, a show was due to happen on Wednesday.

We were kept busy with louse-hunting, or chatting, and a lot of energy was used in scratching and rubbing, undressing, seam-scouring, and louse-killing. When we scratched our legs the devils started their irritating movements in our shirts. However many we killed there were always plenty more. They were fruitful and multiplied, and who was he who could number them in all the land?

And so the game went on. Bullets and shells came and went quickly, but the heat came and stayed. If there was a foot of shadow on one side of the trench we crouched there until it was only a few inches wide; then we got up slowly and cursed the sun, and the heat radiating from all sides and the trench-floor. The sun hit us hard whenever we went into it suddenly from our little bits of shade. Green flies seemed to be fatter and more numerous now, and maggots and the smell from the dead were always with us. We were always thirsty, and we felt more and more miserable. Intestinal diseases were gaining ground, and septic sores were becoming more numerous. At first, only one here and there had a dressing or a bit of rag on finger, hand or arm, and we didn't take much notice; but after a time there were thousands of septic cases. The hospital ships still winked at us at night; but we couldn't go to them yet. If only a gadget-wound would happen—just a little one, to take us away from the hell-hole to a hospital and a bed to rest in! That was all we wanted, all we asked for, all we hoped for.

Near our home a short sap ended on the side of the slope down to Krithia Nullah on our right. From the end of it we saw the open ground round the nullah head. Some artillery men lived at the main trench end of this sap, and a young artillery officer had ordered one side of the sandy sap to be hollowed for the stacking of shells. Men who knew how risky it was to do this warned him; but he wouldn't be warned.

On the morning of Tuesday, August 3, there was an accident. While some of the artillerymen were sitting in the sap, the side collapsed on them. Sergeant Rose of the 7th told us that three of them were killed and the young officer badly hurt.[150] He cried, when he understood what

---

150   Sgt 845 W. Rose, 7th Manchesters.

had happened, so Stanton told me later. We were all depressed after this accident.

One of the 7th had got hold of a coffee-mill from the French, in exchange for some of our rations. This morning we had good coffee for breakfast, for it did not take us long to find something to grind in the mill, and it was a welcome change from never-ending tea. Ogden brought us more rumours of a big bombardment in the near future, and on the near Turks. We could feel it coming. We had rice and prunes for dinner, flavoured with dixie, but that didn't matter—we had not seen either rice or prunes for some time. When that was over, I went for a wash with Stanton and Lawrence. It was an important one for me, as I had not had one for some days. We wandered down No. 12 Sap to a miserable little place which failed to tempt us, and then we thought we might as well go further, perhaps as far as Gurkha Bluff, not knowing how far it was. Suddenly we found ourselves in Dead Man's Gully, near the Eski Line and the ruined Gully Farm. It was the first time I had seen this place since our very early days there, when it was part of the firing-line. A few men were going about their fatigue jobs, and some were knocking about Gully Farm in the open. When I had been there last it was fatal to show yourself in this district. Now it was as safe as London, or nearly so. It made me laugh, to think of that windy night when Hossack and I had been scared by a glow-worm, and how lights and noises, on and off, had frightened me in the dark; and the night when we jumped in a trench-latrine. It was funny now, but it wasn't a bit funny when those things were happening. Jokes like those took a long time to see. We found a washing-place in Dead Man's Gully and had a good swill. There was no equipment in the stream now, and all the bodies had gone. We sat on the top of the bank, and I told Stanton and Lawrence all I could remember of those early nights. I found the place where I had tripped over into the nullah, and the places where we had crouched while bullets swished through the grass on the tops. It was a bad dream of ancient and distant things. We sat with our backs to Achi Baba, listening to the rumble and crash of guns and shells. Looking over our shoulders, now and then, we saw smoke on Achi, and more in Krithia. We wondered when Krithia's windmill would be knocked out. Shells were plentiful to the left of Achi Baba. We felt as if we were at the war but not of it. Before very long we were in it again.

Next morning, Wednesday, August 4, we all had bad tempers. Stanton and I, however, were amicable enough with each other, and went off together to inspect local conditions in the firing-line. Here we discovered a trench mortar, one of the earliest patterns, dropping Garland grenades in a Turk trench a few yards from ours. The charge was smoky but did not make an unreasonable amount of noise; but the burst of the grenade was like a grinding-snarl, and the flying bits made sounds like whip-lashes. They made us shiver. We went to see the new 100-pound bombs, known to us as 'flying pigs.'[151] These were fired from mortars. A flying pig was about 40 inches long, including the bomb and the stem. The bomb was a cylinder eight to 10 inches in diameter and about 10 inches in length. Three blades were fastened to the stem, some distance from the end to allow the remainder to be placed in the mortar. The blades were to steady the descent. The pigs were stored in a recess dug into the side of the sap. We saw many processions of men staggering up the nullah with pigs on their backs, holding them by two of the blades of each pig. Rumours of the new show were now arriving thick and fast.

A white flag had been sent for, so that Major Ross could take a message to the Turks.[152] When the flag arrived and was shown, the Turks fired at it. Between 5 and 6 p.m. artillery was lively on both sides, and some of theirs came to our district, in fact, quite a lot came.

There was a waterfall in Krithia Nullah, near the end of the duplicate firing line.[153] The drop was too great for men to climb up to the higher level, even if there had been suitable foot-holds, so an inclined plank had been placed between the levels, close to the left nullah-side as we went up. We were warned to be careful here, as a sniper was marking our men while they were on the plank. He had already marked several men.

151 Flying pig was the common name for a highly destructive 150mm projectile that was loaded with a 40kg charge of high explosive (Melinite) and fired from a French Dumézil 58T No. 2 Mortar (often corrupted by the British to 'Demoiselle'). To the Turks they were known as black cats.

152 Major Edward Harry Ross, Leicestershire Regt. He had arrived on 10 June, to be attached to the Manchester Regt (probably the 7th Bn).

153 There were several duplicate firing lines at Helles. They were constructed to strengthen particularly vulnerable parts of the line. Riley is referring to the duplicate firing line that ran behind the firing-line and the redoubt that overlooked the east branch of Krithia Nullah. Its left was in Krithia Nullah, about 100 yards from the bifurcation. Its right lay close to where G11 met the firing-line.

Recent casualties were reported as one man killed, and others seriously wounded. In the evenings this particular spot was weird, when the red glow of sunset was reflected on the light earth of the nullah-side, the tortoises splashed in pool or stream, the bull-frogs croaked and the sniper's rifle cracked.

It was a year since war had been declared. We wondered if it would ever come to an end, and how long it would be before we were back in England. We often wondered about it.

Before dinner, next day, Thursday, August 5, I went to the end of the short sap, where the artillerymen had been buried. The sap was full of planks and earth, and we had to climb over these to reach the far end, where Sergeant Rose had a shooting-gallery. Here he kept one or two rifles and plenty of ammunition. We called at the gallery several times for shooting practice at the Turkish lines down the slope to our right front. We splashed their sand-bags often enough, but I don't think we hit anybody. I didn't want to hit a Turk, particularly. Long afterwards, Stanton told me that on one occasion his companion's bullet hit a Turk's spade while he was using it. The Turk popped up and shook his fist. Stanton, scenting danger, said 'Come on!' and he and his companion cleared out of the gallery, quickly, and luckily, for the Turks sent four whiz-bangs which landed close to the gallery. Stanton said that I was his companion but I cannot remember the incident. Nor can I remember the dummy the Turks put up, with a sniper hidden on one side of it, waiting to fire at our men when they shot at the dummy.

Many dead were lying out in front and near the side of the nullah. Some had been in our brigade. There were bodies right up against the Turkish lines. They looked as if they had finished their share of the war quickly and cleanly. It was a strange and gloomy landscape. Yet, at times, this landscape of dead men was one of quiet and rest, rather than of bloody war. It was hard to realise that we had known some of these men, that they had seen Krithia and Achi Baba before them as we did, that they could do no more now, and that they must lie out there, unburied. It was a strange picture, and it had a certain grandeur about it.

The big guns were busy again, and again the Turks sent us a few rounds. The heat was great, and there was no breeze. The only stir in the air seemed to be that made by the green flies as they buzzed round us—when they were not occupied in defiling our food.

That afternoon the 5th and 7th Manchesters changed places, and we were with the 5th once more. Tim came round at tea-time and told us that we must patrol the line to the 7th signal office hourly, and that we must see that the artillery signallers, or others, had not been putting their lines in our staples. In short, that the line generally, was intact. Our lines were laid in nicks in the side of the communication trench, and the artillery people and others had made a habit of interfering with them, tapping in, pulling our staples out and putting their own lines in. I arranged that we should take duties of two hours each, patrolling the line at the end of each duty. The 7th headquarters was near the junction of the communication trench and the reserve line. Once, when I reached the 7th, I found Noble enjoying himself. He had just burnt some holes in his tunic, respirator, smoke-helmet and slings. And not on purpose, either.

Meanwhile, signs and omens told us that the new show was nearly due. We heard that it was to happen the following day. All kinds of preparations were being made. Dummy heads and shoulders were made and placed in readiness to show to the Turks and draw their fire. The REs had made plank bridges over the trenches, and little white flags were placed, to mark the position of the bridges, to guide the infantry when they crossed the front lines. Tim came along and told us that our station would be the most important one in the attack.

The 29th Division was next to ours and on our left.

When we awoke on the morning of Friday, August 6, our trench was full of Worcesters of the 29th.[154] The greater part of that division was on the far side of the communication trench. The Worcesters moved up to where the Munsters were. Then the East Lancashires, wearing red armlets, went up to the firing line.[155] Our lines had gone wrong, but Tim, Vick and Ormy soon had them in order again. Nothing happened until 2.30 p.m., when our bombardment started. Unfortunately, the Turks were of the same mind, and bombarded our lines. Both sides were noisy, and the Turks gave us plenty to be going on with.

154 See VIII Corps Order – Special, 6 August 1915, which Riley includes in his 'Additional notes', presented in Appendix VII.

155 A, B and D companies, 5th East Lancs, provided the 'garrison' for the division's entire firing-line.

At 2.13 p.m., I sent a message to brigade:

Battalion in position.

It was handed in at 2.09, from Colonel Darlington, OC, 5th Manchesters. The noise increased. The air quivered, and the earth shook with explosions. Shells, mostly shrapnel, were bursting unpleasantly close to us. June 4 seemed to be outdone.

Up went our flying pigs. We heard the muffled pops of the mortars, and watched the ugly wobbling pigs go up, and then drop, slowly feeling the steadying effect of the wings and landing nose down. They ascended about 400 feet. When a pig dropped there were three or four seconds of suspense, and then we saw great, dull red horizontal flashes, thirty or forty yards on each side of the burst. Even our own trench rocked and shook with the explosion, while earth and debris fell over us. To the Turks these things must have been devils from hell. They looked terrible to us. Then the Turks shelled us again. Bits of smoking metal, balls singly or in clusters, still in their grease, which smoked in the heat of the explosion, fell in our trench. We might have stopped something at any time. We shouldn't have been surprised. Rifles and machine-guns were hard at work. As usual we were dazed, we couldn't understand much of what was going on. The communication trench passed through ours, and in front of our line, leading off from the CT, a shallow trench had been made. Some of the 5th Manchesters were in it, waiting to go forward, over the smoking ground. Leaving the signal office for a few minutes to have a look round, I happened to be at the end of the shallow trench when the 5th had the word to go. I saw them get up, and as they scrambled over the rough ground, I tried to take a photograph. We had had some rough words with a few of these men, about interference with our line. The line seemed a trivial thing, compared with what these men were facing now. My photograph failed, but I took another of the battlefield.

We had 'priority' on our line, but for some time very little came through either way. Meanwhile high explosives were wrecking our trenches, and we could feel the heat and wind of shrapnel bursting near us. We could also hear the thuds of the showers of balls and fragments of metal, nose-caps, shell-cases.

At 4.10 p.m., Colonel Darlington sent a message to brigade:

> Have captured parts of H11a and H11b. AAA. Will send details
> when I receive them. AAA. Enemy shrapnel heavy.

It took me six minutes to get this through.
At 4.40 p.m. the next message came:

> Have captured H11b. AAA. Attack on H11a failed. AAA. Have not
> enough men left to capture H11a. AAA.

This one was through in three minutes.
At 5.35 p.m. I sent this message:

> Attack on H11b and H11a failed. AAA. H11b was dummy trench at
> north-west end and we could not hold on owing to enfilade fire.
> AAA. Am organising garrison in our original firing line. AAA.
> Cannot get into touch with Worcesters. Turks hold south-west
> end of H13. AAA. Afraid our casualties heavy. AAA. Am putting
> one hundred 7th Manchesters into present firing line.

At 5.55 p.m. I sent:

> Message from Worcesters (88th Brigade) sent from OC
> Worcesters states reinforcements urgently required. AAA. We are
> unable to supply. Adjutant Worcesters confirms this in person.

This was through at 5.55 p.m.
At 6.25 p.m. I sent:

> Remainder of my battalion estimated about 200 strong.
> Fifty 7th Manchesters and East Lancs garrison are holding our
> original firing line. AAA. Position is as before the attack. AAA.
> Considerable number of men missing.

* * *

The dressing station was ten yards from the signal office, at the junction
of the communication trench with ours. A few seats cut in the parapet

of our trench, near the corner, were kept free, as part of the dressing station. Two stretchers were on the trench floor in readiness. The MO and his men waited.[156] His case of instruments was open. A wounded man came down and was attended to, quickly; and then the wounded came down in strength, passing our office. Some had very little clothing on. That of others was torn to shreds. The MO worked quickly. He took his tunic off. But however fast he worked, he could not cope with the numbers who crawled or staggered to him. Amongst them were some of those who had argued the point with us about our line, not long before. We hardly recognised them. They were muddy and bloody, dirty and torn. Khaki was dark with soaked blood. There were bloody dressings on heads, arms, hands and legs. Men sat on the trench-seats, staring but not seeing. They were struck deaf and dumb by shell-shock. Some of them were muttering; others shook in every limb. The MO worked harder; but however hard he worked, he could not keep up with the numbers.

A man crawled past us using both hands and one knee, dragging the other leg along the ground. Another man came past whose face was a bloody mask. Only his eyes showed through it. The MO was as gentle as possible. He did not handle a single man roughly. He might have been attending to children. But he was tiring and needed a short rest. The stretchers were occupied, time after time. It was slow work, carrying them down the narrow winding trench, and then returning with them empty. The trench was crowded, and the dressing station was exposed. Shells burst round us. The trench shook with explosions. Dust and debris fell on the dressing station and on us. Two shells burst near the corner, and the place was full of smoke and dust. The MO went on with his work, looking over his shoulder, now and then, when a shell had burst close by. He was doing his very best. He had been unpopular at times; and we remembered him refusing to attend to a man whose cheek had a scratch by a bit of metal at bomb-practice. That was forgotten now; for, whatever he may have done in reserve, he delivered the goods at the dressing station.

* * *

156 Capt. F.W.A Stott, RAMC, attached to the 5th Manchesters on 16 July 1915.

Above the general noise we heard a loud crash; and peeping over the top, quickly, we saw that the pig had blown up a portion of a near Turk trench. It must have been one of their offices, for papers came fluttering down through the smoke, and a lot of clothing dropped as well.

General Lawrence, our brigadier, came to the telephone arranging for further attacks by 200 of the 7th Manchesters.[157] He spoke to division, and pleaded that our men had done all that could be expected. Again and again, he asked that it should stop. There were tears in his eyes as he spoke. Hundreds of men had been lost. As I was wearing the earpiece, I heard the answer 'No,' from division.

The attacks, as such, had failed. They had, however, held the Turks at Helles, while something was happening elsewhere.

There were some guns a few yards behind our trench, and their shells whizzed over us. Looking round, we saw columns of smoke of all shades, splashed with red flashes. The ground rocked and trembled. We could hear neither the telephone nor the buzzer clearly when brigade was sending anything through. Our heads ached with noise, shaking and strain. I found myself looking at our watch. I dropped it, and the works stopped. I played with it, teasing the wheels with a needle and a safety-pin, and managed to set it going again.

At night there were bursts of rifle-fire, odd shells and flares. We expected attacks, but none came. We were wretched, depressed, downhearted.

A message came in for brigade. It was scribbled on a leaf from a field service pocket notebook. Its office of origin was the 7th and via the 5th. It was timed four minutes past twelve, on the morning of Saturday, August 7. I don't remember when we received it, but I remember that I had great difficulty in reading it. I filled in the details of a message form. It was this:

> A messenger has returned from the OC first party that went out.
> AAA. He says they cannot find the Worcesters trench. AAA.
> He found wounded Worcesters but could get no information to
> help him. AAA. The OC Worcesters does not know where his

---

157   Brig. Gen. Hon. H.A. Lawrence, KCMG, had assumed command of the 127th Brigade on 21 June 1915. See Appendix IV, officer biographies.

battalion exactly is nor has he got into touch with them. AAA. An NCO of the Worcesters had just brought in a party of 12 who were holding a bit of trench about 60 yards north of H11b. They had Turks on their left and right and had to retire. AAA. Our men are in three parties now in the right direction but evidently not in H13 and have been instructed to try and find out by patrols where the Worcesters are. As far as I can gather it seems very doubtful if any part of H13 is in the hands of the 88th Brigade. AAA. The patrols who have come in from our parties report that the Turks hold H13 and are firing heavily from it.[158]

Early that morning we knew that there was to be another bombardment, and assault on H11a and H11b, by composite parties.[159] There was the usual noise, the shaking of the ground, shrapnel on all sides, and the bits of metal, smoking hot, dropping about us. An empty shrapnel-case bobbed over the parapet, dropped on Berry's knee and rolled down between Livesey and me as we were sitting on the trench seat in the parapet. I looked after the telephone until 2 p.m.

The composite parties attacked.

At 11.22 a.m. I sent a message to brigade from Colonel Darlington:

Attempted to take H11b at 10.45 but did not succeed owing to very heavy rifle and machine-gun fire. AAA. Have not taken H11a. AAA. H11b must be flattened by artillery fire before it can be taken. AAA. Would require 200 for H11b. AAA.
Men somewhat demoralised by shelling of our own guns. AAA. Afraid they are not up to another assault today.

---

158 A and D companies, 7th Manchesters, were ordered to attack H11a and link up with the Worcesters on their left. After the Manchesters had gone forward, they lay down in a line in front of H13, supposedly held by the Worcesters. Capt. A.E.F. Fawcus, OC, A Company, went forward to make a reconnaissance of H13, and came under heavy fire from Turkish troops still holding the trench. Fawcus' miraculous escape is recorded in the divisional history: 'That Captain Fawcus returned safely was amazing, his clothes being riddled with bullets.'

159 This composite force was made up of a number of 5th Manchesters and 100 men from C Company, 9th Manchesters, under two of the 9th's officers, Lieut. Samuel Porter and 2nd Lieut. S.W. Ruttenau. Ruttenau had several lucky escapes and survived but Porter was killed as soon as he got over the parapet. Four other 9th Manchesters were also killed and another 21 wounded.

Once more the long procession of wounded, dirty, ragged, torn and bloody men came down to the dressing station; once more those who were deafened, shaken and quivering sat still on the trench-seats, their eyes fixed vacantly; once more the MO worked as hard as he could; once more shells burst about us and the dressing station, filling the trench with yellow, stinking fumes, while dust and earth dropped on all of us; once more our heads ached with the strain and noise, and we were lucky to get away with that.

Some of the 7th Manchesters were lying, wounded, about 25 yards in front of their trench; and they lay there all day, in the hot sun, not daring to move until night, when some of them might be able to crawl slowly and painfully back to our lines. A shell-burst blew Major Cronshaw over, shaking but not wounding him.[160]

We had difficulty, again, in reading our buzzer when heavy firing was going on.

At 12.33 p.m. I sent an urgent message from Captain McLoughlin to field artillery:

> Turkish reinforcements coming down Right Krithia Nullah.
> AAA. Their fire trenches are already very strongly manned.
> AAA. Infantry expecting counterattack. AAA. My line still cut.

I saw Price of the 5th. He looked thin and ill; but the great thing was to be there at all, not how anyone looked or felt. The Manchester Brigade was only a skeleton now, its four battalions unrecognizable from what they had been three months before. The ramble to Constantinople was easy.

A message came through, saying that a division had landed at Anzac. (This probably indicated the Suvla landing.)

We heard that Corporal Stanton had been killed. Our old companion McCartney of the 7th was killed.[161] He had won innumerable medals, daily; but his medal was his identity disc, and everyone had a disc.

---

160   Major (later Lt. Col.) Arthur Edwin Cronshaw, DSO, 5th Manchesters. Mentioned in Despatches.

161   L/Cpl 2409 Harold Spencer McCartney, 7th Manchesters, died 7 August 1915, age 18.

It was Saturday afternoon. The trenches were crowded with dirty, ragged, worn-out officers and men. They sprawled everywhere, many of them asleep, and we trod carefully so as not to disturb them. It is impossible to describe how these men were living. Tall men slouched, thin, round-shouldered, bandaged over their septic sores, dirty, unshaved, unwashed. Men were living like swine, or worse than swine. About these crowded trenches there hung the smells of latrines and the dead. Flies and lice tormented men who had hardly enough strength left to scratch or fan the flies off for a few seconds. The August sun scorched us, for there was no shade. No photograph could show the misery of those trenches that Saturday afternoon. Dressing stations were busy with lint and iodine, helping the innumerable septic cases to hold out a bit longer, for it could not be cured on Gallipoli. Men worked mechanically because they were used to their duties. Discipline and practice had done that much for them.

When we could move I drew some letters from the next battalion headquarters to ours, where they were waiting for me. I heard that there were other letters for me, but some ass had put them on the parapet and I didn't get them. They may have been buried.

Kerby, the chaplain, had been knocking about in the forward trenches during the scrapping. What, exactly, he was doing, I don't know. I met him several times, and we discussed whatever situation happened to be important at the time. Anyhow, he was a change.

At 9 p.m. that night, the Turks attacked, but they had no luck. Our pigs went up, and returned to earth to shatter it, and shake us, and give forth their loud whangs. We finished the day with an issue of BDVs,[162] and the news that the Lancs Fusiliers were supposed to be holding a captured trench on our right, near the Vineyard. The fighting in the Vineyard had been very severe from what we heard; but it was not on our front, and so we did not hear much about it until later.

---

162 BDV cigarettes, manufactured by Godfrey Phillips Limited and sold under the slogan 'Mild and Sweet.'

Figure 15. Photograph taken around 1930 of a trench running through the Vineyard. Twelve Tree Copse Cemetery can be seen in the far distance, on the left of the image. (Alec Riley, *Twenty Years After*)

Flying pigs rang the bells on Sunday, August 8. After breakfast I had a stroll round the firing-line. Many of our own shells had dropped here, and I heard plenty of tales about the damage they had done, and what our men thought about our gunners, and said. Just before we got there a 5-inch howitzer shell had burst in the trench. There was Karno artillery-work going on. The trench was full of bloody debris. The dead and wounded had been removed, but the torn and bloody equipment, most of it bullet-riddled, broken entrenching tools and other litter, mostly brown with blood, told their own tales. From a stained webbing pack I took a spoon and other things I needed. A body lay on a stretcher. As it was covered, we knew it was going to a grave and not a dressing station. The earthy parapet and parados and the traverses were all blown about. I saw a muddy active service pay book lying on one of the tops. I found a heap of field service postcards, took as many as I wanted, and filled in a few of them for various people. Then I captured a supply of AF o.[163] Worth its weight.

Hossack had been at a part of this line where it was blown about and wrecked. Many men, scrambling up the ladders for the charge, were hit before they could reach the top, and one or two of them had fallen back on Hossack. The ladders were blood-stained.

Hossack was with Major Worthington to the left of the Vineyard.[164] Our men wore their cap-comforter in such a way that they resembled the Turkish helmets (which were smaller than ours) and this resemblance was the cause of many casualties—from our own men.[165]

When we had a chance to call an unofficial roll-call we were glad to hear that all No. 4 Section were safe.

* * *

I saw Cronshaw talking to some of his men. One of them was a thin pale lad, ragged and dirty. Cronshaw was doing his best to cheer the boy. He asked him how he liked soldiering. He was only seventeen. I heard Cronshaw say 'Poor lad.' The other men standing about, dirty, ragged, tired, all looked badly in need of cheering up. A few of them were wearing helmets, but the usual head-dress was a cap-comforter, folded into a queer-looking two-cornered cap. Everyone wore them, at times, like this. There was very little talking, and what there was came almost in whispers. No one by any chance laughed. We saw that the eyes of most men were dull and vacant. We came to the stage of quiet speaking, except on the telephone when we were angry and shouted at the man at the other end of the line. When we left the trenches we livened up, and lost some trench-heaviness.

When we were back at the signal office we found that Berry had boiled some bacon. With this, coffee with sugar in it, and dried figs, we began to cheer up.

Two officers came to us. They were exhausted. One of them could not drag himself further without a rest. I had a word with him, and gave

163 Toilet paper, also known as 'Army Form Blank.'

164 Major (later Lt. Col.) Claude S. Worthington, OC 6th Manchesters. See Appendix IV, officer biographies.

165 Riley attributes this information to Hossack in his diary. The note is dated August 6–7.

him some small packets of boric powder I had removed from someone's dug-out. His feet were sore, and he could only limp slowly, so he was grateful for the powder. Another officer came along, and asked if we could give him some food. There was none in his part of the line. We gave him all we could, at short notice, water, jam and broken biscuits. He was a very young subaltern.

There was little to distinguish officers from men, now. Junior officers wore men's tunics, and carried rifles and packs. Their responsibilities included the enduring of hardships, and the sharing of them with their men. However, when the Manchester Brigade was on Imbros, there was saluting-drill, just to remind all ranks that they were soldiering.

Candles and pads of message forms had been sent up to us during the day, and Noble gave us another spare candle.

That night I heard Major Knight, our brigade major, tell Capt. Saunders, the 5th Manchesters adjutant,[166] that the Turks in front were from Adrianople. They had found out how weak we were, and would probably attack us. They shelled us, and left it at that.

Early next morning, Monday, August 9, our patrols crawled out and heard the Turks talking and chattering. From the amount of noise, it was concluded that H11b was more strongly held than before. The day passed quietly. Lawrence brought me a new water-bottle, a towel, papers and a letter from home. Stanton and I had a walk to Dead Man's Gully. We also had words about the signal service and the infantry signallers attached to it. This argument followed the general rules and got rid of the time nicely. It was the old story:

> God made the bees. The bees made honey.
> The infantry do the work. The REs get the money.

Well, we couldn't help it.

We explored some old trenches. Bully and biscuits littered this place. I found another razor and some rifle-oil.

Evenings, now, were rather damp, and on the damp breeze came the smell from decaying bodies. In some parts of the line the smell was so

---

166 Capt. (later Lt. Col.) John Malcolm Brodie Sanders, MC, Leinster Regt, attached to 5th Manchesters. Twice Mentioned in Despatches. See Appendix IV, officer biographies.

strong that we seemed to be eating it. An extra puff of damp air brought it over at double strength. This awful stench is beyond description. It is bitter, horrible, sickening.

Our guns opened fire at 7.50 p.m., and kept at it for twenty minutes. The Turkish answer was feeble. Then came very heavy rifle and machine-gun fire on the left, continuing for some time. When it died down, we heard our men yelling and cheering, again and again. This was a welcome sound. Something good must have happened. It had. The Gurkhas had taken a trench, and the Munsters made the noise; to mislead the Turks, we heard.[167]

At 7.50 p.m. we sent this message to brigade:

> Captain Syers' trench mortars have bombarded G11a and communication trenches at intervals during day. AAA. G11a has been practically dismantled, traverses blown in. AAA. MG and snipers were able to get at Turks bolting in open. AAA. Mortars' pits were found by Turk artillery about 1515 and pits partially blown in. AAA. Mortars undamaged no casualties. AAA. Please inform 29th DA and ask for instructions for Capt. Syers.[168]

On the morning of Tuesday, August 10, a heavy gun, placed behind our lines, opened fire. It was in a trench just behind ours. Whenever it was fired it gave us every benefit of the discharge except the shell. Otherwise, the day was quiet. Stanton and Berry went to several dressing stations and hospitals, to find news of Stanton's brother, but they heard nothing about him. Noble came up for sight-seeing purposes. Many dead were lying in the open, the results of charges, some near the Turkish parapets; but it was better not to look at some of the little heaps of khaki too curiously. So far we had heard nothing more about

---

167 The 29th Indian Infantry Brigade had been attached to the Australian and New Zealand Army Corps. On 9 August, the Gurkhas were fighting below Chunuk Bair.

168 Probably Capt. (later Major) Thomas Scott Syers, MC, Royal Field Artillery. Died 14 November 1918. Syers was using a heavy French Dumézil 58T No. 2 Mortar that fired 'flying pigs'. Col. Darlington mentioned this episode in a letter to his wife: 'Yesterday [9th] we had what is called a "combined hate," our machine-guns and snipers and the gunner officer in charge of 3 trench mortars, a most infernal machine which throws an enormous bomb of 100 lbs. full of high explosive. The Turks have a trench in the nullah which we enfilade and which is below us only we can't get at them because it is cleverly and heavily traversed. The trench we wanted to strafe is called G11.H …'

events on the Aegean coast; but we were pleased when we heard that we could expect to be relieved the next day. We heard, also, that Ridings at brigade headquarters had been wounded the day before. Full details were given me later by a disinterested party. It seemed that nature had called upon him to go a certain distance, just after he finished his duty in the signal office, and he was standing in a low trench when the bullet caught him in the back. Thomas tied him up. Tim came along to see if Ridings would have brandy or whisky. He preferred whisky, and then he was taken away on a stretcher. Noble told me that he had been amused. Riding's parting instructions concerned the disposal of a pair of spurs, of which he was proud, and he asked Ormy to look after them. They found a resting-place in the nullah, however, Ridings got through safely.

We heard very heavy gun-fire that evening, both near and distant, and in our left-front direction. Joe Cummings told us about strange and wild doings in the charges. Some of them were very strange. He told us about some of our men firing at a wounded Turk as he crawled back to his lines in no man's land. This fed us up, but we allowed a little for exaggeration. Then we heard that the Turks had found one of our batteries hiding behind a hospital on one of the cliff-tops, and they sent word that the battery must be moved within twenty minutes or they would fire at it. The battery was moved.

Several of these stories were going the rounds, and I include a few of them.

One of our wounded was lying in the open. Two Turks crawled up to him, at night, apparently to see what they could find in his pockets. Thinking they were going to murder him, he called out 'Mercy!' The Turks jumped up and ran away.

When the Turks recaptured some of their old trenches on June 4, they found some of our wounded in them, bandaged them and fed them.

One of our wounded, hidden in a little bit of cover, was found by a Turk who looked after him and gave him water. The fellow drank it and then shot the Turk as he was going away. If this was true, we hoped our man died.

Our men were always waiting to snipe Turk ration-bearers going to their lines, and many were caught as they passed certain marked spots. Our snipers often used Turk rifles on their old owners. They were accurate weapons. BSA aperture sights were used by some members of our old rifle clubs. I had left mine in my kit-bag at Alexandria, and never saw either again.[169]

There were stories creditable and discreditable to both sides; and I noticed that discreditable stories about our men were not forgotten.

A letter from home told me that Poole's brother had called to see if they could give any details about his death. I had not mentioned it. I did not mention anything of that kind. The letter also enquired about Humphries who had now been transferred to another section.

On Wednesday, August 11, I heard harsh words on the telephone. Two well-known officers were arguing. Captain S—— did some plain speaking. Major K—— answered 'That'll do S——,' in an even voice, one with mischief in it, if S—— didn't let it do.[170] I also heard that AF E.624, which we had signed at Hollingworth, meant that we were had for the duration of the war.[171] I didn't know this before. At least, I had not considered it particularly. This bit of news was interesting, if not good, and we gave it close and careful attention, and discussion. We heard that Ridings was in hospital. And that Joe, too, had gone to hospital. Then we heard about an officer of the 29th signals who had been killed near our brigade headquarters. He was going down a road toward Helles, on a motor-cycle, when a shell burst behind him. The nose caught him in the back and passed through, killing him on the spot. One or two of our men ran down to him when he was hit. The sight was horrible.

On Thursday, August 12, when Noble came up, we had a look around, through periscopes, at the remains of recent fighting. The dead were on top, and we, the living, were below the general ground-level. The usual order of life and death were reversed. The trench ended in a wall of loopholed sand-bags. In one loophole there rested a loaded and cocked rifle. A sentry sat by it, on the watch for a shot at anything unusual. This

169 Riley struck out the passage which follows, but it is still legible. It reads: 'Ormy told me about a place where the Turks had to cross an exposed gap in the Turkish line. The 6th Manchesters snipers were marking it, and Turk after Turk was hit as he crossed the gap. At last, Captain Holberton, the 6th adjutant, got so sick of the sight that he cried "For God's sake, stop it, now!"' Another version of this incident is related in Chapter 6, 'Additional notes on the night of June 4/5.'

170 Probably Capt. J.M.B. Sanders, the 5th Manchesters adjutant, and Major H.L. Knight, Brigade Major to 127th Brigade. See Appendix IV, officer biographies.

171 Army Form E.624, the agreement to serve overseas, signed by the men of the 127th (Manchester) Brigade while at Hollingworth Lake Camp, in early September 1914.

bit of trench was covered over at the top, in case the Turks sent some bombs over. Through the loophole we could see the end of the trench on the side of the rise, and the open country beyond, sloping down to the nullah.[172]

A dead Turk lay at the open end of the trench. We were told he was the 'latest bomb thrower' (presumably the last one caught); he was late enough.

Abe Williams was with the Lancs Fusiliers. A doctor was inoculating the men in the trench, and the method was simple and rough. The doctor grabbed a man's arm and jabbed the needle in. Abe got the needle before he had time to tell the doctor that he was RE and not LF. It did him no harm; but from the way he talked about it, he had the needle in both ways.

Between 6 and 7 p.m. that evening, and just about our mealtime, the Turks bombarded our lines, firing salvos of four and six shells at once. We had a bad half-hour while the bits and pieces dropped in the trench, or smacked the parados. Then came news that the Turks had re-captured part of the Vineyard.[173]

I was looking forward to more parcels from home. We wanted all we could get; for they helped us through the hot uncomfortable days, disgusting days, blood-and-thundery days, and the days when we felt like walking louse shelters.

Next day, Friday, August 13, we were relieved by some Scots. They had Stevenson telephones; whose chief point seemed to be that they went out of action on the slightest provocation. We tried one of them,

172 Probably the trenches H11 or H11a.

173 The battle for the Vineyard had been raging since 7 August just a few hundred yards from Riley, and in the days that followed was truly 'the hottest corner at Helles.' The final consolidation of 100 yards of trench that ran across the middle of the Vineyard represented the only reward for eight days of intense battle. As such this tiny piece of territory took on an almost totemic significance as the British troops struggled to hold on to their meagre gains. During the fiercest fighting, a 9th Manchesters' officer, Lieut. William Forshaw, defended the north-west corner (where three Turkish trenches converged on the British firing-line) with a small party of 9th Manchesters for 41 hours without relief. He was later awarded the VC. He had chain smoked throughout the action, using his cigarette to light his jam tin bombs which he lobbed continuously, and became known as 'The cigarette VC.' In addition, another 9th Manchesters' officer, 2nd Lieut. C.E. Cooke (who many felt had himself earned the VC) was awarded the MC, and three of Forshaw's platoon, Cpl 180 Samuel Bayley (who had remained with Forshaw throughout the time), L/Cpl 2148 Stanley Pearson and L/Cpl 2103 Thomas Pickford, received the DCM for their actions between 7 and 9 August.

and tightened a screw with candle-grease. These Scots were a queer crowd, but we did some business with them. They gave us enough milk for three mess-tins, and in return we gave them one and a half loaves and three and a half tins of jam. Tim told us to come in at 6.30 p.m.

We crawled down the nullah very slowly, and when we reached the old brigade headquarters we found it deserted, and no one could tell us where the new one was. We looked for it until we were too tired to look further, but we knew several places where we could have food and rest by asking for it, and that night I slept in the orderly room dug-out of the 7th Manchesters. I slept soundly, thankful to be away from the damned trenches, with their innumerable shellings and constant attention to the telephone. It was only when we got away from them that we realised how much we needed a change, and most of us were wearing out.

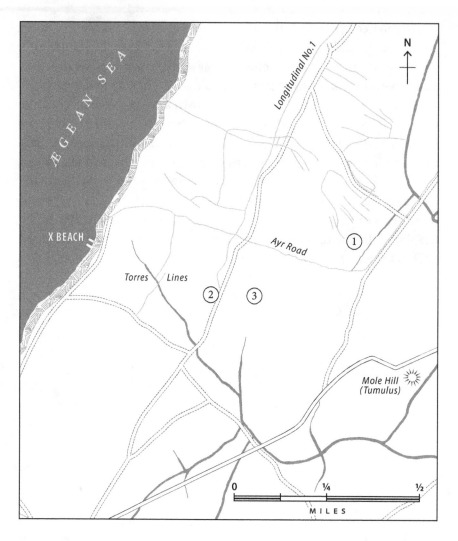

MAP 11

(1) Centre of 'Shell Bivouac'—42nd Division's main 'rest' area until 19 August

(2) 42nd (East Lancs) Division HQ (GN/YDB) until 19 August

(3) 6th Manchesters HQ

CHAPTER 12

At rest

On the morning of Saturday, August 14, we tried to find brigade head-quarters again, but we failed until an orderly of the 7th told us where it was. We had some tea at the 7th's kitchen, and then went to brigade which was only 200 yards away. I shared a dug-out with Abe; and we lay low all morning, when I had been for a lonely bathe. We had a rifle inspection at 2 p.m. and then I went with Pearson to GN, our divisional headquarters, to try to get a shirt from old Campbell, the CQMS. Campbell was short and shirty. A mail came in the afternoon bringing me five letters and two newspapers.

After that, Ormy and I retired to the cliff-edge above X Beach. Here I read my letters, and Ormy told me all about QG's shortcomings, with particular reference to cadging. On these cliffs we were as much at peace as we could hope to be on that hell, and we went up there, evening after evening, when the heat had gone, and there we sat, watching the splendid sunsets over Imbros and the Aegean. We sat there until the red glow faded, dark side-wings closing over it; and then, feeling cold, we went home to our burrows like the animals we were.

There was nothing to be said about those sunsets. All we wanted was to watch them. The spectacle of fire and water was one of the grandest imaginable. Space and distance cleared our minds a little, and cleaned up some of the dirty effects of living in trenches. Imbros and Samothrace, which was beyond and partly hidden by Imbros, with their dark hills, looked desirable islands. There was no war on either of them.

Figure 16. A row of six or more 100-foot-long dugouts close to where the 42nd Division's headquarters were situated between May and August 1915. Taken in May 2017. (Michael Crane)

Figure 17. Photograph taken circa 1930 of the road and ground above X Beach. Achi Baba can be seen in the top right of the picture. (Alec Riley, *Twenty Years After*)

I have already mentioned that we watched the monitors firing over the cliffs, and the Turkish shells from Asia or the Krithia front, splashing the sea as they dropped near the monitors.

From this high ground behind X Beach, we could, by turning away from the Aegean coast, overlook the Dardanelles beyond Morto Bay, and the plain of Troy on the far side. Down on Morto Plain was the tumulus, where we spent some of our first nights. We could see De Tott's Battery, and the abrupt cliff, the sandy fringe of Morto Bay where we first bathed, and the old water-towers. To the left was Achi Baba and the country of the nullahs, and, to our right, the wooden slopes of the inland rise to the high ground behind Sedd-el-Bahr and Cape Helles. From this distance we could see little detail in the battlefields area. A letter reminded me that Paul had been somewhere near this corner of the Mediterranean;[174] but Paul was of no importance as far as we were concerned. Now and then we amused ourselves, when we were on the cliffs, by aligning sticks and stones on what we supposed to be the direction of England, wondering when we should see it again.

There was a rough road on the cliff-top, a few yards inland. Near it, and near our look-out on the cliff, there were gun-pits. The muzzles of the guns were just above the ground-level, and branches of trees had been used to hide the guns as much as possible. From their higher ground, the Turks were always after these guns on the exposed cliff-tops. One evening, when Ormy and I were on the cliff, a wagon came along the road, going towards Helles. We heard a distant pop, a second pop, and soon after, the cracks of shrapnel about 100 yards behind the wagon, and we heard the smacks of the pattering balls as they dropped on the road and hard-baked earth below the thin scrub on either side. The driver, seeing what was happening, drove like hell, and made his horse gallop. We heard more pops, and each shell was nearer the moving mark than the last. The noise of the pattering balls made us feel weak in the stomach; but we were so interested in the race that it needed a shell-nose, coming straight for us and ripping through the scrub, to make us take some kind of cover. We made for the cliff-edge and crouched behind it. We wanted safety, and not to be mixed up with shrapnel. The wagon was some distance down the road by this time. The Turks

174 Saint Paul, the apostle.

could not catch it, and when they had wasted a good proportion of the equivalent value of the wagon, they gave it up. In the distance we saw that the driver, finding that no more shells were following him, had pulled up his horses, and was continuing his journey at his previous rate. He had won. The race had been exciting to watch. It must have been unpleasantly thrilling for him. A race against shrapnel.

On the night of Saturday, August 14, the Turks shelled Lancashire Landing, or W Beach. Night was very noisy, one of the noisiest we had known, for artillery fire. The Turks seemed to have more guns now. They thundered and lightned, and their bolts shook the earth.

Next morning, Sunday, August 15, we were up and about by 5.30 a.m. Mall was annoyed and wanted to argue the point about such early rising. I was tired and lazy, and stayed in my dug-out, dozing and scratching. Later on, I walked over to the 6th lines and met Teddy Walker.[175] I had heard he was back from Egypt. He told me that, on June 4, his job had been the placing of an artillery-screen. These artillery-screens were oblongs of red cloth with a stick at each end. Their purpose was to mark our positions in advance for the benefit of our gunners' eyesight. He received two wounds, and had been sent to Alexandria. He had only just returned, and he was expecting a commission. We discussed the above in detail. I was glad to meet someone from Eccles, and we talked scandal about it for some time. We had an extra rum-ration at night, and Noble entertained us with his mouth-organ. We heard heavy firing, and the news that our side had taken a trench and lost it again.

Meanwhile, septic was gaining on us. I had it on hands and legs. Various forms of dysentery or enteric were common, and many of us spent quite a long time in the latrines. I don't think we realised that there was anything seriously wrong, or that there was a chance of getting away from the place with disease. We had settled to monotonous routine and had lost all hopes of being sent away, unless, of course we stopped something in its flight. That was always a possibility. We felt rotten; but, as everyone looked more or less the same, and we were going down the nick at the same time, we had no standard to judge from. The parched and dusty peninsula was a good germ-breeding ground. We lived in dust, and, at times, the winds spread it in clouds; at others, there was a

---

175   Pte 2121 Frederick James Walker, 6th Manchesters.

dust-haze hanging over the place. By now, it would be hard to imagine a more dreary and colourless landscape than that of Helles. It had the appearance of a desert. The greens had gone, and the buffs and browns had replaced them. Our bodies and faces were thin. No. 4 Section, as we had known it in its prime, had ceased to be. It could never be the same again, and it never was. It was curious to remember that these companions of ours, all becoming invalids together, were the men we had camped with and drilled with, in times when we did it because we liked and enjoyed it, and their company.

We bathed before breakfast next morning, Monday, August 16, and then had a rifle inspection. Karno came round, so, scenting mischief, we decided to be as absent as we could. I persuaded Ormy to come with me, for a ramble. We went to V Beach. As we were going through some thin trees on a slope behind Helles, we found a battery of 75s. A rail had been laid to this position for bringing up shells from the beach. Looking towards Achi Baba, we had a good view of both sides, theirs and ours, for we were looking down and over the hollow of the peninsula-tip. We watched the 75s firing for some time. Being near the guns, the noise was sharp and harsh, but we were interested in the tiny puffs, three miles ahead, where the shells were bursting. The French artillerymen were not pleased to see us while they were busy; but we took some photographs, and agreed that the first part of our walk had been well spent.

We were soon close to V Beach. On the ground above it we found a French canteen. Here we had a good rest, bought chocolate and wine, and had a talk with the man in charge. He was a reservist, and he told us about France in 1914. He had also been a chef and had travelled the world. We had our water-bottles with us, so we filled up with wine. It was only French ration wine and not very strong, but it warmed us up. His descriptions of 1914 were mostly about villages with plenty of 'Obus' and 'Pouf!'[176] We explored Sedd-el-Bahr village, walked along the one street where every house had been shelled down by our naval guns before the landings. The cellars were habitable, however, and we went down into some of them. The French troops were using them for dug-outs. In one of them we tried to do business with the Frenchmen living in it. We had brought some tins of jam for bartering purposes. We had no luck in this

176 *Obus* – explosive shells and projectiles.

one, but later on we exchanged some tins for chocolate and coffee which we carried away in our handkerchiefs. The French were very fond of apricot jam, or what the labels called apricot, and when we found out about this, we saved all the apricot labels, removed the plum-and-apples and replaced them with apricots. The insides didn't matter, they were all much the same. We wined again, and then explored the burial-grounds and the wrecked mosque. The stones in the burial-ground, mostly long, round and slender, were tumbled around like a lot of ninepins caught, and stuck, in falling. We took a few photographs. Fighting had been heavy here in the early days.

We went to Sedd-el-Bahr fort, passing some obsolete guns, but we could not get inside. Then we went round the walls on the stony, rocky shore. Here we found a few old Turkish field-guns and some round and empty bombs. The guns were wrecked by our shells. The sea-ward walls of the fort had been shelled and blown about and the place was littered with bits of masonry. Having inspected the debris, we continued along the shore towards V Beach. To the right of the fort, facing the sea, a rough jetty had been built out for some distance. There were several lighters here, and at the end of the jetty was the *River Clyde*. This was our chance to explore her. A military policeman on the jetty told us about what he had seen on the first landing at V Beach on April 25, and, like children, we listened to the exciting little stories he told us as he pointed out the places of importance to the men who landed and those who did not. In that forked tree, at the top of the left slope, a sniper had done some accurate shooting before he was spotted. Then the *Queen Elizabeth* had stopped him. We had seen the great bastion at the near corner of the fort, or what was left of it—for now it was a crumbled mass of stone. There were snipers here, until Lizzie sent them a 15-inch shell. The tree-sniper had been particularly busy on our wounded as they were being returned to the *River Clyde*. It is, however, difficult to understand how they could be taken on board in the early hours of the landing. Still, that is what this MP told us.

We were close to the *River Clyde* and saw that the iron plates were chipped and pocked by rifle and machine-gun bullets. It was like poker-work. Here and there a few inches had been missed, but not many. We saw the large square holes in the side. Through these, the landing men had come out, to run down some planking and on to the lighters, which were soon full of dead and wounded. Later on, in Netley, one of the Dublin Fusiliers who was in the next bed to mine, told me that he had been on the *River Clyde*, and had landed at V Beach from a boat. As he was jumping on shore he was hit through the shoulder and chest and fell in the sea. His sergeant major saw it, grabbed him and dragged him on to the sand, where he lay for hours. Then another bullet caught him in the knee. Later, he was taken on the *River Clyde*, quickly in use as a hospital ship of sorts, when the shortage of surgical stores and attention was one of the scandals of the war.

We went on board the *River Clyde*. After inspecting the shell-holes in the deck, we had a general look round. We were on board one of the most famous boats in the world—an obscure 'collier' until April 25, 1915. We found that some of the shell-holes were of later date than April 25. They had sliced through the iron deck, at an angle, before exploding, if they did explode. There were iron plated machine-gun shelters on the bulwarks, approximately 5' × 6' × 6', and in the sand-bagged bows. Looking up at the bridge, we saw that one of the glasses had been shattered by a bullet which, we were told, killed an officer who was looking through at the time. What we could not understand was why all the glass had not been shattered. Looking down the hatchway we saw that there was a lot of water in the hold below. We stood in the bows, trying to imagine what V Beach, the fort and village, and the easy slope behind the beach must have looked like from the point of view of those who made the landing—if they were interested in anything, beyond getting ashore at all. It was an easy place to defend, and we wondered how a landing had been done there while the Turks played hell with our men. We could see their trenches on the slope in front. We looked round at the busy life of the beach, disembarkation of men, stores, planks, food, ammunition, from lighters, men rambling about, tents and marquees. Just as we were leaving the *River Clyde*, a military policeman came to us and asked what we were doing, and told us we were not allowed to go on her. We had seen all we wanted to see before he knew we were there, so we thanked him and went away.

Having found a boat conveniently moored to the jetty, we entered it, undressed, and bathed with some Frenchmen. There was a sandy bottom and safe diving. We were enjoying ourselves and feeling merrier and brighter than we had done for some time. While we were dressing,

Ormy said he was sure he had washed off all his lice. I bet him that he had not, and I won the bet. We had dried our bare skins in the sun. The noise of something blowing up on the beach made us jump. We inspected a big French gun, and some long red painted torpedos lying on the shore near the sandbank. Then we went back to the canteen for our wine.

It was time to be going home, but we did it leisurely, taking the path to the top of Cape Helles, the headland and cliff on the right of V Beach, facing seawards. From the cliff we looked down on the beach and along it to the fort, the *River Clyde*, the village, the Dardanelles beyond them, and the Asiatic side. Seawards we saw warships, transports, hospital ships and smaller craft in great variety. We explored Fort No. 1. This was on the cliff, and we overlooked V Beach from it. In the ruins were two 24cm guns blown from their mountings. Fort No. 1 was not an enclosure. It consisted of artificial mounds with bricked chambers inside, and the embrasures for the guns were between the mounds. The masonry was a yellowish stone. The heat was great, still, so we went along to find a bit of shade in the ruins of old Cape Helles lighthouse. We sat on some rough stones and, feeling tired, dozed for a time. Then we talked—mostly about home-affairs in England. We had nothing to say about the war. It had ceased to interest us. Now and then, when business was slack, we would call up one of our stations on the telephone, and ask the operator this question: 'Have you realised it yet?' Pearson was fond of putting this question to me. The answer was usually given in a few well-chosen words. We had realised it; and that being allowed, Ormy and I had nothing to add. When we had finished resting, we moved on again to a place where we overlooked W Beach, or Lancashire Landing. There, on the far side, near the cliffs of Tekke Burnu, was the jetty where we had landed on that dark night in early May, and we were near the place where we spent our first hours in cold and shallow pits. It seemed a long time ago, now. We passed a great pit on the cliff-top. Men had been buried here and only partially covered. Here and there we could see their boots sticking out of the soil. Near this pit we found a little group of graves, with crosses sticking in the mounds. Here we found Captain Bazley's grave. We photographed the cross. About us were innumerable other graves, crosses, memorials to men and groups of men, killed in the early fighting. From this place we went straight home for tea and an expected issue of lime juice. We were tired after our long day. We had not been far, but it had been a change to amble about and see something new to us.

I felt wrong, on Tuesday, August 17; I may have had too much chocolate and/or wine. Up to now we had kept our long rifles; but the time having come for these to be given up, we went to GN for that purpose, and to become real soldiers with short guns.[177] While we were there, we called on Hell-faced Bill, the postman. 'Hell-face' was always ready to discuss the situation in general, and rumours and the goings on at YDB in particular. It was about this time that I awoke to the fact that the brigade sections of the Signal Company were being received on equal terms with REs of older standing. Up to now, we had not taken any particular notice of REs of any standing; and although we had become REs ourselves, in the natural course of events, we didn't care a damn about REs, either in general or particular. We did not mix, nor were we interested. We had plenty of good friends in the brigades. A remark once made about us, more in sorrow than in anger, we used between ourselves when we felt amiable; but it was not counted against the one who made it, seriously. Both sides had learnt something about each other.

A general inspection was rumoured for this afternoon, and not wanting to be generally inspected, my ragged breeches and general appearance being what they were, I arranged to be absent. In lieu thereof, I was detailed to proceed to a dump in the valley and to collect a Begbie lamp,[178] thereafter, taking it to CQMS Campbell at YDB. Withington and Hopkinson came with me. Near YDB we saw the armoured cars stabled in long open dug-outs to rear of a bit of ground rising above the local level.[179] We collected it, knowing it to be incomplete, and took it to Campbell. I had almost persuaded him to have it when he had the bright idea of looking at it carefully. Of course, we knew nothing about its deficiencies, but we had to take it back and bring 'lamps, Begbie, 1' that was complete.

177 The 42nd Division was armed with the Long Lee Rifle, a Boer War relic, while the regulars had SMLE rifles.

178 A type of lamp used for signalling.

179 YDB, the 42nd Division's HQ, was at this time situated close to the Torres Lines, around 600 yards east of X Beach.

We met Lawford and had some conventional conversation with him. He was showing signs of wear and tear.

We returned to our homes. These were on the lee side of a slight rise, and were not visible to the Turks. But they knew all about them, for they sent occasional shells to share amongst us. The bursts had very nasty sounds. Lumps of metal flew about, whining and whirring and screeching horribly. The noise gave us a sickly feeling.

We spent our evenings paying calls. Ormy, Claude, Hopkinson, Pearson, Greenbank, Abe, Mall, Noble, Haworth and I would gather in one or two groups, brewing tea at dusk. Then we gossiped. Our dug-outs were arranged in lines. The loose earth from them was piled up behind each line and between the dug-outs. Paths had been trodden over the long mounds at intervals. When we were lazy, we jumped over a dug-out instead of going around by a path. All our possessions, rifles and equipment, were, of course, in the holes. We sat in the open for talk and tea, close to the holes.[180]

That night, Pearson and I were in the same party. It was nearly dark when we saw a body jump over Pearson's dug-out, and then we heard a lot of loose earth rattling down on his things. Pearson remarked 'That's it, you great clumsy devil!' We laughed. We laughed more when we saw that the great clumsy devil was Major C——. Having heard Pearson, he came to us and asked if Pearson belonged to decent society. No. None of us did. Surely Major C—— did not suppose he was in a draw-ing-room, where a remark with the same meaning would be pleasantly camouflaged? 'You great clumsy devil' had a vogue. It was useful on the telephone. Major C—— was fond of 'souvenirs.' He had them in sand-bags, and was therefore responsible for the words his men used when they had to lug his bags of old iron about. And C—— was a good churchman. The language was thrilling, and, according to custom, included more adjectives than nouns.

Next morning, Wednesday, August 18, we bathed before breakfast. For me, this was followed by a duty from 9 a.m. to 3 p.m., and then Ormy and I went for another bathe. On our way we inspected a new draft for the 6th Manchesters, and very entertaining it was. One of the

---

180   The remains of these dugouts can still be found within woodlands about 750 yards east of X Beach.

draft told us that he was certain it wouldn't be long before we captured Achi Baba and Krithia. We were glad to hear it. Before we had finished with him, he knew that at least two of the scroungers who had been on the peninsula longer than ten days or a fortnight did not believe him. It amused us to hear what new drafts were going to do. They were going to put things right in a few days; but we knew very well what would happen—if they were still lucky enough to be alive they would be chatting as well as talking.

We explored several by-ways, near this bivouac. We rambled about, poking our noses into anything we thought worthy of investigation. There were some pine trees at the foot of a small rise, to our left and near the bivouac, and in them was placed a battery of our divisional artillery. We came here to watch the battery at work. As the guns were of old pattern, shell and cordite were loaded separately. A telephone operator called out the necessary alterations in range and elevation, and the number of the next gun to be fired. These, of course, were received by an officer, and repeated by a NCO. Shell and cartridge were popped in the breach, a lever pulled, a yellow flame leaped out of the muzzle, and a harsh crash hit our ear-drums.

We had seen that deep and narrow communication trenches had been made on each side of Krithia Road. One on each side, close to and parallel with the road. They were only wide enough for men to go along in single file. The road was in full view of the Turks, who would send a shell if they saw two men on the road. Guns and wagons went up it at night. By the roadside, a shrapnel had burst low, and as its contents had not space to scatter, they lay all together—a collection of balls, bullets, nails and old iron. The heap was there for days.

From the high ground behind the X Beach cliffs, we watched a battalion of infantry going up in extended order, several lines of them. The Turks spotted and shelled them. Shrapnel puffed and flashed over them, and here and there men staggered or sank to the ground as they were struck.

By night we saw curious silhouettes of wagons and their drivers, going up the road, against the dull red sunset-glow, or against shell-flashes, or flares from the lines.

I have mentioned our news-sheet, the *Peninsula Press*. I kept a number of copies; the earliest, dated Tuesday, May 18, 1915, was issued by GHQ Printing Section, Med. Exp. Force, and the others by the RE Printing Section, GHQ, MEF. I don't know the date of the first issue, but that of May 18 was the first one I got hold of, and kept. The *Peninsula Press* gave us what was supposed to be news about atrocities, frightfulness, the *Lusitania*, Italy, Dutch opinion of Germans, fall in German peace stock, submarine feats in the Sea of Marmora, Greek elections, war loan, munitions, and other things our Wise Men thought it good for us to know and believe. Some of it was good propaganda. We suspected everything we saw in print, however.

Campbell, our CQMS, had gone into business. We interviewed him, unprofessionally; for he was retailing grub of a more luxurious kind than we were used to. No one bothered about the prices. We bought eggs, tinned fish and cheap Egyptian gelatine, charitably called Turkish Delight. Eggs were five for a shilling. When I reached a certain stage of decline, I swished eggs in diluted condensed milk. By this time we were expert judges of the relative merits of various brands of condensed or tinned milk. Ideal, which had a creamy taste, was popular. Nestle's Swiss was known as Swistle's. When we did this kind of business with Campbell, our relations were those of merchant and customer. For the time being he forgot that he was our CQMS, and the dignity attached to that rank.

When I called at Campbell's for more eggs and milk, on the morning of Thursday, August 19, I was received with such politeness that I felt overcome with emotion. Could such things be possible? They were. While I was at divisional headquarters I heard a rumour that it would move at 6 p.m. and when I returned to brigade I found that we, too, had to be ready to move after dinner.[181] A mail had brought me a parcel of grub. I took this with me, unopened, when I went to the 6th Manchesters with Stringer and Gorman, to move up with the 6th when they did. It took me some time to collect Stringer and Gorman and all our belongings. The 6th headquarters was about 200 yards from

181 The offensive at Suvla had virtually stalled and it had been decided to send the 29th Division to Suvla to take part in a renewed attack. A reorganisation of the line at Helles was required, with the 52nd Division taking the right sub-section, the RND the centre and the 42nd Division taking over the left subsection from the 29th Division.

brigade, to our right and when we got there we were told to wait until Major Worthington was ready, and to follow him when he moved.

While we were resting and counting our candles, Winn came up, with a lot of noise and fuss, and told us to help one of his men to put on his webbing equipment. We didn't wear webbing; we knew nothing about it and we said so. Winn got excited and made reflections on REs in general, and on us in particular. We gave him some of his own back, on the spot, and later as well. We did not like him. We did not like being with the 6th Manchesters, either, although it was our old battalion. From our point of view it was the most unpopular battalion in the division. Just before we started a man came and spoke to me. He was an Eccles man. I didn't know him, but he knew me. He had come with the third draft.

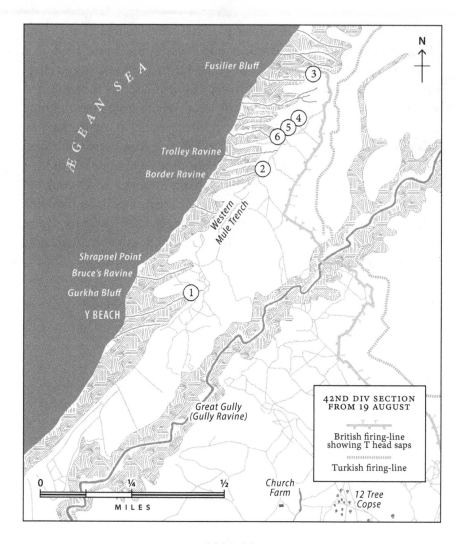

MAP 12

1. 127th (Manchester) Brigade HQ from 19 August–2 September

2. HQ position for the battalion manning the left sub-section firing-line:
   6th Manchesters, 19–22 August; 8th Manchesters, 22–25 August;
   and 5th Manchesters, 25 August–2 September

3. Visual signalling station at Fusilier Bluff

4. Bury Echelon

5. Rochdale Echelon

6. Salford Echelon

CHAPTER 13

With the 6th Manchesters

While we talked, I kept my eye on Worthington & Co. I saw Walker again and had a word with him. At last we made a start, following Worthington and Dr Norris down to the beach and along the shore-road under the cliffs to Gully Beach. Then up Saghir Dere, the Great Gully. We couldn't keep up with Worthington for long. We were tired, and had not much strength left. In Great Gully we followed the dusty road as it passed between high cliffs, and bluffs, twisting and turning with the course of the gully. Dug-outs had been made in the steep sides. Scrub and bushes grew wherever they could find earth enough to hold them. Here and there trees grew precariously on the crumbling edges. We passed great bluffs of white-yellow earth. Paths led up to the cliff-tops, where they were not too precipitous, or to shelters of all kinds— holes in the ground or merely suspended ground-sheets. The hot sun scorched us as we kicked up the loose dust of the road. We mopped our sweaty hands with our handkerchiefs, or with our tunic-sleeves. Now and then we saw white puffs against the blue of the sky, when shrapnel burst over the gully, and then we heard the patter of the balls, and saw the dust they raised. The pattering sounds made us windy, but none of them were caused by balls falling near enough to catch us. Sometimes we saw clouds of brown smoke and dust rise high in the hot air of the gully, when a high explosive shell dropped and burst. The gully-sides glared at us, making us screw up our eyes. We were tired and had to keep resting. We were thirsty and we called at every drinking-place we could find; drinking until we did not want any more, and then we

Figure 18. Great Gully, better known as Gully Ravine. From the album of a soldier in the 8th Manchesters. Taken after 19 August 1915. (Editor's collection)

Figure 19. The Gurkha Mule Trench. Taken in May 2015. (Michael Crane)

were thirstier than before. Our lips and mouths were dusty, dry and parched. By this time we had lost sight of Worthington. Tim passed us, looking very excited about something, but he didn't see us. We passed a dead man, lying along the side. We passed horses, wagons, water-carts, pack-mules carrying ammunition boxes, and stores, dumps of SAA, dumps of boxes of bully and boxes of biscuits. We passed men going up, men going down, men standing still, men resting. Dirty, ragged, lousy-looking, most of them. Men looking thin and worn-out, and a few who looked comparatively fresh. We saw many graves on the sides.

At last we came to a bend in the gully where a path ascended to the left. The short path was steep and took us into a narrow trench.[182] As we went up it, climbing slowly, we looked down on the wild, dusty gully scenery on our left. At times we had to stand still, when the trench was blocked with mules carrying water *fanatis*,[183] and their Indian drivers who pulled, tugged or pushed the struggling, kicking mules. These men made strange little sounds of encouragement or abuse. We were carrying our telephone, blankets and full equipment. I had not brought a blanket, however, as I didn't need one just then. We crawled slowly upwards. We didn't know where the 6th were or where their headquarters would be.[184] All we could do was to ask men who passed us if the Manchesters were anywhere about; and being told that they were, we thanked heaven and went on.

At last we reached the top and the Western Mule Trench. It was easier for us, now that we had left the heat and dust of Great Gully and our path was more on the level. The thought of that gully was like a night-mare. We still had some distance to go, but at last we came to the head of Y Ravine, where our brigade headquarters was fixed on a wide ledge, high up on the side of Gurkha Bluff, to the right of the ravine, and a short distance from our trench path. A good path led to brigade head-quarters and the signal office. This was palatial, with a seat of planks and overhead shelter. We passed behind the top of Gurkha Bluff, to our left, now, and we passed the top of Bruce's Ravine.[185] Although we

182 The Gurkha Mule Trench.

183 Metal tanks, for carrying water. An Arabic word adopted by the British Army.

184 The 6th Manchesters took over the right half of the division's left sub-section on Gully Spur.

185 Riley also names it Bruce Ravine in some parts of his text.

Figure 20. Y Beach, Y Ravine and Gurkha Bluff. From the album of the widow of Captain H. Hargreaves Bolton, 1/5th East Lancs Regt. Taken after 19 August 1915. (Editor's collection)

were tired, we did not fail to notice the differences between the kind of country we were in now, and all we had seen before. It was a relief to look down at the sea and at the wild scrubby steep slopes and ravines, for we were several hundreds of feet above the sea-level; and the air was cooler up here. This trench was made along the cliff-tops.

About 9 p.m. we found the 6th Manchesters headquarters in Border Ravine, to which a short trench branched from the one we had come along. A path led down the ravine to the shore. Battalion headquarters consisted of a few rough shelters scraped in the ravine-side, on the left, and about a quarter of the way down the steep slope. The incline was about 50 degrees. The shelters faced the sea. When we were in them, we seemed to be right over the sea. Imbros was in front of us. We were very tired when we took over from the Royal Fusiliers, 29th Division. We heard they were to embark at midnight for a place further north, up the Aegean coast. Before they left us they repaired a break in the line. Then we dumped all our belongings and settled down. About 11.15 p.m. there was another break, and in the early hours of Friday, August 20, while

Stringer was on duty, Tim and Thomas came to see about it. We had not done anything about it. I was too tired to bother with it. It was all I could do to reach the place at all. When my turn of duty came, I opened my parcel and had some grub from home.

The line was broken again, later on. Some artillerymen were tapping in. I went out and found them looking for a break in one of their own lines. I found ours near brigade headquarters and Thomas found it at the same time, so we sat down together for a rest and a talk before going back, when we had repaired it. The rations supplied by the 6th Manchesters were the worst we had known. There had been a time when we thought the 6th were the last word in all that was good, and when we wanted to work their line. Now, we judged battalions by their rations and the 6th let us down every time. They let themselves down, too. I felt so weak that I had to steady myself, at times, on the trench sides. Eggs and milk kept me going. That evening I managed to reach Abe's visual station, on Fusilier Bluff, perched high over the Aegean. Abe was in touch with the navy, with helio and electric-lamp. The firing-line was a short distance in front. In one grand sweep it ran down-hill to the shore which it met at right angles. The scenery about here reminded me a little of the Devonshire coombes. To right and left we looked down a steep concave slope on to the rugged and hillocky sand dunes, where fighting had been hard, on June 28, when these wild and picturesque gullies, ravines and cliffs had been captured. After the flies and heat of the day, it was very pleasant to spend an hour at Abe's station, at sunset and in the twilight. One part of the path to it was on the edge of a steep and dangerous bit of ground, and here a hurricane lamp was kept. It was moon-light when we went back to Border Ravine.

As we sat in our office, looking down and seawards, our view was confined to the inside of a large V, made by the ravine-sides as they converged below; but from our height we could see many miles of the Aegean. Now and then, particularly at night, we saw our destroyers slink into sight in the V, approach the shore, and fire a few rounds. The noise over the water and up the ravine sounded peculiar.

In a *Weekly Times* of July 16, we read Ashmead-Bartlett's account of the capture of this area on June 28.[186] We did not know much of what

---

186 Ellis Ashmead-Bartlett was an English war correspondent.

was happening on the larger scale until we read about it, weeks later. We knew quite a lot about what happened on the small scale. There was very little bathing about this part of the coast. We were all very dirty and very tired. My shirt was dirty and torn. The sun was strong, the flies innumerable, and with these about us letter-writing was hard work.

On a small shoulder of hill, to the right of our headquarters, there was a wooden cross. Seen from the landward side, against the background of the red Aegean at sunset, it gave, perhaps, the most striking effect of all the crosses of Helles. It was the most striking of all those I saw.

This headquarters had a luxurious kitchen, but roots, and odds and ends of wood, for fuel, were scarce. We pulled up all the roots and scrubby bushes we could find. The 6th rations improved slightly.

On the morning of Saturday, August 21, I went round to the 6th headquarters. Here, I heard Sergeant Wells say that a man had been hit in the head early that morning, and had no chance of getting over it.

I asked who it was.

'A chap called Walker.'

'F.J.?'

'Yes.'

It was Teddy Walker, and he had stopped a bullet while he was peeping over the parapet, just before he was relieved from sentry-duty, on the morning when he was to have gone home for his commission.[187] I went to see Sergeant Stirling about him. He had been taken down to a dressing station. Everything possible had been done. Stirling said it was hopeless. He was an old school-fellow.

We were half a mile from our sources of washing and drinking water. The REs had made a deep well in Bruce's Ravine. They had made the top large and square. When we went down to it we took a canvas bucket and sluiced ourselves, emptying the water over our heads; and making as much of a holiday of it as we could. Thomas and Withington came to see us, and brigade gave us some cigarettes. We heard a new story. Shells dropped in Krithia Nullah while a stretcher-case was being taken down. One shell dropped close by. The bearers dropped the stretcher

---

187   Pte 2121 Frederick James Walker, 6th Manchesters, died 25 August 1915.

and made for some cover. The case sat up, found himself alone, got up, and ran for cover too.

While we were sitting in our office, that afternoon, a TBD came into the V and started firing over our cliffs. The noise was harsh and clanging, making the cliffs echo and rattle. Three TBDs looked after our seafront, the *Scorpion*, *Wolverine* and *Coventry*.[188]

Our menu that night included tender steaks, rice-pudding, cocoa, and bread with grease on it.

I must repeat some description of the sunset-picture as we saw it from Border Ravine. Nature repeated it time after time, and we watched it evening after evening. It is a picture so striking that none who saw it in 1915 can forget it. The sun is setting. The sea is an expanse of shining red. Imbros and its mountains are black against red clouds. We are looking at a grand panorama of fire and water, space and distance. For a short time we have turned our backs on the trenches and what is happening in them ... Then a destroyer slinks into sight and opens fire. The guns flash brightly and clouds of smoke rise from them. The Turks answer the fire, and their shells throw up great fountains of sea. Splashes and smoke are tinged red in the sunset-glow. There is no peace, even at sunset.

* * *

We went up and down the Western Mule Trench and the Echelons, between Border Ravine, Fusilier Bluff and brigade headquarters, many times; so often, that we knew it as well as we knew our streets at home. When possible, we liked to go along it in the cool of the evening. We will go through it once more.

We are on our way back to Border Ravine from brigade headquarters with our letters from home. The heat of the day has passed and the sun has set, leaving a pearly green light, a mysterious ghostly light. The moon has risen. Lightning flashes occasionally. We are quite alone; we cannot even hear a voice or a foot-step. There is no need to hurry, so we walk slowly. The moonlight gains over the green tint and stars are

188 Riley is wrong here. HMS *Coventry* was not launched until 1916. The third ship was probably another Beagle class destroyer like *Scorpion* and *Wolverine*. These destroyers were armed with a four-inch gun and three 12-pounders. Part of their work was to provide naval artillery support.

beginning to twinkle. Bits of metal buzz or hum between us and the stars. They sound like noisy insects overhead.

We reach a place where we see a cross on the top of the right parapet. It is made of pieces of packing-case. It marks the grave of a sergeant. To the usual statements of date and name, and 'killed in action,' number, regiment, one word is added, 'KISMET.' By this we remember it. Kismet is a commonplace over-worked word, but we remember this grave. Perhaps it is the surroundings, the rugged ravine close by, its effect by sunset or moonlight, or its loneliness; it may be any of these, or all of them, but we remember this grave. We are superstitious now; we have gone a long way back towards the primitive—if we have ever really left it. We like to have a companion with us in the Western Mule Trench at night.

The trench is haunted, where twelve inches of overcoat sleeve projects from the left side. There is a skeleton arm in it, and a skeleton hand dangles from the cuff. In the pearly green light or moonlight, those thin white ghostly bones make us creepy. They belong to some long-buried body, partially uncovered when the trench was widened. We squint at them sideways, when we pass the place at night, and we are brave enough to say 'Saida' to them,[189] or even shake hands with them, when we have company. There is buried clothing near a corner of the trench. Some of it is more uncovered than when we passed it last. We have pulled pieces out, looking for Turkish buttons in case it is one of theirs. We may see more of its owner when this place has been knocked about a little more.

We are very brave by day, or with a companion.

*   *   *

Sunday, August 22, was uneventful. The 8th Manchesters took over from the 5th and 6th. Gorman left us and Robinson and Greatorex came in his place. We were all very lousy. I hung my tunic on a root sticking out from our back wall. Soon, a lot of little black ants were running about on it. They brought the lice out of the seams and carried them away to their nests. It must have been hard work for the little creatures to carry such big lice and I helped some of them with a twig. This kept me busy

---

189 'Nice to meet you.' Arabic greeting picked up in Egypt.

for some time. Someone had sent me some lemon-squash crystals, and I mixed them with lime juice to vary the old flavour a little.

I spent the evening at Abe's visual station on Fusilier Bluff. Noble and Haworth were there as well. Abe's cup of joy was running over. He had done his first visual business with the navy, sending map-references for the TBDs to fire on. Abe was overflowing with interest in his job. Thus was visual justified of her children. Abe told us all about it. His best line was the electric lamp, a compact oblong box screwed on a tripod. It could be worked from a distance of a few feet, by a long wire with a key at the end. I sat in Abe's dug-out, leaning back comfortably, and playing with the new toy while Abe made sounds of pleasure as he explained it. Except for a small amount done by the Signal Company headquarters section, visual signalling had been a wash-out at Helles.

By this time we were finding it hard work to be pleasant with our companions. Most of us were really ill, although we didn't realise it. There were no serious rows, but there were innumerable squabbles over details of no importance. Three months before they would not have been noticed. Three months later they were forgotten. They were natural under the circumstances.

My mouth was full of flies when I woke up on Monday, August 23. I cursed the green devils as I spat and spluttered them out. The day was quiet. We did our work mechanically. There was little interest in it now.

Murphy, now the adjutant of the 8th Manchesters, was good to us.[190] I spent many an hour with him, and as I mentioned previously, he always had something to offer me. It was a pleasure to take a message to him, for there was always a rest and a talk, sitting in his dug-out. His remarks about certain Ks officers, replacing old territorial officers who had been killed with the 8th, or who had left the peninsula, were worth hearing. Their heads were of large dimensions, apparently. Murphy gave one of them such a stiff dose of logic that he could not answer it. We had no time for Ks, and we lost no opportunity of saying so.

We had plenty of tinned milk. Robinson dealt with it and made a good rice pudding. I took a walk as far as the water-carts in the gully. Later, and having nothing to carry, I managed to get to ZLG and down

190 Second Lieut. Peter Murphy, former A/RSM of the 8th Manchesters. See Appendix IV, officer biographies.

to Y Beach below, where I had a bathe of sorts; but the sea-water made my septic places smart. Down there I met Stanton and Berry and we walked round Gurkha Bluff along the shore—a very narrow strip, here. We turned left and up Bruce's Ravine, passing a great bastion of sandstone on our right as we went up. High up, on the yellow face of the rock someone had carved a large crossed khukris, the Gurkha sign, and other hieroglyphs. This was a wild place. One of the wildest corners of Helles and the fighting in it must have been difficult before it was captured. We had heard tales about Gurkhas decapitating Turks, and about headless Turks' bodies lying about, but I never saw any of them. We took plenty of time in climbing up the steep path in Bruce's Ravine, and we had numberless rests. Even in going down Y Ravine I had to rest frequently. It took me all my time to reach the Mule Trench, but I got home to Border Ravine at last. All we could find for tea was bully, but we made some toast on our own small fire to go with it. As usual, we watched the sunset, and a duel between a destroyer and a Turkish gun which placed some shots very near its mark.

Tuesday, August 24, was more remarkable for food than for war. Stringer and I had parcels. Mine contained chocolate, and a cake stitched up in linen. The cake had crumbled, so we put it in our mess-tins, mixed pineapple chunks and Ideal milk with it, stirred well, and served cold. It was quite a good trifle. I went to brigade in the afternoon, arriving just before a dust storm blew up. For half an hour the air was thick with grey dust and we breathed and ate it, as we sat in the signal office, resting.

That night the *Scorpion* sent us the news that the Russians had sunk the *Moltke*, three cruisers and seven destroyers in a naval action in the Baltic. We wondered how much truth, if any, this contained. Also, that Italy had declared war on Turkey and that Venizelos was now the Greek premier. What we wanted to know was how all these good things, if true, were going to help us. Such news items seemed futile when the receipt of them synchronised with a few shell-bursts over Great Gully. How soon would these events have a beneficial effect on us, individually; how soon should we be able to get away from this lousy peninsula? Lice were biting my left arm at that very moment. And what about seeing the last of Tickler's bloody jam-tins? And Paxton's as well. We didn't care two spent shrapnel-balls who the premier of Greece was, so long as we could get away from the hell-hole.

Now and then the Turks sent shrapnel over our ravine and over the mule trench. Otherwise we were quiet. I met Tim in the trench. He was as clean and neat as usual. He was carrying his fly-whisk at the trail. For that fly-whisk I envied Tim. We discussed various marriages and scandals we had heard about from the home front, and then, a staff-officer coming along for a word with Tim, I left them to get on with it. I was considering the idea of reporting myself as sick, but couldn't imagine anything better than a No. 9 as a result.[191]

By this time we had heard about an incident connected with the arrival of our people at brigade headquarters. Whenever that body moved its position, J—— was in the habit of having plenty of blankets taken to the new place for him by one or other of the attached men.[192] This was noticed, and at last orders were given that each man must carry all his own blankets and kit, and not dump them on others. J—— arrived at the Y Ravine office, after the longest and most tiring walk we had had, expecting to find that his belongings had walked there too. It had not. Enquiring about it, he was told that, for all anybody else knew, it was where he had left it. He used several adjectives while he wiped the sweat off his face, and said it wasn't playing the game. He couldn't leave an old signal office with the rest of the staff, and someone ought to have looked after it for him. But he went down the gully, found his things and brought them up. And it must have been a hell of a walk.

On Wednesday, August 25, the 5th took over from the 8th Manchesters and we had a change of employer once more. The usual period up here was three days per battalion. We explored Rochdale Echelon and a few deserted trenches. Between Trolley Ravine and Fusilier Bluff were Salford, Rochdale and Bury echelons. Evenings were delightful. We spent odd hours at the 6th Manchesters headquarters, at the junction of Mule Trench and Y Ravine.

On the morning of Thursday, August 26, while I was on duty, sitting in our shelter, which was covered by a ground-sheet, a spent bullet dropped on the sheet. It had made such a curious noise in the final flutter that all who heard it looked round to see what had happened.

191 A No. 9 pill was a 'universal laxative pill,' mockingly depicted by troops as a cure-all given when no other remedy was deemed suitable.

192 Probably not Joe (Sgt 262 Graham Royle) as he was evacuated sick on 12 August.

Fletcher shouted loudly, asking where it had gone to, and Morrison came to us and picked it up. It had not even scratched the ground-sheet, let alone gone through and hit me, and it must have had hard work to keep up as long as it did.

Tim wanted to know who had been on duty at 2.05 a.m., and a report from me as to why calls from brigade had not been answered. I found that Q—— was the man. Jerry, who had been down the line during the night, had also to make a report. I asked him to come round to see me. He did so and we agreed that our reports should be sufficiently alike to clear Q—— of any great misfortune. That is, we cooked our reports. Q—— had been asleep. We made it clear to him that he was a damned fool, and that we did not want him if he couldn't make a better job of it then he had done. All the same, it is doubtful if there was a single one of us who had not been to sleep on duty, and more than once. It was nothing to boast about, but a difficult thing to avoid. Tim saw Holberton about it. Q—— was sent back to his company, Holberton telling him to report again in fourteen days. Mallalieu, however, told us that Tim did not want Q—— back. Hartland, who was ill with something or other, came to us in Q——'s place.

Although we were so fond of sleep, some of us were beginning to lose the art of sleeping at the proper time, and we had very little that night; but we had a wonderful show of lightning over the Aegean, both sheet and forked and both at once. I sat in the office, watching it for a long time. The effects were beautiful.

Next morning, Friday, August 27, we had a row with the 6th who were using Abe's wire for battalion purposes. Abe came to see me about it, and we decided on a plan of campaign to beat the 6th. We reported it to Tim, and the affair ended by the 6th supplying two orderlies to take messages to and from our office. Holberton was annoyed at the idea of RE signals dictating the way to run his battalion communications, but what we wanted we got and everything worked easily. We tried to get some creosote to put on our clothes in the matter of lice, but we couldn't, so cigarettes were in demand.

Dr Norris had seen Abe with two tins of condensed milk, and, being in a bad temper, had told Abe that they had been pinched. What it had to do with Norris, pinched or otherwise, was not clear, and we resented his interference with us. Abe had said quite a lot to Norris in return.

We were in the habit of taking anything we needed when we could find it, except private property; although I had done that more than once, when the need was great, but never from my companions.

I heard from home that more cake was due to arrive, and that certain men I knew were home on leave. Enviously, I hoped they would have a complete change and rest. Enviously and cynically.

After breakfast, on Saturday, August 28, I was feeling wrong again. I spent most of the day resting in the shade of the ground-sheet. We heard that four Turk transports had been sunk, but we had no proof. Somehow, our success never seemed to do us any good and we were losing interest in these newsy items.

Sunday, August 29, was a lazy day. I spent most of it trying to read, and trying to write letters. I couldn't think of much to say in them, and I hadn't much energy to think at all. Ormy rang me up, telling me to get to YDB to draw some pay. The thought of that walk down the Great Gully and the narrow sap, if it happened to be full of kicking mules, was enough to frighten me and I managed to have that silly business cancelled.

That evening, a Turk prisoner was brought to our headquarters. He was blindfolded. He was well-clothed, but hungry. Our men fed him, gave him water and cigarettes. I saw him with a tight clutch on half a loaf. He was taken to brigade and then to the base.[193]

News came from Anzac, that 'object was attained and position consolidated.' That night the destroyers did a lot of firing and the sausage was up observing, just in front of us.[194]

This part of the line ran almost due north. Fusilier Bluff, where the line turned due west, was north by west of Krithia and our firing line crossed Great Gully due west of Krithia. Great Gully was shallow up here compared with the lower stretches. We noticed these points as we went about our work, for there was a certain amount of interest in locating our positions, for some of them were curious. For instance, it

---

193   The Turkish prisoner had surrendered to C Company, 8th Manchesters, at the Beach Barricade at 9 p.m. The 8th Manchesters war diary, 29 August 1915, recorded: 'He was hungry and ate a loaf of bread and a pot of jam in very short time. He was very well dressed, we passed him to Brigade. Received message from Brigade to the effect that the surrendered Turk had told them many more were willing to come in and therefore keep a good lookout. No more came in however.'

194   Kite balloon of either HMS *Manica* or HMS *Hector*.

Figure 21. Firing-line trench. From the album of a soldier in the 8th Manchesters. Taken after 19 August 1915. (Editor's collection)

Figure 22. Troops of the 42nd Division 'stand to' at Fusilier Bluff. Probably taken between September and November 1915. (Ross J. Bastiaan collection)

was strange to us to be actually north of Krithia even if we had gone slightly west at the same time.

Next morning, Monday, August 30, I called on the RAMC in Y Ravine. The MO said I was unfit for duty, and that I must stay in my dug-out, and in the shade as much as possible. He gave me a pill to be going on with. It was not a No. 9. The lice seemed to multiply themselves by themselves. They prevented us from resting. I had put my tunic on the dug-out floor. When I picked it up, there was a centipede under it, a great yellow thing with black curved legs. It was about eight inches long and was S shaped as it wriggled about. The heat was great. It came from all sides and from the ground-sheet overhead. In front the sea, yellow in the sunlight, glared at us. We cursed the lot, as we tossed about, unable to settle comfortably. Now and then the buzzer irritated us, so we cursed that as well. Feeling dizzy and weak, I lay as still as I could, dozing occasionally. Someone had sent me *The Professor at the Breakfast Table*. What I wanted was the MO, not the Professor. I took a turn at the telephone that night.

On the morning of Tuesday, August 31, I saw the MO again, and told him that it had taken me all my time to get there. He awarded me half an ounce of castor oil, and orders as before. I went back to the dug-out.

Berry came over to see us, and told us about one who had clothed himself in more than his regulation allowance of authority, so we arranged to have it stopped, and I would pass the word to brigade to that effect. We finished the day by telling the tale in the proper quarter and so getting hold of four spare candles.

Abe was having trouble with M——, whose objections to going for water and rations were famous. The sight of that man annoyed us as much as his never-ending grumbles wearied us. Abe and I took council together, to find a way to make him work. The jobs all got done, somehow, but not without a lot of arguing. It was like the clucking at a hens' tea-party. Of course we could have ended it at any time, but that way was the last thing we wanted to do. We did not want to have any man sent back to his company.

I was up and about again on Wednesday, September 1. Green, one of our attached men, made a magnificent custard. We had plenty of tinned milk and we had some eggs brought up for it. The custard, however, was counter-balanced by what we saw in the mule trench, where a body,

Figure 23. Battlefield cemetery above Y Beach and below the field ambulance at Y Ravine. From the album of the widow of Captain H. Hargreaves Bolton, 1/5th East Lancs Regt. (Editor's collection)

buried in one side, had become exposed, and what we saw was as ugly as sin. It needs no description.

Bits of equipment, and other odds and ends, were lying about the scrubby slopes near the ravines. They had been there since the fighting at the end of June. The sight of them annoyed us, but we picked up a few things we needed for use or comfort. I found a small Turk grease-tin, with the crescent stamped on the lid, but I lost it shortly after.

Thursday, September 2, was our moving day. We were relieved by Straddling & Co., pushed up, and went to the brigade signal office, where parcels were waiting. There was one for each of us. They were Lady Douglas's Gifts.[195] Mine contained a small towel, a khaki hand-kerchief, bootlaces, socks, toilet-paper, louse-bag, Spanish-root, writing

---

195 Lady Douglas, the wife of the division's commander, had created a fund for the supply of comforts to her husband's troops.

pad, and a pencil. This was the only distribution of parcels of this kind made to the section while I was there. We were nobody's children. In any case these were far too late to be any real use, and I think that most of us opened them in cynical curiosity. Cynical, because it had taken nearly four months to put us in the running for such things. Most of us were well supplied with parcels from home, and opening these, just as they had come from the hands of our own people in our own homes, was our greatest pleasure. They were links with a life where women had a place, and where there were chairs and table-cloths, where buzzers did not worry, and where you could sleep in a clean bed, free from lice and flies.

We packed our parcels in our haversacks and went down Y Ravine to the beach, and along the coast road to the left. We had many rests on this road, with the sea lapping the stone on our right. We walked two to three hundred yards at a stretch. The sea glared at us. It had a kind of dull leaden glaze, instead of being cool or blue-looking and it was not pleasing to look upon. Now and then it swished over the rocky road-side. It seemed all wrong, somehow.

Odds and ends floated in it, bits of the war; and dead mules were lying on the rocks. Men, in single file, were going along this narrow strip of road, under the steep cliffs and slopes, or resting, with their backs to the cliffs. Some were asleep, others were staring at the glassy sea. At last we reached a place where pure sparkling water filtered through the rock to a little basin in the cliff-face on our left. Some Moses must have struck the rock and made us a present of this clear, clean water. We drank as much as we could and as much as we wanted. We had become used to water from the carts, with a strong flavour of chloride of lime; or from wells, where water tasted like rubber, and where dead men had been rumoured in the early days. We neither knew nor cared whether there were bodies in them or not. We wanted water and we took it where we could get it.

We went on again, reaching and passing Gully Beach, until we came to the entrance of a small ravine in the cliff to our left, about 250 yards beyond Gully Beach, and at the end of a low and narrow trench we came to a rocky hollow with a rocky wall in front of us.

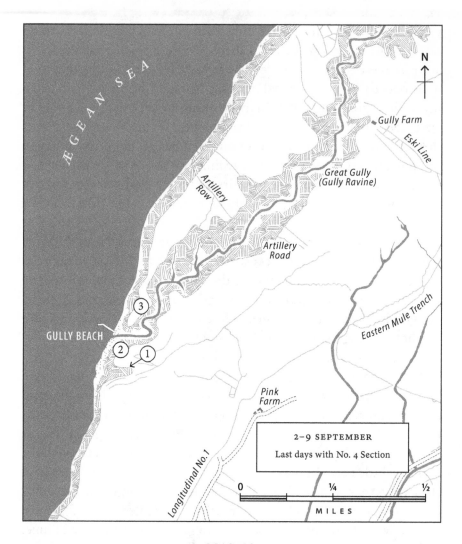

MAP 13

① Little Gully

② Dressing Station

③ 42nd (East Lancs) Division HQ from 19 August

CHAPTER 14

Little Gully

We called this place 'Little Gully.' The section lived in it for some days. It was a blind alley, but there were steep paths up the sides near the head. The ledges in the cliff face were strata of harder rock than that above or below which, in places, was sufficiently far back to give us room to walk and work on the ledges, the lower one in particular. We could reach this ledge by climbing up a heap of stones. The place was really a shallow cave. Vick lived in it, and here our lines were overhauled for breaks and bared places. Several miles of wire were man-handled in this cave. We lived in shallow holes in the gully floor. Our kitchen was on the right, near the heap of stones. I lived in a small hole on the left. Ormy and Claude had adjoining holes, opposite. About 20 feet up the gully-side there was a shelf of rock ten feet wide, and we could walk round the head of the gully on it. Brigade headquarters, where Tim lived, and the signal office, were high up on the left of the gully. On the ground above these, by going a short distance, we reached a place where we could look down on Great Gully, just inside the entrance. Immediately below, and nestling at the foot of the slope, was our Signal Company headquarters. We reached them by this route, sometimes, instead of going the longer way round, via the beach and Great Gully. On the top, also, we found a quiet scrounging-place in some deserted trenches. Two parcels had come for me. They were of little value to me, for all I could eat now was bread and milk, made with Ideal.

Figure 24. Signal section at Little Gully 'overhauling wire for breaks and
bared places.' (Alec Riley collection)

On Friday, September 3, I bathed in the afternoon. Sea-soap had been issued to us, so now we could make more elaborate toilets than we had known for some time. With several septic places, I found bathing awkward; but I did what I could about it. Fish-bombing was popular at Gully Beach. The fishermen took their boat out a few yards from the shore, and dropped bombs in the sea, killing or stunning any fish near the boat. Near the beach an oversea latrine had been made from long poles; a high skeleton of a latrine it looked from the shore. Life moved slowly, except when very odd shells burst behind Little Gully.

As I was still taking my turns in the signal office, I went on duty from 4 to 7 p.m. There was a quaint and curious arrangement of calls from the brigade officers' dug-outs. When I was off duty, I took to using the upper shelf for my bed-room, as it was within easy reach of a latrine, the place most frequented by several of us now. I had half a blanket, a dirty, dusty old rag. It felt and smelt like a large duster and was the only one I had kept for any length of time. My British Warm, and ground-sheet, had been all I needed in the hot weather.

Next morning, Saturday, September 4, I felt more tired than usual, but went over to the company headquarters to buy eggs and milk from Campbell. Townshend and his partner, our RAMC men, gave me plenty of iodine, lint and bandages. Sometimes they put the dressings on for me. Townshend was liberality itself with iodine. We paid a few calls, and compared a few notes with the washed-out crews in their dug-outs on the lower gully side. We wished Turkey and the Kaiser were frying in hell. Another parcel came. It contained, with other things, a tin of 'fly-ointment.' The rumours that there were flies on Gallipoli must have reached England; but the ointment, good or bad as it might be, had come too late.

Now and then Tim appeared. He asked Ormy what Claude meant when he shouted 'Chai up!' Ormy translated it. I tried to write letters but couldn't remember whether I had already answered letters and parcels or not. Then I had some rum to send me to sleep. SRD was our very good friend; and evil be to him who thinks evil of rum.[196]

---

196 SRD was the abbreviation for Supply Reserve Depot, commonly dubbed 'Seldom Reaches Destination.'

At this point my diary runs dry for a time. We spent the next few days lazing, or going to the gully for dressings. I wondered how I was going to get up to the trenches again. Somebody was blasting the ledge of rock not far away, and bits of it rattled down in Little Gully. We ourselves had finished damning and blasting. Most of us were past it.

* * *

On Wednesday, September 8, I went to the dressing station with a sick-report. This station was on the road-side facing the sea, between Little and Great gullies. The MO in charge ordered a milk diet, dressed my limbs, and told me to call again the following day for more dressings. I had a septic place on my right heel, and was walking with the back of my boot doubled in and the boot tied on. I was not wearing my tunic, my shorts were ragged, my helmet dirty and battered—for it had been my pillow for weeks, and with the top bashed in, it made a good one— my hands, legs and foot bandaged. I saw Tim eyeing me as he stood outside his home on the side of Little Gully. A disgrace to his section. That was the last time I saw Tim.

Figure 25. Headquarters of the 42nd Division in the entrance to Great Gully, better known as Gully Ravine. (Ernest Brooks)

CHAPTER 15

RAMC

When I went to the dressing station next morning, Thursday, September 9, the MO asked me a few questions, ordered me to be 'detained' and told me to get down on a stretcher. I had obeyed many orders, but never one like that before; and at first I could hardly realise what it meant. That it might be the end of Gallipoli for me seemed impossible and unnatural. I was not surprised, and yet it seemed as if the impossible had happened.

One of our attached men had come with me. When I was detained, I sent him back for my kit, so that I could select what I wanted. When it came, I kept my camera, films, diary, papers of all kinds, woollen-helmet, body belt and, of course, *Our Mutual Friend*, which had its use later on. I kept, also, one or two fragments intimately concerned. I lost my purse and about forty piastres, and a few other relics. I had my British Warm, and needed it shortly.

It was strange to lie there, enjoying the luxury of having somebody to look after me; but I couldn't sleep or even rest comfortably, for shorts, shirt and tunic were full of lice. Hell, doubly heated, was not hot enough for them.

On the morning of Friday, September 10, the MO labelled me for Mudros. As this meant getting away, even if only for a short time, I was content. He said I had jaundice. I packed all my small kit and private possessions in my overcoat pockets. Then, on a stretcher, I was carried to the road up to the cliff-top, on the Helles side of Little Gully, and up the rather steep path to a bend of the road. Motor ambulances could

Figure 26. The road down to Gully Ravine which runs past Little Gully. Taken circa 1930. (Alec Riley, *Twenty Years After*)

not come right down, the road not being fit for them. At the bend I was placed in a waiting ambulance. Ormy and others of No. 4 Section came to say good-bye. I had seen the last of No. 4.

We were taken to a field hospital on the cliff above W Beach, near the place where we had spent our first night on the peninsula. There were several marquees and we were carried to one of them, where my stretcher was dumped on the dusty ground inside, mine being one of a row of stretchers. The dust was thick. Clouds of it rose whenever anybody walked past us. I wondered how long it would be before I had some good food and a clean bed. We heard we were to have been taken to a hospital ship but the sea was too rough. A doctor came round, had a look at my eyes and teeth, and he, also, wrote 'Mudros' on my blue ticket. This was fastened to one of my tunic button-holes. I heard him tell another doctor that I was the 84th case of jaundice he had seen that morning. We lay there, like rows of addressed parcels. The day ended with a supper of milk, bread and jam, and dust; and I didn't like the taste of the dust, which was grey and gritty. Clouds of it.

Next morning, Saturday, September 11, we were given more milk, and then we were taken down to W Beach in ambulances, to one of the jetties, and here we were shipped on an old barge. When this was full of cases, it set off for the *Glasgow*. I had left my stretcher, and made myself as comfortable as I could.

At last I had left the peninsula, that hell-hole of bloodiness, and some odd sporting events. The red and green lights, which had given us the glad-eye for so long, were about to materialise.

It was not a particularly bright morning. A little sunshine would have cheered us up, and we needed cheering, for the passengers on the barge looked sick with themselves and with everything else. Amongst them I saw a few of the officers we had worked with, but no one bothered about anyone else. We were all too busy thinking about ourselves. Personally, I was not doing much thinking at all; although I had a good and last look at what we were leaving.

CHAPTER 16

Last thoughts

As our barge drew away from W Beach, most of us turned to look at the shore and the headlands with their Red Cross flags and marquees. There was now a little sunshine and in this the place looked brighter and more lively, as the flags fluttered in the wind ...

The shore and cliffs no longer filled the landscape. As they appeared lower, we could see the high ground beyond, and up to nearly six miles away. The country looked brown, parched, ugly and uninviting, and very different from what it was in early May, when it was green and fresh.

We had left many old friends there. Some were buried, others were still working. What was No. 4 Section doing? I thought of them making that long dreary journey up Great Gully, in the dust and heat, while an odd shrapnel or two was bursting overhead. Just then we could not hear any guns, and the sound of a distant rifle shot was so faint that it was hard to believe it might have been dangerous for somebody. No. 4 was probably still resting in Little Gully. I wondered if anybody had taken over my dug-out. 'Whatever else they may be doing; they will certainly be catching lice.' It was unbelievable that I should not be going with them up Great Gully or to Krithia Nullah again.

I did not know, then, that before many days had passed, the greater part of No. 4 would have followed me. I should not have been surprised, knowing the state some of them were in.

We reached the *Glasgow* and were taken on board. I sat on deck. We were soon on our way to Lemnos. Helles, now, could be seen in one piece, and very soon I could not distinguish men on shore and cliff from the backgrounds any longer. But I could fill in all the unseen details. Then, I could no longer make out more than very general features of the long, low peninsula, except, of course, Achi Baba.

At last I got tired of looking at it, and went below, wondering about the future. The past could take care of itself.

Hamilton's introduction to 'Return to Cape Helles'

Here is a little book which ought to sell very well although it was not (I happen to know) written with that as its chief end.[197] The reason? Well; thousands of dead are lying at the Dardanelles and although they can buy no books they can sell them. The story, too, though told for sheer romantic phantasy has turned out to be something quite practical; a guide-book to the cemeteries and their surroundings at Helles in Gallipoli; and, as the years roll by the demand for a sentimental guide-book will grow.

The late Lord Balfour said to me that he hoped never again to hear the word 'Gallipoli'. That was a natural enough wish on the part of one whose calm, well-balanced, fastidious outlook on life shrank away in sheer horror from anything which reminded it of the contrast between the whole-hearted devotion shown on the Peninsula and the hateful propaganda and half-hearted trimming at home; and yet, even to him, the story had only been half-told. Now, at last, the days of Revelation are at hand; and, if ever the world settles down again and exchanges render travel possible, one hundred pilgrims will travel to Helles compared to the one who manages to make his way there now.

---

197 This introduction was written by Sir Ian Hamilton for one of Riley's manuscripts that failed to find a publisher. The manuscript is lost but the two appendices that follow are probably excerpts from that work.

Meanwhile, there are the survivors of the Helles Landings and subsequent terrible struggles up to the Evacuation which left the Turks in possession, no doubt, but so beaten, so demoralised, that they could not, despite the frantic efforts of their officers and the strongest Artillery support, be whipped up into delivering an attack even upon the last few thousands. These men will want to possess a book of this kind, for Mr. Riley has personal knowledge of Helles as it was in 1915.

Also, surely, there are those who, as relatives of the dead, have seen, or—exchange or no exchange—are about to visit these cemeteries on Gallipoli, the most beautiful cemeteries imaginable, and who will need a keepsake to remind them of their pilgrimage.

Here they have it! But, because it was written for love rather than for money, its word-sketches and the photographs mean far more than any mere guide-book or keepsake. A gentle sentimental flavour emanates from its pages; a quality of wistful melancholy and an aroma of sweet flowers.

IAN HAMILTON.

11th November, 1932.

The silent nullahs of Gallipoli

Here is a picture of Gallipoli as it is twenty-two years after. The writer, who served with the 42nd Division, has made more than one pilgrimage to Gallipoli since the War ended and knows the Peninsula better than most. As he could tell you, it is an eerie business wandering alone up and down the deserted gullies and nullahs, places which at one time were scenes of bustling activity, but today are once more mere features of that rugged peninsula which has mounted guard over the narrow waters of the Straits since the days of Troy.[198]

A fellow-passenger, on a steamer going through the Dardanelles, pointed to the Peninsula and said to me, 'That place—it is not good'; and many people will agree with him, for, in 1915, the men on Gallipoli had but one wish—that they could get away from it and never see it again.

Comparing Past and Present

As time has passed, the hatred of those days has changed to curiosity to see the country under pleasanter conditions, and to compare the present with the past.

For these and other reasons I have revisited Helles twice, independently, living near Sedd-el-Bahr for several days, tramping the country systematically and alone, and photographing what I thought

---

198 *Twenty Years After: The Battlefields of 1914–18, Then and Now* edited by Major General Sir Ernest Swinton, KBE, CB

Figure 27. 'A bluff in Gully Ravine. This picture is typical of the southern portion of the ravine. Notice the scrub-covered bottom, with further dense scrub on the tops of the cliffs. Here the ravine is stern and narrow, but further up, in the Krithia section, it widens as it rises toward the open country, and becomes quite pleasant to look upon.' (Alec Riley, *Twenty Years After*)

to be of interest and importance. From the narrative of my rambles, three sections have been chosen for *Twenty Years After*, dealing chiefly with the two great highways of Helles, Great Gully and Krithia Nullah, and with the Helles Memorial and cemeteries. For purposes of contrast, some recollections of 1915, based on my notes for that year, have been included.

Certain parts of Helles can be reached easily enough, many of them by car; but the trackless country to be found in other areas is a different matter. It often means slow progress over or through natural obstacles, and it always means exhausting labour; for, although map-distances appear short, the same distances on the ground may include the full Helles variety of country.

As the reader comes with me, in imagination, over some of the ground he once knew so well, we shall find relics of a lost civilisation, we shall see and hear much that was familiar in 1915, and we shall recall the past; but, I must remind him that we shall be alone, day after day, in a land where thousands of men once lived, where thousands died, and where on headstones in the cemeteries and on the tablets of the Helles Memorial we shall find many names we know.

Great Gully and West Helles

Every man who knew Great Gully in 1915 will remember his tramps up and down the dusty road through this winding ravine. He will remember the dumps of bully and biscuits, water-tins, and ammunition; the dug-outs on the slopes, the scrub and trees growing on the precipitous sides, the yellow bluffs, the paths, leading to higher shelters and tops, and the places where he could find drinking-water. He will remember the scorching heat, the blinding glare from the gully sides, the white puffs of shrapnel overhead, the sound of pattering balls, and the clouds of brown smoke and dust where high explosives had burst in the gully.

He will remember processions of stretcher-bearers, and of sweaty, ragged men tormented by flies, going up with heavy loads of rations, or to relieve others in firing-line, birdcage, or sap, for he saw them often enough as he rested by the roadside. He will remember that steep and narrow path up the west side leading to the Mule Tracks; how it was blocked by mules loaded with SAA boxes and *fanatis*, and how the Indian drivers cursed or encouraged the struggling, kicking mules; for he passed them many times. And he will remember his relief when he reached the top and breathed cooler air.

Although Gully Road no longer exists, there are paths through the ravine, and on these we can make our way slowly, for the shallow-stream must be crossed several times, and there are places where thick and high vegetation blocks the tracks.

Winter rains have washed down loose earth from the steep sides; but, apart from such small changes, and the newer growths, Great Gully has not altered, and in the deeper sections where there is no breeze, the heat is as hard to bear now as it was in 1915. In this wild place the only sounds we hear are the rustling of scrub or bushes as we break through them, the croaking of bull-frogs by the stream, and the songs of birds.

Those who lived on the gully sides in 1915 would hardly know their old homes now, for only slight traces of dug-outs and shelters can be seen; but there are other signs of the occupation, and, on a slope near the Zig Zag, I found buttons from British tunics, webbing, broken rum-jars, and shrapnel and bullets from both sides. In the Turkish gully lines, between Krithia and Fusilier Bluff, two large and live shells lay by the side of the stream; and close by I came to a clean trench, 10 feet deep and crossable only where the sides had given way.

A short nullah from the north joins the gully near the final positions, and beyond this point the main gully and its offshoots shallow gradually to the open country near Krithia.

Today, Geoghegan's Bluff and the Boomerang are deserted; and are places without meaning to the few local people who pass them.

Figure 28. 'What story is there behind this bullet-pierced water-bottle, lying after more than twenty years as though dropped but a few months ago? Only the absence of its felt jacket, which alone has been obliterated by time, betrays the length of its sojourn on the lonely spur-top between Gully Ravine and the sea. Not far from this bottle were two or three others, their blue enamel easily seen amid the green and brown of the landscape.' (Alec Riley, *Twenty Years After*)

Figure 29. 'Gully Beach, as all who were in Gallipoli in 1915 will remember, is situated between X and Y Beaches, slightly less than a mile north of the former, which in this view is behind the central cape. The coast road used to be a great highway for troops going to and from the Great Gully, but nowadays the cliff has fallen in many places, and walking over the heaped stones is far from easy.' (Alec Riley, *Twenty Years After*)

A Pilgrimage to Fusilier Bluff

Gully Beach is a convenient place for starting a walk to Fusilier Bluff by way of the Aegean cliffs and ravines. Readers who were here in 1915 will remember that the spur separating the coast from Great Gully ends in a sharp point. Today it is difficult to descend this slope, once full of dug-outs, and it is necessary to go down by a series of jumps on to uncertain footholds of loose earth and grass. To climb it is not worth the trouble, as the top can be reached by stone steps and a path, a short distance up the gully.

From this high ground we look down on a narrow ridge where a path leads to the end of the spur, and our view will include the beach, gully-entrance, and Helles Ridge and Monument in the distance beyond the cliffs. To our right we look down on the remains of a jetty, and a derelict K lighter.

Figure 30. 'This again is typical, but typical of the handiwork of Man in Gallipoli rather than that of nature. The picture comes from Gully Beach, and shows the ruined jetty, with a derelict "K" lighter lying off it. On the night of the evacuation, General Maude—later of Baghdad fame—was to have left the Peninsula on this lighter, but it ran aground, and he had to walk, with a small party, by the coast-road to W Beach.' (Alec Riley, *Twenty Years After*)

A wide track on the cliff-top leads to the head of Y Ravine; and as I went forward, crossing and re-crossing the spur, so that I could overlook sea and gully alternately, I saw that the scrub was full of litter. There were bayonet-scabbards whose brittle leather was no longer held by the bleached and rotted stitches; rum-jars—broken as usual—bits of webbing, boots whose leather was in shreds, nose-caps, a mess-tin which may have been used as a brazier (for it was riddled with bayonet stabs), shrapnel cases and balls, and hundreds of Turkish bullets. Here and there the blue enamel of water-bottles caught my eye.

Gurkha Bluff, rugged and lonely, dominates this part of the coast. Before reaching it, I followed a broken path down the slope of Gurkha Ravine to Y Beach, a strip of sand at the foot of Y Ravine and Gurkha Bluff. Over large stones I made my way round the foot of the Bluff, past

Bruce's Ravine to Shrapnel Point; and from this corner I could look along the coast to Sari Tepe.

Y Ravine is a gutter where the rains wash down mud and sandy clay, and where a few old tins have settled. As I climbed up it I saw patches of scrubless earth on the sides of the ravine, and these were the only signs of our old resting-places. On another walk in this area I found a ruined shelter, nearer the cliff-top, where a mess-tin lid and a rotting ground-sheet were both half-buried in the floor.

In 1915 a popular evening's entertainment was to look down on the Aegean, where our monitors cruised, and to watch them firing. When the monitors had finished, we waited for Nature to show a picture of fire and water. Night after night we sat on the cliffs watching that crimson glow and its reflection, until Imbros and Samothrace vanished in blackness.

Figure 31. 'Y Beach and Y Ravine. A photograph taken from the side of Gurkha Bluff. Today a rough place to climb or descend, Y Ravine led in 1915 to a bathing-place for men in the north-west sector of Helles. As to the bluff, the best view of it is to be had from the top of the projection in the centre of the photograph. The feature owes its name to the climb which the Gurkhas made up its rugged flanks from Y Beach on the night of May 12th, 1915.' (Alec Riley, *Twenty Years After*)

Figure 32. 'Fusilier Bluff and Sari Tepe. Unlike Gurkha Bluff, Fusilier Bluff is not a prominent feature. This part of Helles is very exposed, and the rains have washed down much of the soil—the terrain being in any case of an exceedingly friable nature. The scrub is thick, and walking consequently difficult. In 1915 the extreme left of the British firing-line ended on the lower slope of Fusilier Bluff, which in this photograph is in the foreground, with Sari Tepe beyond.' (Alec Riley, *Twenty Years After*)

Sounds Amid the Solitude

Today the ground at the head of Y Ravine is full of crumbled trenches, and is crossed slowly and with difficulty. On Gurkha Bluff I found a level patch, and here I had lunch in the ruins of a shelter, thankful to find a few inches of shade under a bit of overhanging scrub. From this lonely place it was cheering to see a passing steamer when I looked down on the Aegean, and still more cheering to hear the distant siren of an unseen ship as it left the Dardanelles.

But, however lonely these cliffs and bluffs may be, they are the most delightful places at Helles. The scenery is wild, and the surroundings are full of litter, but the sky is blue, there is a pleasant breeze, and from below come the sounds of wavelets breaking on the shore.

From the top of Gurkha Bluff we can skim the surface of Helles and see the Dardanelles and the high ground at the end of the peninsula in the hazy distance. From one side of the bluff we look down on Y Beach and Ravine, and along the cliffs; and from the far side gaze over Bruce's, Essex, Border, and Trolley Ravines, and their separating ridges, to Fusilier Bluff and Sari Tepe.

Continuing my walk to Fusilier Bluff, I passed Douglas Street and Essex Street West, and went along the tops of the Western Mule Track. Behind this track are Inniskilling and Forward Inches, Manchester Street, Colne Street and Post; but, well known as these and the other trenches at Helles were in 1915, today they are deserted and crumbling, with nothing to distinguish one from the other.

The Western Mule Track is four-feet deep, and too rough for walking along. I found nothing to remind me of those evenings in 1915 when we

Figure 33. 'A trench near the Echelons. There were three "echelons," named respectively "Bury," "Rochdale," and "Salford," all situated between Trolley Ravine and Fusilier Bluff. They were reached by the Western Mule Track. In this photograph a coil of barbed wire can be seen near the skyline, with sundry posts, still upright, to left of it. In the bottom of the trench are a sniper's shield and a broken SAA box.' (Alec Riley, *Twenty Years After*)

Figure 34. 'The stream in Krithia Nullah.' (Alec Riley, *Twenty Years After*)

passed through it on our way home: when sunset was followed by pearl-green twilight, and a full moon was rising; when summer lightning flashed, and 'strays' whined between us and the stars. Some readers may remember how the Western Mule Track was haunted, where a coat-sleeve and the thin bones of a skeleton hand, white in the moonlight, stuck out from the side.

I came to Salford, Rochdale, and Bury Echelons, disturbing a snake on my way. Behind the echelons, Sikh Road led to the Western Birdcage and various saps. Litter was thick round the Echelons. There were bombs, periscopes, tin linings of SAA boxes, mess-tins, Maconochie tins, other tins, rum-jars—broken or whole, but empty—curls of barbed wire, a sniper's shield, pickheads, shovels, a long, thin bayonet bent and twisted, rotten leather pouches and scabbards, shell cases, bullets, shrapnel balls, iron splinters, rifle-barrels, and some water-bottle corks whose deficiency-returns used to be demanded by unimaginative Staff-Captains at inconvenient times.

The western section of the British firing-line passed over Fusilier Bluff, and ended on the shore below. Apart from that, the Bluff is not remarkable in any way, and has no striking features. From it I could see the Anzac Hills and Suvla Point away in the distance beyond Sari Tepe.

Those who passed the high places of Western Helles, in 1915, saw many wooden crosses silhouetted against Aegean sunsets; but the remains of the men whose resting-places these crosses marked have been taken from the wild bluffs, and today lie in gardens of peace and beauty.

Krithia Nullah

We will start this walk from Clapham Junction, and go through one mile of the water-course to our objective—a small corner of the August battlefield near the Fork—comparing, on our way, Krithia Nullah as it is now with the Krithia Nullah of 1915, when it was one of the main roads of Helles, with trenches on either side.

The reader knows that Eski Line crossed the nullah a quarter-of-a-mile from Clapham Junction, that No. 2 Australian Line and Redoubt Line touched it further on, that between Redoubt and the Fork were Ardwick Green, Great Western Road, and Clunes Vennel on the west, and Wigan Road and Renfield Street on the east, and that the nullah served them all.

Today Clapham Junction is deserted, and its features are overgrown with vegetation. But in 1915 ... It is the Market-place of Helles. A large wooden cross, with smaller crosses round it, stands at the point where the nullahs meet. Close by are dumps of ammunition, stores, clothing, and equipment from dead and wounded. Near some horse-shelters in the nullah-side are the water-carts of local units, where men wait in queues for their turns to fill their own water-bottles, and as many others as they can carry; for in trenches where no air circulates there are many parched lips caked with dust, waiting impatiently to drink warm water flavoured with chloride of lime.

Ragged bandaged men go along the path, in the yellow dusty heat of a summer's day at Helles. When shrapnel bursts over the nullah, more dust is raised by the scattered balls. In the low nullah-sides there are shallow dugouts, open at the front and top, or with ground-sheets pegged over them. Here live quartermasters, staffs, and others who have business at the Junction ...

Figure 35. 'Another reach of the stream ... Springing from the neighbourhood of Krithia, the nullah runs southward, parallel with the equally small Kanli Dere, or Achi Baba Nullah, and ends up in the vicinity of Morto Bay.' (Alec Riley, *Twenty Years After*)

Choked with Vegetation

Today, in our mile of nullah, there is a small trickle of water in the stream, and by its side there are traces of a path which we can follow; but, where it is not continuous we must make our way through scrub on the sides or tops. Trees, bushes, and tufts of coarse grass cover the rough banks, and in places the nullah is choked by thick growth. We are going through wild country, where the rains and torrents of winter and the growth of spring have done much to help Krithia Nullah to return to its natural state.

In all this desolation it is pleasant to find small pools where the stream has widened, and to see in them the reflections of blue sky and green surroundings. I found only one sign of human activity in the nullah—a patch of cultivation where a few olive-trees were growing. Close by were tins, rotted and half-buried ground-sheets, and a piece of wire-netting holding up the crumbling side of a shelter.

In open country, Eski, Redoubt, and other trenches are easily found, but in Krithia Nullah, where the sides are overgrown and crumbling, identification is difficult, even with the help of a map. I noticed several depressions in the bank-tops, near the sites of trenches well known in 1915, but nothing to remind me of our lines when we knew them as clean cuttings. Near Redoubt there is a waterfall and also a deep pool where frogs splash and swim, where tall rushes grow from the muddy slime, where flies swarm round us, and there is a stagnant, unpleasant smell. The surroundings are full of tins, and above the fall a piece of rusty iron lies in the water.

The Nullah in 1915

In 1915 we know this same nullah from many points of view. It is a highway, where battalions of weary men crawl along the narrow path, going up to the front line. Almost every man is bandaged on hands, fingers, and legs. They carry picks and spades, or boxes of rations, as well as khaki bandoliers, rifles, and equipment. Some carry 'flying pigs' on their backs, to a trench mortar dump near the firing-line; and others are carrying boxes of SAA.

Down the nullah come stretcher-bearers, peering through sweat as they seek level bits of ground. Their wounded burdens are wrapped in brown blankets. Sometimes the victim rests his head on his hands and smokes a cigarette; sometimes his face is covered with his helmet, or a cap-comforter is pulled over his eyes, and all we can see is the lower part of a grey face. Sometimes he turns his head to look at those he is leaving, but not as though he can see them; and sometimes he lies quite still. If the blanket covers him from head to foot he will soon be buried.

There are many graves on the nullah-sides marked by crosses made from twigs and bootlaces or string, and better ones made from strips of packing-case, so that the name can be carved neatly with a penknife, or printed with indelible pencil.

In an hour there will be a new cross further up the nullah, where some ragged figures stand near a stretcher, and a shallow grave holds the body of a friend. In the scorching sun these men are holding their helmets over their necks while the padre reads a short service.

Figure 36. The remains of two 'flying pigs' photographed by Riley in the 1930s. (Alec Riley, *Twenty Years After*)

We are always thirsty; but we know some springs where water trickles from the nullah-banks. Going up or down, we call at each watering-place, even at those marked by boards with 'Unfit for Drinking,' where we can smell the dead buried close by. We splash through mud to one of these springs, where the water fills a hollow in the soil. Someone has left an old jam-tin by the side. As we ladle a tinful of water, the rest is muddied; but we drink it, thick or clear. We clean ourselves in shallow pools of dirty nullah-water, and sometimes we pretend to bath, soaping our bodies and throwing water over one another from a mess-tin, or a canvas bucket found and kept.

Here and there we know deeper pools fed by small waterfalls, and to stand under one of these falls is the height of toilet luxury at Helles; but there are times when we hear a crack, and looking up see a puff of smoke against the blue sky, while the balls splash the water; and feeling very naked we make for the side and our lousy clothes, for we may be unlucky if the Turks should send another round. There are places where the nullah is marked by Turk snipers; and one of their favourites is the side of a waterfall, where a plank takes the path to a higher level.

The Chill that Follows Sunset

The chalky cliff is tinged with a delicate pink in the sunset glow. After sunset the air may be chilly, and we shall need our tunics. Those who have cut off their shirt-sleeves above the elbows, or cut their trousers down to shorts, wonder if coolness by day is worth coldness by night.

It is dusk. Lights twinkle on the nullah-sides, and in the still air blue smoke ascends from tiny fires of pinecones and heather-roots. There is a pleasant smell from these wood fires. Round them sit little groups of men drinking their evening tea, and talking about matters of importance.

We belong to one of these groups, and we set about discussing rations, unfounded rumours of relief, and still more unfounded rumours about going home. As we drink our tea we hear a splash. A large water-turtle has dropped from his cliff to the stream below, disturbing the frogs, which for a time croak louder and more insistently.

It is dark now, and glow-worms show their lights. We hear the clink of picks and shovels, from a working party coming up the nullah. A few hours ago these men had gone down to rest—and now they have come back to spend the night digging near the firing-line. Some of them will not come down again, but will stay where they are buried, and new crosses will be needed in the morning.

Now and then we hear the rattle of machine guns and the crackle of rifles. Bullets whine over the nullah, tearing through scrub or ripping up the ground. The nearer trees are black against the glow of flares in the front lines ...

Thus it was in 1915.

A Host of Relics

Continuing my recent walk through the nullah, I came to the fork, where East and West Krithia nullahs diverge; and here lay two rifle-barrels, bent and twisted, bombs, a live shell, lead, and litter. Beyond the fork the country is wild, and there are waterfalls in the sides of the branching nullahs, where cliffs, trees, and scrub make it difficult to explore the surroundings.

For a quarter-of-a-mile the two nullahs are 200 yards apart; after that the distance between them increases. The last Turkish firing-line is 200 yards north of the Fork, crossing both nullahs.

To the left of West Krithia Nullah are two trenches, known officially as H11a and H11b. H11a follows the course of the nullah until it meets the shorter H11b at right-angles. In the August battle, the last one of importance at Helles, some of the hardest fighting concerned these two trenches and the Vineyard, 400 yards away on the far side of the nullah-fork.

Near H11b, I found a shallow depression, with barbed wire still hanging on posts, backed by a seven-foot bank. As I sat near H11a, smoking a cigarette in this quiet spot, where the light earth of ancient parapets was the only sign that I was on the battlefields of June and August, I looked back toward our old lines, and recalled the inside of a trench ...

August, 1915: on the parapet-midden are tins, coils of barbed-wire, clips, bits of wood and other rubbish. We hear metallic clinks when bullets hit the tins. The heat is intense, for the sun reaches every corner of Helles, and a man is lucky if he can find six inches of shade cast by a trench-side. Fat green flies buzz round our faces, or defile our food. By day no breeze comes to this place; by night, damp air brings the smell of corpses. When we look over the parapet we see a brown and ugly landscape; and we see, also, many of the dead lying in the open.

Friday, August 6th, 1915

It is Friday, the 6th of the month. Our guns open fire at half-past two. There is a whizz of shells and bullets overhead; and when the Turks answer, the air about us quivers and the ground shudders with explosions. We hear the muffled pops of our trench mortars, see the 'pigs' wobble upwards, steady themselves, drop on Turkish positions, and burst with long, horizontal crimson flashes. Then, while we shake and rock in sympathy with our surroundings, bits of hot metal, clusters of balls in smoking grease, showers of earth, and slower dust fall into our trench. White smoke hangs over the torn foreground, and through it our men go forward. Coils of barbed wire appear and disappear in the smoke.

There is a dressing station at a trench-junction 10 yards from us. When the attacks start, the MO and his orderlies wait for such of the wounded as can manage to reach it. A few seats have been cut in the trench-side, and the MO has opened his case of instruments.

Wounded men come down, singly at first, and then in one long procession—many of them supporting others more badly wounded than themselves. Most of them have been in mud and water; some have little clothing on; that of others is torn to shreds, hanging from shoulders or waist. All are bloody, and there are blood-soaked dressings on heads, arms, hands, and legs.

The MO works hard and quickly, but he cannot cope with the numbers. Men sit on the earth seats, staring, but not seeing; others are deaf and dumb; others are muttering or shaking in every limb. One crawls past us on one knee and his hands, dragging a useless leg. Another's face is a red mask, and only his eyes show through it. Stretchers are filled time after time, and carried slowly down a winding narrow trench crowded with men. Shells burst close by, and the dressing station is full of smoke and fumes. The MO looks round, but no one has been hit.

The noise is deafening, but there is a louder crash when a 'pig' bursts in a nearby Turkish line, throwing up clothing, timbers, and papers, which flutter down in the smoke.

Saturday, August 7th: another bombardment, and an assault by composite parties, on H11a and H11b. Once more heads ache with noise and strain. Once more the sun glares through stifling air. Once more light cases come to the dressing station, while earth descends through yellow stinking fumes. Once more wounded men lie in front of the trench they have left, scorched by the sun, and not daring to move until night, when some of them may be able to crawl back to our lines.

Laughter Rarely Heard

It is Saturday afternoon. Trenches are crowded with worn-out men, lousy and unwashed for days, who sleep where they can find room to lie; and we must tread carefully so as not to disturb them. A few men slouch past, thin, round-shouldered, eyes dulled, bandaged on hands or legs, full of septic sores. They cannot be cured on Gallipoli, but dressing stations are busy with iodine and lint. There is little talking, and, although Helles has had its humour, laughter is rarely heard now.

A young subaltern comes to us asking for food, and while we give him all we have—broken biscuits, jam, and water—he tells us that there is no food in his part of the line.

We know the results of the fighting on our small front, but nothing about events on either side of it, until news comes that our men are holding a captured trench alongside the Vineyard, and a good part of the Vineyard itself, where bombing and fighting have gone on day and night, and where Helles has indeed been hot.

On Sunday morning the firing-line tells a plain story. Between its shattered walls are broken entrenching-tools, bullet-riddled equipment torn and stained, jagged iron, shell-cases, broken ammunition-boxes, clips of SAA, stained stretchers; and from this bloody litter we take such things as we need. Then, on field service postcards, we cross out those statements which do not apply ...

In the future, a visitor to Lala Bala Cemetery at Suvla will find these words inscribed on the gate-piers:

> Near this spot the IX Army Corps landed on the night of the
> 6th–7th August, 1915.

For that is what has happened while those at Helles have been fighting ...

But in the trenches of central Helles there is no shade from the August sun, and the men who hold them are tormented by flies and lice; while over them hangs the heavy scent of death ...

The Monument at Helles

My cigarette was finished, and it was time to leave the solitudes of nullah and disappearing ditch, where now the only life is that of wild creatures, and the only changes are those of the seasons.

On Gueji Baba, a hill 150 feet above sea-level, and the highest point in this part of Gallipoli, stands the Helles Memorial. This is an appropriate site, for near it the original British landing was made and the last troops were evacuated.

The monument is more than 100 feet high, and consists of an obelisk rising from the centre of a square platform nearly eight feet above ground level. The platform is reached by steps on the south, and is enclosed by a parapet-wall. The sides of obelisk and platform face north, south, east, and west.

Four panels on the lower sides of the obelisk are inscribed: Royal Navy, Anzac, Suvla, and Helles, followed by names of ships, divisions, and brigades concerned in those areas; and each panel faces the general compass-bearing of the area whose name it bears at the top. The detailed compositions of these larger formations, and the names of smaller units, are inscribed on the parapet-wall facing each side of the obelisk.

Carved on panels set in the outer side of the wall are the names of some 21,000 sailors and soldiers from the Home Countries, India, and Newfoundland, who were lost or buried in Gallipoli waters, or who died on the peninsula at Helles, Anzac, and Suvla, and who lie in unknown graves. Names of 248 Australians who fell at the Second Battle of Krithia are included. The Australian and New Zealand dead are commemorated by their own memorials in other parts of Gallipoli.

The Helles Monument, therefore, serves two purposes. It is a record of the whole campaign, so far as the forces of the Empire were concerned, and a memorial to many thousands of those over whose bodies headstones cannot be placed. Designed by the firm of architects, Sir John Burnet, Tait, and Horne, it is to Gallipoli what the Menin Gate is to the Ypres Salient; and on this carefully chosen site it is seen to advantage from both land and sea.

Evening is the best time to inspect it, for then the stone no longer reflects the sun's glare. From the platform, surrounded by names of ships, regiments, and men, we look over the parapet to the blue Dardanelles, the roadsteads where fleet and transports lay, Lancashire Landing Cemetery, the tops of gully, bluff, and ravine, Achi Baba and the nearer country of nullahs and battlefields, and to black Imbros and Samothrace between red sky and red shining sea.

Gallipoli Cemeteries Today

Strategic and spectacular characteristics made the Gallipoli Campaign stand out from the rest of the Great War, of which it was as much a part as the fighting on any other front; and today, memorial and cemeteries, although different from those of other fronts, are links in the same world-wide chain of Empire graves.

Pilgrimages to Gallipoli have been made, tourists have landed from steamers to spend a few hours on the peninsula, and occasionally someone has found time and opportunity to visit it alone; but, apart from these, there are few who know what the architects and the Imperial War Graves Commission have done on this rugged corner of Europe.

The reader is asked to recall the graves of Helles, isolated or in groups, on battlefields, shores, and gully sides, as they were in the early days of the campaign, when they were marked by crosses made from any bits of wood obtainable; and how these primitive crosses were replaced by others of regulation pattern, also of wood.

Instead of these scattered groups, there are today six British cemeteries, known as V Beach, Lancashire Landing, Pink Farm, Twelve Tree Copse, Redoubt, and Skew Bridge, each having its

Figure 37. 'V Beach and V Beach Cemetery. This cemetery was begun and ended, so far as burials in 1915 were concerned, during the period April–May, but a few other graves were added after the Armistice. The burials include those of 500 United Kingdom soldiers and sailors and a number of unidentified dead. Cypresses, pines, and tamarisks now grow outside the cemetery walls on all but the shore side.' (Alec Riley, *Twenty Years After*)

Figure 38. 'Redoubt Cemetery ... looking toward Helles, whose memorial may just be discerned on the skyline to the left of the nearest cypress. Many of those killed in the Third Battle of Krithia, on June 4th, 1915, are buried here. The cemetery is beautifully laid out, and its immediate vicinity is also orderly and trim; but further afield the country is wild and untouched—a strong contrast.' (Alec Riley, *Twenty Years After*)

name inscribed on the gate-piers. There were small cemeteries on or near these places in 1915, and how they were made and increased by concentrations is described in the official records of the Imperial War Graves Commission.

Except from certain beaches, gullies, and low ground, there are few places in the British area from which the obelisk and one or more cemeteries are not visible; and as their pines and cypresses grow taller, the cemeteries grow more into the landscape. It is difficult to realise the time, skill, and labour spent in planning and construction; but if we stand on the walls at Pink Farm or Redoubt, and look over the scrubby wastes of trenched battlefields on all sides, remembering that out of such chaos these places have been made, we begin to understand what it has meant to change the wilderness into gardens of cultivated beauty.

Similar in general outline, each cemetery was specially designed and given its own characteristics. The gates of Indian teak were made in

England, where also the headstones of Hopton Wood stone were cut and inscribed.

Water has to be carried to these spots; and through severe weather and parching summer heat they have every possible attention from the gardeners, and constant supervision by the Area Superintendent. English grass is not suitable for the lawns, so local couch-grass, which is green in summer and brown in winter, has been planted.

By Krithia Road

I will now ask the reader to imagine that he is standing on high ground off the rising bend of Krithia Road, looking down on Skew Bridge Cemetery, which stands between Krithia and Kilid Bahr Roads, 50 yards from the Dere over which the former was carried by a wooden skew-bridge.

Figure 39. 'Krithia in ruins looks like the remains of some huge feudal castle, and is a desolate sight indeed. Fallen stones, hidden in the thick undergrowth, make it a difficult place in which to wander, and care is also needed to avoid a number of deep wells. Outside the confines of the village, there is still to be seen the stump of one of the round windmills which were so well known (from a distance) in 1915.' (Alec Riley, *Twenty Years After*)

Figure 40. 'Achi Baba from Krithia.' (Alec Riley, *Twenty Years After*)

The cemetery is just behind the centre of the Allied line across the peninsula of April 27th, 1915, and it came into being after the Second Battle of Krithia, May 6th–8th. Although used throughout the occupation, it contained only a few bodies until after the Armistice, when others were brought in from certain points and battlefields. Outside the walls are belts of ilex, while cypresses, rosemary, and blue irises grow among the graves. In the afternoon the sun shines full on the Memorial against its background of pines.

To this contrast between white stone and the dark and light greens of trees and lawn, the reader must add a deep blue sky and the colours of wild flowers and butterflies around him. He must hear the sounds of the countryside—the songs of birds, the lowing of cattle, the call of a peasant, the barking of dogs in the distant village, and the nearer rumble of a country cart; for these make up the setting of Skew Bridge Cemetery in springtime.

In the still evening air we hear the tinkle of cattle-bells, and the footsteps of country people coming down the track in Achi Baba Nullah with their donkeys, cows, and goats. It is dusk in the quiet nullah, and in the west Pink Farm ridge is black against the red glow of sunset.

* * *

Figure 41. 'Although Krithia and Achi Baba Nullahs are not widely separated, they are noticeably different in character, and, of the two, Achi Baba Nullah is the pleasanter. Its southern portion is, in truth, a delightful place in spring; the grass is shorter and greener than in most parts of Helles, there are plenty of trees and flowers, and the trickle of the stream may be heard. This photograph comes from higher up, where the nullah is wilder.' (Alec Riley, *Twenty Years After*)

Figure 42. 'Main street, Sedd-el-Bahr. It will be noticed that Sedd-el-Bahr bears little resemblance to what it was in the early days of the campaign. The houses in this street have never been properly rebuilt, and few of them are more than poor shelters. Two cafes are the only centres of (masculine) social life. Strongly fortified by the Turks in the 17th century, Sedd-el-Bahr—village, fortress, and ancient castle—was stormed on April 26th, 1915.' (Alec Riley, *Twenty Years After*)

Gallipoli under tranquil skies

Revisiting beaches and battlefields with the eye of an old campaigner

The landings in Gallipoli of April, 1915, are commemorated this week-end, when a new Gallipoli exhibit will be staged at the Imperial War Museum. Mr. Riley, who describes below his visit to the Helles battlefields in later years, has contributed photographs to the exhibit.[199]

On an April morning in 1915, British soldiers landed on the beaches of Helles; and although the survivors of those landings, subsequent battles, and months of occupation cannot forget their adventures, their recollections of the country itself are fading. Nearly twenty-three years have passed since most of them saw it.

My first glimpse of Gallipoli since 1915 was from a steamer approaching the Dardanelles. Across the blue waters were the light, grass-topped cliffs of Helles and Achi Baba's distant slopes. The Cape, W and V beaches and Sedd el-Bahr fort were there in their old familiar forms. The *River Clyde* had gone, there were no lighters lying off the beaches, no signs of activity on shore, no smoke rising from the hill; but there were two new landmarks: the white lighthouse on Cape Helles, and on Guezji Baba, the obelisk of the British Memorial, which the steamer saluted with three siren blasts.

---

199 *The Daily Telegraph and Morning Post*, Saturday 23 April 1938.

Identifying Dug-outs

From each of several famous viewpoints on Helles Ridge the inland prospect is similar: Achi Baba, five miles distant, spreads his green and attractive terraces along the horizon, dominating the apparently featureless central country. By a track through olive orchards on the rear slope of Helles Ridge, I descended to Morto Plain, crossed it, and made my way up to Pink Farm. A short walk from Pink Farm took me to Twelve Tree Copse Cemetery, where three grassy terraces command a wide panorama of central Helles.

Survivors of countless digging parties may be interested to know that the average depth of their trenches was four feet when I saw them last, and that it was possible to walk a few yards in parts unchoked by weeds, brambles or young fig trees. Even certain lines could be identified from memory or a map, but others had changed beyond recognition.

Here and there I made out the grassy blocks of traverses and the hollows of trench recesses. Many dug-out sites were patches of sandy soil with tufts of grass, but some of them could be identified by local landmarks.

In 1915 we could walk along the Western Mule Track to the Ravines and Fusilier Bluff, through Sauchihall-street to White House, to Leicester-square, via Oxford-street, Piccadilly-circus and Regent-street; we could follow Nelson-avenue, St. Vincent and Argyle streets, or reach Birdcage and Barricade from Essex-knoll or Hampshire-cut. We knew, also, the two Australian lines, Oldham and Wigan roads, the Gurkha Mule Trench and Ardwick Green. Much of the story of Helles was told by its trench-labels; but these trenches, now, are unnamed and silent ditches.

Littered with Relics

Although copper, brass and the large forms of war material have been cleared away, innumerable relics survive. In certain areas the ground was littered with what were known as 'shell-cases,' bullets, clips, odd rounds of SAA, shrapnel-balls and fragments of bombs, with tins, tunic and trouser buttons, and such details as a broken tooth-brush and the metal frame of a small mirror. There were shards of that popular pottery which is stamped 'SRD'; and a jar-neck with cork intact told its story of deliberate destruction—and waste.

The first of my return visits to Helles included June 4. Recalling some of the events of June 4, 1915, I allotted that day to Achi Baba and places of interest within reach of the Krithia road.

This road descends from Sedd el-Bahr to Morto Plain, and rises, near Skew Bridge Cemetery, to the spur-top between Krithia Nullah and Achi Baba Nullah, where it is sandy and rutted, but level for some distance and parallel to the track of 1915. It crosses Eski Line and then Redoubt, where a left-hand path leads to Redoubt Cemetery.

The Vineyard, a small area of flourishing but untended vines, 300 yards from Redoubt, was more fruitful in grenades than grapes in 1915. Here I had difficulty in penetrating close, overgrown trenches, where the air was stifling, and where bombs with short fuses lay in soft earth. The last British firing-line ran through the Vineyard. Like that of the Turks, it is shallow and bushy.

A Derelict Lighter

Achi Baba lies almost half-way between Dardanelles and Aegean, his spurs and terraces extending and declining in all directions. I recalled restless nights and hopeless dawns in the country below; and noisy days such as that other June 4 when the hill was shrouded in the smoke of blasting shell-fire. It was easier, however, to remember the lighter misfortunes of a time when I hoped that my stay would not last much longer—though I feared that it might.

My recollections of Achi Baba on this later June 4 are those of a hill-top silence, only broken by birds and the soft rustle of leaves; and of a hillside farm, where kindly Turks brought water and refreshment, while they invited me to rest in the shade of the olive trees.

I made an expedition to the beaches of Western Helles, by way of Pink Farm and Great Gully; following the winding gully to its shallow extremity near Krithia, inspecting Fusilier and Gurkha Bluffs with their surroundings, and descending Y Ravine to its beach. This broken and scrubby country was littered with relics; and, on the slopes of Y Ravine, I found traces of the primitive shelters of 1915. Beyond the rocky foot of Gurkha Bluff I came to the shore-end of Bruce's Ravine—rugged enough in the past but even wilder now.

Figure 43. 'Zighin Dere, usually known as Gully Ravine or Great Gully, is deep and wild for most of its three-miles' course. It runs north-eastward from Gully Beach, making several sharp turns, and shallowing as it approaches Yazy Tepe. The photograph shows the end of Gully Spur, a long ridge, varying in width, which divides the ravine from the Aegean.' (Alec Riley, *Twenty Years After*)

From the far end of a path along the spur, between coast and ravine, I surveyed Gully Beach. To my left was Great Gully, with its scrubby slopes and yellow curving cliffs; to the right, on the spur-shore and close to the concrete and rusting iron of a broken pier, lay a derelict K lighter which ran aground on the night of the evacuation. There were traces of dug-outs on the face of the spur-point, but only a sandy and weedy bank, behind the beach, marked the site of what I knew as an overworked field ambulance.

I planned a further walk, to cover W and V beaches. The first objective was Lancashire Landing Cemetery, 300 feet above the beach and 1,000 yards behind it, where the gate-piers bear these words: 'The 29th Division landed along the coast on the morning of April 25th, 1915.'

Lancashire Landing, or W Beach, lies between Tekke Burnu and the NW end of a precipitous and cliffy slope which continues to Cape Helles, and it is backed by an irregular slope and small gully. Surveying the shore from each cliff in turn I looked down upon partially buried lighters and the remaining stones and iron supports of piers.

From the south-eastern cliff I made my way to Cape Helles, where the coast bends eastward sharply, and followed the cliff-line to a point below Fort No. 1 for the best view of V Beach.

Below me lay the cemetery, a few feet above the sands, with its memorial facing the sea and its gate facing the beach. Then came the low earth cliff, by which V Beach is backed, and a central jetty. Near the Old Fort were the remains of the *River Clyde* pier. Land adjoining the shore had been cultivated; a field near the fort was being ploughed, on the long slope behind the beach, sheep were grazing between old trenches where village children played.

I recalled the *River Clyde*: her bullet-chipped bows, the shell-holes in her deck, the water in her holds; the broken glass of her screen, and the large ports through which, during the landing, men had passed to gangway and lighters, and many to their deaths—for, in the cemetery, several headstones bear this date: 'April 25, 1915.'

Only the murmur of lapping wavelets disturbed the silence of V Beach.

Figure 44. 'W Beach and Cape Helles—Now. Utter desolation is the modern keynote of this once animated scene—as, indeed, it is the keynote of all Gallipoli.' (Alec Riley, *Twenty Years After*)

The Shadows Lifted

Sunset reddens the Aegean and blackens Imbros and Samothrace, while colours fade from the darkening landscape and stars shine with increasing brilliance. In the cold glare of a full moon Krithia road wavers across hazy contours into shadowed obscurity. The Helles night-choir of howling dogs and hooting owls is augmented by a chorus of bull-frogs. No 'strays' whisper over the battlefield, but the echoing sound of a farmer's gun-shot is strangely familiar.

Grey dawn streaks, mirrored in Morto Bay, widen slowly as they change to pale yellow, gold and red. The olive-trees take shape; and calls of wakening life sound over field and valley. Then, the rising sun floods the early mist with his light, while he turns Achi Baba from grey to green and lifts the shadows from the dark country of the nullahs.

* * *

Figure 45. 'Morto Bay restored to loneliness ... In the foreground is the Krithia Road, passing the cypresses of the old Turkish cemetery.' (Alec Riley, *Twenty Years After*)

Figure 46. 'Krithia Road, though rough, is used for motors between Helles and Kilid Bahr. The country on both sides of the road is typical of this part of central Helles. Olive trees, dwarf oaks, brambles, and innumerable varieties of shrubs, weeds, and wild flowers, make up the scrub. Krithia is on the extreme left of the skyline in the photograph.' (Alec Riley, *Twenty Years After*)

Biographies

Alec Riley

Second Corporal 10, Alec Riley, Royal Engineers (TF), formerly Private 10, 6th Manchesters, later Sapper 426899, Royal Engineers

Alec Riley was born in Salford, Lancashire, on 24 March 1887, son of Thomas Riley, age 50, and former schoolteacher Mary Ann Riley (née Dobie), age 33. He was baptised on 24 March 1888 at Manchester Cathedral.

Alec grew up with two siblings—his half-brother, Thomas Alfred, 16 years older than Alec and from his father's first marriage, and a younger sister, Margaret, who was born in 1893.[200] Riley's father owned a well-established dry salt business and was comfortably middle class. He brought up the children in a substantial detached Victorian villa, Rosthwaite, attended by two servants.

Tragedy struck in 1894 when Alec's mother died while he was seven years old. One year later, Alec's father married his third wife, 48-year-old spinster Eliza Cowley, giving the six-year-old a new stepmother. Little is known of his early years, but it is probable that Alec received his secondary education at Eccles Grammar School.

---

200 The 1881 census shows two other children by Thomas Riley and his then wife Sarah—Elizabeth, age 13, and William T., age 6. Neither of these children are present on the 1891 census, nor are there any records showing their birth, death or marriage, and it is likely that both died in childhood.

Alec joined the 2nd Volunteer Battalion of the Manchester Regiment on 16 May 1905. When the Territorial Force was formed on 1 April 1908, he re-enlisted in the retitled 6th Battalion of the Manchester Regiment. In the same year Riley served as a member of the Honour Guard when Sir Ian Hamilton unveiled the Manchester Regiment's South African war memorial in St Ann's Square. His records show he was a committed amateur soldier who attended all his two-weeks-long annual training camps between 1908 and 1912.

The 1911 census of England shows the 24-year-old Riley employed as a clerk in a salt warehouse. This was probably his father's business, at No. 3 Arch, Hulme Locks, Egerton Street, Hulme, Manchester.

Riley was an enthusiastic cyclist and was on a bicycle tour in the south-west of England when war was declared. Cutting his tour short, he returned to Manchester on 5 August 1914 and reported to battalion headquarters at 3, Stretford Road, Old Trafford, in the afternoon to be embodied.

On 20 August, Riley moved with the battalion to Hollingworth Camp, near Littleborough, and on 2 September, by now a lance corporal, he signed Army Form E.624, volunteering for overseas service.

On 10 September 1914, the East Lancashire Division sailed from Southampton for Egypt. On the same day Riley was attached to the 1/1st East Lancs RE Signals Company which embarked, together with the Lancashire Fusiliers Brigade headquarters and the 6th and 7th Lancs Fusiliers, on the Donaldson liner SS *Saturnia*. After an uneventful passage, the fleet carrying the division arrived at Alexandria on Thursday 25 September. Riley and his company disembarked in the early hours of the following morning and, after a delay, entrained for Cairo. They arrived at Abbassia sidings after a journey of six and a half hours. 'The men, hot and tired, tramped across a stretch of sand to their barracks, where there shone a light. It came,' wrote Riley, 'from a canteen. Where there was beer there was hope.' Now a member of No. 4 Section, Riley had arrived at his new home in Polygon Barracks, Cairo.

For the next five months the East Lancs Division undertook a program of training designed to raise the men's fitness and turn the amateur soldiers into an effective fighting force. The men of No. 4 Section took part in some of this training, but the greater part of their time was occupied in operating various communications facilities in and around Cairo and on the Suez Canal. On 18 January 1915, Riley and the other members of No. 4 Section were transferred into the Royal Engineers. In April 1915, Riley's aptitude was recognised with a promotion to 2nd corporal.

By the beginning of May 1915, the East Lancashire Division had been allocated as reinforcements for the MEF. Riley embarked from Alexandria for Gallipoli with No. 4 Section on 3 May, landing at W Beach on 6 May. During his time at Helles he was attached on various occasions to the 5th, 6th, 7th, 8th and 9th Manchesters and briefly to the 4th East Lancs Regiment, giving Riley the opportunity to have close personal contact with many of the key personnel within these units and to see a great deal of the Helles battlefield. He was present in the forward trenches for both the Third Battle of Krithia and the Battle of 6–7 August,[201] and later wrote vivid accounts of both battles and their aftermath.

Riley was medically evacuated on the morning of Saturday 11 September 1915 and taken from W Beach by hospital ship *Glasgow* to Mudros Harbour where he was transferred to the hospital ship *Simla*. He remained on board *Simla* for three days, during which time he was diagnosed as suffering from jaundice, enteritis and diphtheria, with nine septic wounds. On 14 September, Riley was transferred by launch and motor ambulance to 'the infectious section' of an Australian hospital. By now Riley was unable to walk, due to paralysis caused by diphtheria. He was taken to a 'battered old bell tent', which gave no protection when a great storm swept over Lemnos that night—Riley thought it the worst night he had experienced at Gallipoli. In the morning, after being examined by a 'tall, fat and pig-like' Australian doctor called Johnson, he was designated an acute case and, in a brutal form of triage, moved to an isolation tent with two other men. Riley felt the move was to allow them to 'finish our time—that is, to peg out.' One of the men died but Riley confounded Johnson by surviving the ordeal, and a few days later was moved into a large marquee where he received better treatment and began to recover.

201 Also known, in acknowledgement of the battle's only gain, as the Battle of the Vineyard.

By Wednesday 20 October, Riley was considered strong enough to be sent home, and he sailed for England aboard the converted passenger liner *Aquitania*. He arrived at Southampton Water on 27 October and was taken by motor ambulance to the Royal Victoria Hospital Netley. Riley spent the next 11 months at Netley, and its auxiliary hospitals, Shirley and Shorne Hill, recovering from his various ailments.

In September 1916, his discharge was confirmed, prompting Riley to send a telegram to his family from the hospital's post office: 'Kill fatted calf. Prodigal son returns Friday.'

After a spell of home leave, a still less than fit Riley was posted on 25 November 1916 to the 71st Division Signal Company RE to be employed on clerical work (C class). On 17 July 1917, he was reduced to the rank of sapper, possibly due to his disability. Also in 1917, in common with all other territorial soldiers, Riley was issued with a new six-figure service number, 426899.

It is unclear if Riley ever served in France, but he finished his army service with the 67th Division Signal Company RE. On 17 April 1919, he was granted 28 days leave before being demobilised on 15 May 1919. On leaving the army, he returned to Rosthwaite to live with his father and stepmother. Later that year he was awarded the Territorial Efficiency Medal and in 1920 was issued with the King's Certificate and Silver War Badge with reference to King's Regulations paragraph 392 (xvia) which designated Riley as 'surplus to service requirements having suffered impairment since entry into the service.'

Although his records show reference to a pension application there are no records of its actual award. However, it does seem likely because Riley's entry in the 1939 census described him as having retired in 1919 with his last employment being the 71st Division Signal Company RE. Nonetheless, Riley began to look for a career in writing and enrolled as a student at the London School of Journalism, established by Max Pemberton in 1920.

Family tragedy struck again at the end of 1920 when Riley's 49-year-old half-brother, Thomas Alfred, went missing on 21 December and was found dead on Barton Moss on New Year's Day 1921, leaving a wife and two children. The relationship between Alec and Thomas Alfred had been close. Alec had often stayed at his home and the news must have shocked and distressed him. Until his death, Thomas Alfred had worked in their father's business and was named successor and inheritor of the business in his will. A year and a half later, on 7 August 1922, Alec's father died aged 86. It is unclear what became of the business, but he left the net sum of £21,970 in his will. Probate was granted to his three executors—his widow Eliza, Alec (recorded as having no occupation) and Robert Isherwood (Alec's brother-in-law).

In the early 1920s, Riley began a decade-long correspondence with Sir Ian Hamilton, which included exchanges of personal recollections and several photographs. The letters are friendly and informal despite a significant difference in the rank and social position of the correspondents.

In one letter, dated 15 December 1923, Riley encloses two photographs taken during the campaign. Hamilton's reply on 17 December is wry: 'Thank you for your letter of the 15th and for your interesting photographs. I suspect you were defying my regulation when you snapped them!' Riley also informed Hamilton that he was in the honour guard when the General unveiled the Manchester Regiment's Boer War Memorial in St Ann's Square in 1908, adding, 'you were exactly opposite to me when a press photographer snapped the inspection. I have a copy of the photo.'

The correspondence appears to have ended after Hamilton had written, then re-written at Riley's request, an introduction—dated 11 November 1932—for the book 'Return to Cape Helles,' a manuscript for which Riley was unable find a publisher and which is now lost.

Riley made two pilgrimages to Gallipoli, 'independently, living near Sedd-el-Bahr for several days, tramping the country systematically and alone, and photographing what I thought to be of interest and importance.'

He sent some of these photographs to Brigadier General Aspinall-Oglander, two of which—'The Anzac Front' and 'The View of the Dardanelles from Chunuk Bair'—were included in Volume II of his *Official History of Military Operations Gallipoli*. Riley also provided Aspinall-Oglander with 'an odd note or two made for him at the hold-up place in Krithia Nullah.' Later, he sent a copy of his manuscript to Aspinall-Oglander in the hope of enlisting his help to find either a publisher or a newspaper interested in serialising the narrative.

The pilgrimages to Gallipoli had given Riley a rare view of the battlefield 'from the Turkish and our own points of view.' These visits provided the basis for 'Return to Helles' and were also key in getting some of his work published.

Around 1935, Riley had a lengthy article published in *Twenty Years After,* a weekly magazine that recalled major events in the First World War, and featured articles written by veterans revisiting the site of battle twenty years after the event. 'From the narrative of my rambles,' wrote Riley, 'three sections have been chosen.' He added some of his recollections of 1915 for context. Riley also contributed a total of 41 photographic images for use in his own and other Gallipoli-related articles in *Twenty Years After.*

Another of Riley's articles, written to mark the 23rd anniversary of the Gallipoli Landings was published in *The Telegraph and Morning Post* on 23 April 1938. This article included two photographs taken by Riley and a caption under one of them drew attention to a 'new' Gallipoli exhibition at the Imperial War Museum, recently opened and featuring photographs and artefacts donated by Riley.

Riley never married and his later life is something of an enigma. The 1939 census shows Riley, now approaching 60, staying with the Treoaskis family in Falmouth, Cornwall, where he is described as a 'traveling photographer and occasional writer dealing with the Near East' of 'private means.'

It is clear that Riley possessed a lifelong fascination with travel and had the means to indulge this passion. In 1932, he joined the Royal Geographic Society and may have travelled with the Society on a tour of Scandinavia which he described in a letter to Hamilton 'as a complete change from the Near East and Mediterranean: where most of my travels have been.'

Nor was Riley's interest in travel dimmed by age. Ocean liner passenger lists show that he visited South Africa at least three times in his later years. In 1953, he sailed on the SS *Braemar Castle* (namesake of the troop carrier which served in the Gallipoli campaign) from London to Cape Town and then on to Durban and Port Elizabeth.[202] On the return leg of the cruise, *Braemar Castle* stopped at a half dozen East African ports, going on to dock in Aden and Port Sudan, before sailing

202 On 23 March 2021, Port Elizabeth was renamed Gqeberha, the Xhosa name for the Baakens River.

through the Suez Canal to Port Said. Both would have been familiar to Riley from his army service. In 1955, Riley's travels took him from Southampton (another port with great significance to Riley) on board RMS *Edinburgh Castle* to the South African ports of Durban, East London, Port Elizabeth and Cape Town.[203] Finally, in 1956, when he was 69 years old, Riley took another cruise around the African coast, sailing from London on board the SS *Kenya Castle*. The first part of the journey retraced that taken by Riley and the East Lancs Division in September 1914, sailing through the Mediterranean to Port Said then passing through the Suez Canal before stopping at various East African ports. The cruise continued on to Durban, Port Elizabeth and Cape Town before returning to London via St Helena and Las Palmas.

It may well be that Riley took these cruises for the same reasons as other tourists, but it seems likely he sought itineraries that would return him to where he had served in the First World War. And his choice of South African destinations may have been inspired by Riley's fascination with the Boer War, to which he alluded in his correspondence with Hamilton many years earlier.

Riley died aged 71 on 17 October 1958 at the Highfield Hotel, 141 High Street, Chorlton on Medlock, Manchester.[204] It had been his home for at least five years.

* * *

Riley had made his will some twenty years earlier in 1936, including legacies and bequests to various family members. The will also references the content of certain boxes held at the Midland Bank and the YMCA on his behalf. He instructs his executors—the Midland Bank, referred to as 'the Company'—'to dispose of the contents of such boxes in accordance with the instructions contained in the written memorandum or schedule deposited by me with the Company...' Although it is impossible to be sure at the time of writing, it seems likely that these boxes contained the three unpublished manuscripts

---

203   Riley passed through Southampton at least twice during WW1, the first time on 10 September 1914 en route to Egypt and the second on 25 October 1915 on his way to the Royal Victoria Hospital, Netley.

204   The death certificate gives his cause of death as (a) Coronary thrombosis, (b) Coronary arteriosclerosis, and (c) Hypertension.

subsequently donated to the Imperial War Museum. Two are inscribed on their covers: 'For the Imperial War Museum (if it is of any interest).'

The first covered the events around Riley's mobilisation in August 1914, and subsequent service in Egypt from September 1914 until his embarkation for Gallipoli on 3 May 1915.

The second diary recaps Riley's last few days in Egypt and his time at Gallipoli from his arrival on 6 May until his medical evacuation on 11 September 1915.

The final diary describes his evacuation from the peninsula, suffering from diphtheria, jaundice, enteritis, dysentery and nine septic sores. It goes on to describe his time in hospital on the island of Lemnos, his onward evacuation aboard *Aquitania* in October 1915, and his treatment and 11-month-long convalescence in Netley Hospital.

Riley set down the arrangements for his funeral and the disposal of his remains. They indicate what a modest, self-effacing, pragmatic and perhaps lonely man Riley was in later life.

'I wish to be cremated at the Crematorium nearest to my place of death ... but I do not desire my ashes to be kept and I direct my funeral to be as simple and inexpensive as possible and that no mourning shall be worn ...'

* * *

No. 4 Section (Manchester Brigade), 1/1st East Lancs Divisional Signal Company, RE, and men attached

Abe – Lance Corporal Williams

Probably Sapper 664 Richard Williams, Royal Engineers (TF)

Fitter and tool maker of Collyhurst, Manchester. Born 18 October 1889, in the parish of St Michaels, Manchester, fourth of seven children. Son of Samuel Williams, warehouseman, and Rebecca Biggar.

Enlisted East Lancs RE on 23 March 1911 when 21 years of age and working in the fitting shop at British Westinghouse Electrical and Manufacturing Company, Trafford Park. Married Mary Susan Gascoigne, aged 27, a core maker, on 4 October 1913 while both living at

42 King William Street, Salford. Was in 2nd Field Company East Lancs RE (TF) when he signed Army Form E.624 volunteering for overseas service on 2 September 1914.

Embarked with the East Lancashire Division for Egypt in September 1914. Served with No. 4 Signals Section in Egypt in 1914–15. Landed at Helles on 6 May and remained there until the 1/1st Signals Company was evacuated (28 December to 3 January 1916).

Returned to England from Egypt in March 1916 and was discharged, time expired, on 14 April 1916. Had four children, Dorothy (1916), Richard (1918), Stanley (1920) and Hilda (1922). Died 11 February 1958, Headington, Oxfordshire, age 68.

Barlow

Probably Sapper 800 Frank Barlow, Royal Engineers (TF), later Sergeant 444030, Royal Engineers

Electrical draughtsman at the British Westinghouse Electrical and Manufacturing Company, Trafford Park. Born 20 June 1891, Ashton-Under-Lyne. Son of Arthur Yates Barlow, electrical motor maker, and Mary Elizabeth Canfield.

Enlisted East Lancs RE, Territorial Force, on 21 November 1912 when 21 years of age and living at 51 Derwent Road, Stretford. Attended the annual training camps. Signed Army Form E.624 agreeing to overseas service at Bury camp on 1 September 1914.

Embarked with the East Lancashire Division for Egypt in September 1914. Served with No. 4 Signals Section in Egypt in 1914–15. Landed at Helles on 6 May and remained there, apart from two periods of sickness, until the 1/1st Signals Company was evacuated (28 December to 3 January 1916). On 16 June 1915, Barlow was admitted at No. 11 Casualty Clearing Station with general debility, and was taken by hospital ship to No. 16 Stationary Hospital on Mudros. It seems he returned to the peninsula a few days later, attached to the 29th Division artillery. On 30 October, he re-joined 1/1st Signal Company. On 8 December 1915, Barlow was admitted with influenza at the 1/3rd East Lancs Field Ambulance at Gully Beach, then sent to No. 17 Stationary Hospital near Bakery Beach. He re-joined his unit from hospital on 29 December 1915.

Served with the 42nd Division in Egypt 1916–17. On 29 August 1916, while in Egypt, Barlow was promoted to lance corporal, then to acting 2nd corporal on 16 November 1916. Mentioned in General Sir Archibald Murray's Despatch of 1 March 1917.

Went to France with the 42nd Division in March 1917. Appointed acting corporal on 10 May. Was gassed—like many others in the divisional signals company—on 10 September 1917, and was evacuated to England. Treated at the 1st Western General Hospital, Fazakerley Liverpool, then at Whiston Infirmary. Awarded the Military Medal on 12 December 1917.

Returned to France on 30 April 1918 and served there for the remainder of the war. Had a short spell in hospital in May. Promoted sergeant on 28 October 1918. Returned to England in January 1919, and demobilised the following month. A medical examination recorded symptoms of weakness of the chest and occasional heart palpitations but the doctor noted that Barlow felt generally fit and as such did not qualify for a pension.

In 1939, Barlow was an electrical draughtsman living at 23 Hilton Street, Salford, with his wife, Elizabeth Mary (born 12 April 1893), a licensed victualler. Died Flixton, Lancashire, 25 December 1961, age 70.

Berry

Probably Pioneer 1339 John Berry, formerly D Coy, 6th Manchesters, later Sapper 1923, Royal Engineers (TF)

Manufacturer's clerk of Levenshulme, Manchester. Born Kidsgrove, Staffordshire, 16 October 1893. Son of John Curtis Berry, a gardener, and Jessie Berry.

Enlisted 6th Manchesters, Territorial Force, 1 March 1911, at age 17.

Signed Army Form E.624 volunteering for overseas service in early September 1914. Embarked for Egypt with the East Lancashire Division in September 1914, transferring to the 1/1st Signal Company on 1 April 1915 and was allotted to No. 4 Section. Landed at Helles on 6 May and probably remained there until the 1/1st Signals Company was evacuated (28 December to 3 January 1916).

Embarked for England on 22 March 1916. Discharged 14 April 1916, time expired.

Married Norah Chorlton on 22 June 1929 at St Margaret's, Burnage, when a resident of Heaton Chapel. The 1939 census shows him as grocery shop keeper, living in Levenshulme, Manchester. Probably died either in Stockport, in the last quarter of 1945 age 52 or in Manchester in the last quarter of 1956 age 63.

Caldwell

Probably Driver 1364 William George Caldwell, Royal Engineers (TF), later 2nd lieutenant, 7th Lancs Fusiliers, afterwards lieutenant, Machine Gun Corps

Travelling salesman in the cotton trade. Born Manchester, 18 March 1881, the second child of Alfred, a landscape gardener, and Annie (Anna).

Enlisted in the East Lancs Royal Engineers (TF) at Manchester on 19 September 1914 and was sent out to Egypt on 3 March 1915.[205] Served with No. 4 Signals Section in Egypt and landed with it at Helles on 6 May 1915.

Caldwell's Active Service Casualty Form B.103 shows him being re-embarking on to HMT *Cuthbert* on 19 May 1915 and arriving back in Alexandria on 21 May but it is assumed he re-joined No. 4 Section at Helles sometime later. The next entry on his Active Service Casualty Form B.103 shows him being admitted into No. 15 General Hospital (Alexandria) on 9 September 1915 and then onto Mustapha Convalescent Camp, Alexandria, on 11 September. Caldwell presumably returned to Helles as he was evacuated from Mudros suffering from dysentery on 21 October 1915 on board the SS *Aquitania* (Alec Riley was also evacuated on the same vessel on the same date). He reached Southampton on 27 October and was admitted to Highfield Military Hospital, Liverpool on the 28th.

By 21 December 1915 he had recovered sufficiently to be was granted seven days home furlough, with his pass confirming he was now

---

205 Many of Caldwell's records give contradictory information causing the author to make a number of judgement calls. Both his Medal Index Card and 1914–15 Medal Roll give his date of disembarkation in Egypt as 29 September 1914. This is very unlikely, given he had only been embodied (without previous service) 10 days earlier. Additionally, Caldwell's Active Service Casualty Form B.103 has a note stating he embarked from Southampton, at the same time as the division, on 10 September 1914 ... nine days before his enlistment!

considered fit for light duties and was likely to be fit for service overseas within three months. However, it was not until 11 May 1916 that Caldwell was finally discharged from hospital (2nd Western General Hospital, Manchester) and was ordered to report to the East Lancs RE depot at Old Trafford, Manchester.

On 25 September 1916 Caldwell was discharged from the Territorial Force. He re-enlisted the following day and was commissioned 2nd lieutenant in the 7th Lancs Fusiliers (his Medal Index Card suggests that he may have served previously in the 7th Lancs Fusiliers as Private 9364). On 4 December 1916 Caldwell was seconded to the Machine Gun Corps (LG 8 January 1917). He remained attached to the MGC and was promoted to temporary lieutenant on 26 March 1918 (LG 4 September 1918) later made substantive lieutenant (LG 25 October 1918).

At some stage while attached to the MGC Caldwell received a gunshot wound to his foot which eventually caused him to relinquish his commission on 20 May 1920 (LG 19 May 1920) and was granted a pension.

Following his discharge Caldwell may have briefly lived his parents at Lynwood, 39 Richmond Grove West, Longsight, Manchester, but shortly afterwards moved to the Wirral. There he met and married Eleanor May Hatton with whom he had two sons, Eric and Alan Alfred. He also had a third son, Reginald by another partner. Caldwell died at West Kirby, on 13 February 1938 age 56, and was buried at St Bridget's Church, West Kirby on the Wirral, Cheshire.

Claude – Corporal Hague

Probably Pioneer (later Corporal) 3614 Ernest Houghton 'Claude' Hague, Royal Engineers (TF), later 267953, Royal Engineers

Estate agent's clerk of Prestwich. Born Ladybarn, Lancashire, 19 February 1883, the first of three children of John and Jane.

Signed Army Form E.624 volunteering for overseas service in early September 1914. Embarked with the East Lancashire Division for Egypt in September 1914. Served with No. 4 Signals Section in Egypt in 1914–15. Landed at Helles on 6 May and may well have remained there until the 1/1st Signals Company was evacuated (28 December to 3 January 1916).

Hague's main service records appear not to have survived, however, his entry on the 1914–15 Star Roll confirms he served for the duration of the war. Transferred to Z Reserve 4 June 1919.

May have married, but was single in 1939 and working as an estate agent's cashier. Died Rochdale, 2 January 1956, age 71.

Cooper

Probably Driver 1155 Reginald Cooper, Royal Engineers (TF), later Driver 444069, Royal Engineers

Judging by Cooper's service number he probably enlisted a year or two before the outbreak of war. Few of Cooper's service records survive but his entry on the 1914–1915 Star Roll gives his date of disembarkation in Egypt as 5 March 1915. He was probably attached to No. 4 Section in Egypt and arrived with it at Helles on 6 May 1915, and may well have remained there until the 1/1st Signals Company was evacuated (28 December to 3 January 1916).

Two references to Cooper by Riley in his diary (one on 19 June and the other on 23 July) make it probable that Cooper was attached to the East Lancs Signal Company headquarters sometime between early May and mid-June.

He survived the war and was transferred to Z Reserve on 21 March 1919.

Dale

Probably Private 3629 Wilfred Dale, Royal Engineers (TF), previously Private 2489, Manchester Regiment, later 2nd Corporal 444567, Royal Engineers

Brass moulder (gardener in later life). Born in Chorlton, Manchester on 25 April 1892. Son of John and Alice Dale, oldest of six children.

Originally enlisted in the Manchester Regiment, he later transferred to the Royal Engineers (TF). Signed Army Form E.624 volunteering for overseas service in early September 1914. Embarked with the East Lancashire Division for Egypt in September 1914. Served with No. 4 Signals Section in Egypt in 1914–15. Landed at Helles on 6 May. Wounded on 4 June and may have been medically evacuated. Transferred to the regular RE. Dale's main service records appear not to have survived, however his entry on the 1914–15 Star Roll confirms he served for the duration of the war. Transferred to Z Reserve 16 April 1919.

He married Catherine McGrath in April 1916 and together they had one child, also named Wilfred. Died in 29 April 1942 in the Royal Infirmary Manchester and was buried in Southern Cemetery (Catholic Plot) on 2 May 1942.

Darlington

Probably Driver 1228 Clifford Darlington, Royal Engineers (TF), later Sapper 440184, Royal Engineers

A bricklayer by trade. He gave his age as 23 years and one month when he enlisted in the Royal Engineers (TF) on 4 September 1914. Although his Medal Index Card and his entry on the 1914–1915 Star Roll give Darlington's date of disembarkation in Egypt as 26 September 1914, it is possible he arrived with later drafts in November 1914 or in March 1915. He was attached to No. 4 Section and presumably arrived with it at Helles on 6 May 1915.

On 4 June 1915 Darlington was hit by a large piece of shell fragment which fractured the bones in his left elbow. He was evacuated to the Floriana Hospital, Malta, and then on to England, arriving on 18 August 1915 by which time his arm had developed acute rheumatism.

His injury effected the rest of his war service. On his discharge from hospital in October 1915 he was declared fit for general service at home or abroad. However, in June 1917 he was re-examined and his fitness accessed as C2 (able to stand service in garrisons at home), and in October 1917 he was examined again and reclassified B2 (fit to stand service in lines of communication abroad). He remained classified as B2 for rest of the war and was transferred to Z Reserve on 17 March 1919.

His wound left permanent damage, impairing his grip and restricting movement by about 30 percent. When Darlington attended a Pensions Board in Manchester on 6 July 1920, his overall disability was accessed at 19 percent and he was granted a limited pension.

Dean

Probably Driver 1568 William Dean, Royal Engineers (TF), later 444604, Royal Engineers

Born in 1891. Probably enlisted in the East Lancs RE around 1911. Joined the division in Egypt in November 1914. Served with No. 4 Signals Section in Egypt 1914–15. Probably landed at Helles on 6 May and may well have remained there until the 1/1st Signals Company was evacuated (28 December to 3 January 1916). Transferred to the regular RE. Admitted to hospital in Egypt (probably Alexandria) on 20 November 1917 suffering from Renal Calculus (kidney stones). Dean's main service records appear not to have survived, however, his Medal Index Card and entry on the 1914–15 Star Roll confirms he served for the duration of the war. His pension and medical records indicate he was awarded a pension on 20 April 1919 due to Renal Calculus and was at the time single and living at 499 Liverpool Road, Peel Green, Manchester.

Feddan

Probably Private 1881 Frederick A. Fedden, 6th Manchesters, later Private 3300, RE (TF), finally Private 444520, Royal Engineers

Electrician. Born in Barton, Salford 15 October 1896, son of John and Ellen Fedden, third of four children.

Probably enlisted in the 6th Manchesters sometime prior to the outbreak of war. Signed Army Form E.624 volunteering for overseas service in early September 1914 and embarked with the East Lancashire Division for Egypt in September 1914. Served in Egypt in 1914–15 and was at some time attached to No. 4 Section. Probably landed at Helles on 6 May and remained there until the 1/1st Signals Company was evacuated (28 December to 3 January 1916). Was transferred to the RE (TF) and later to the regular RE. Fedden's main service records appear not to have survived, however, his entry on the 1914–15 Star Roll confirms he served for the duration of the war. Transferred to Z Reserve 1 April 1919.

Emigrated to the United States in the early 1920s, and became a US citizen. Married Evelyn Rees in Seattle, Washington, on 5 September 1927. Returned to UK with Evelyn, July 1936.

Gorman

Probably Private 1626 (1686 on MIC and 1914–15 Star Roll)
David William Gorman, 6th Manchesters, attached No. 4 Section,
later Lance Sergeant 250166 Gorman MM

Clerk. Born Plumstead, Greenwich, London, 15 October 1896. Son of
James William and Ellen Gorman. Family living in Cheshire by 1901.
Enlisted 6th Manchesters on 3 March 1913 as Private 1626, when age 18,
living in Hale, Cheshire, and working as a shorthand typist.

Signed Army Form E.624 volunteering for overseas service in early
September 1914. Embarked with the East Lancashire Division for Egypt
in September 1914. Served in Egypt in 1914–15 with the 6th Manchesters
and landed at Helles with the battalion on 6 May 1915. Wounded (slight
gunshot wound to right shoulder) on 8 May. Detached for duty with the
1/1st Signals Company and was at some time attached to No. 4 Section.
Returned to the 6th Manchesters on 27 August 1915 and remained at
Helles until the division was evacuated (28 December to 3 January 1916).

Promoted to lance corporal on 3 January 1916. Served with the 42nd
Division in Egypt 1916–17. Promoted corporal (temporary) on 7 February
1916. Promoted signalling corporal on 1 September 1916 having successfully completed a technical course. Went to France with the 42nd
Division in March 1917. Appointed acting lance sergeant (unpaid) for
special duties on 8 March 1918. Severely reprimanded 27 May 1918 for
neglect of duty ('answering Staff Parade incorrectly'). Awarded Military
Medal (LG 27 June 1918). Posted 3 September 1918 to Royal Air Force
No. 8 Cadet Wing at West Sandling Camp, Shorncliffe, where pupils
received basic military training and technical instruction on map
reading and Morse code. Posted to the School of Military Aeronautics,
possibly as a trainee observer. Posted to the 8th Reserve Bn Manchester
Regt on 21 December 1918 and was disembodied on 18 February 1919.

Lived at 9 Cedar Road, Hale, Cheshire. Freemason, member of
Assheton Egerton Lodge, Hale. Worked as a reporter at the *Daily
News & Reader*. Married Muriel Moody in April 1926 and was living in
Whitchurch, Shropshire, in 1939. Died Shrewsbury, 1970, age 73.

Greenbank

**Probably Sapper 257 Arnold Greenbank, Royal Engineers (TF),
later Sapper 194716, Royal Engineers**

Telegraph clerk at the General Post Office, Manchester, living in Stretford. Born Stretford, 8 May 1888, second of four children. Son of John Greenbank, shoemaker, and Harriet Elizabeth Bland. Older brother Frank West Greenbank was also a territorial and served in Egypt with the Army Service Corps.

Judging by his low service number Arnold Greenbank must have enlisted several years prior to the war. Signed Army Form E.624 volunteering for overseas service in early September 1914. Embarked with the East Lancashire Division for Egypt in September 1914. Served with No. 4 Signals Section in Egypt in 1914–15. Landed at Helles on 6 May and may well have remained there until the 1/1st Signals Company was evacuated (28 December to 3 January 1916).

Greenbank's main service records appear not to have survived, however, his entry on the 1914–15 Star Roll confirms he served for the duration of the war and it is probable that he served with the 42nd Division in Egypt 1916–17 and went to France with the division in March 1917. Transferred to the Z Reserve on 30 April 1919.

In April 1919, married Margaret Holden. The 1939 census shows Greenbank employed as 'Overseer Postal Telegraph' and living with Margaret at 76 Warwick Road South, Old Trafford, Stretford. In 1948, Greenbank was promoted to Assistant Superintendent of the Post Office, Manchester. Died 8 August 1967, age 79.

Haworth

**Probably Pioneer 1102 James Haworth, Royal Engineers (TF),
later 2nd Corporal 444595, Royal Engineers**

Judging by his service number he probably enlisted around or a little before the outbreak of war. Joined the division in Egypt in November 1914. Served with No. 4 Signals Section in Egypt in 1914–15. Landed at Helles on 6 May and may well have remained there until the 1/1st Signals Company was evacuated (28 December to 3 January 1916).

Transferred to the regular RE. Haworth's main service records appear not to have survived, however, his entry on the 1914–15 Star Roll confirms he served for the duration of the war. Disembodied 9 April 1919.

Holmes

Possibly Private 2336 William Done Holmes, 8th Manchesters, later CQMS 202048, 19th Bn Rifle Brigade

Judging by his service number he probably enlisted around or a little before the outbreak of war. Joined the division in Egypt in January 1915. Landed at Helles on 6 May and may well have remained there until the 1/1st Signals Company was evacuated (28 December to 3 January 1916).

Served with the 42nd Division in Egypt 1916. On 16 November 1916 transferred to the 19th Bn Rifle Brigade and continued to serve with it in Egypt until 31 October 1918 by which time he had reached the rank of CQMS.

Hopkinson

Probably Pioneer 1883 Harry Hopkinson, Royal Engineers (TF), later Sgt 444595, Royal Engineers

Judging by his service number he probably enlisted a year or two before the outbreak of war. Signed Army Form E.624 volunteering for overseas service in early September 1914. Embarked with the East Lancashire Division for Egypt in September 1914. Served with No. 4 Signals Section in Egypt in 1914–15. Landed at Helles on 6 May and may well have remained there until the 1/1st Signals Company was evacuated (28 December to 3 January 1916).

Transferred to the regular RE. Hopkinson's main service records appear not to have survived, however, his entry on the 1914–15 Star Roll confirms he served for the duration of the war. Disembodied 15 March 1919.

Hossack

Probably Pioneer (later Sapper) 2119 Ernest Frank Hossack, Royal Engineers (TF), later 444256, Royal Engineers

Mechanical engineer and draughtsman. Born Gorton, Manchester, 4 November 1888, son of John, a mechanical engineer, and Lettice Hossack.

Worked in the United States of America 1911–1914, including as a jig and tool designer at the Studebaker Company, Detroit.

Enlisted 6 August 1914. Signed Army Form E.624 volunteering for overseas service in early September 1914. Embarked with the East Lancashire Division for Egypt in September 1914. Served with No. 4 Signals Section in Egypt in 1914–15. Landed at Helles on 6 May and remained there until September 1915 when evacuated sick with diphtheria. Admitted Mtarfa hospital, Malta, on 4 October 1915. Transferred to Ghajn Tuffieha convalescent camp on the island from 11 November. Invalided to England in December 1915.

Served on the Western Front from August 1916 with 36th Divisional Signal Company. Gassed Ypres, August 1917. Gassed again March 1918 and evacuated to England. Discharged 13 February 1919. Suffered general debility and stomach trouble.

Married Agnes Mary Egan, April 1920. Works manager, Glasgow. The 1939 census shows Hossack working as a mechanical engineer and living in Ilford, Essex, his wife Agnes a principal in a preparatory school. Died 15 February 1962, age 73.

Joe – Sergeant Royle

Probably Sergeant 262 Graham Royle, Royal Engineers (TF). Formerly 6th Manchesters, later Lance Corporal 238056, Royal Engineers

Sorting clerk and telegraphist at the General Post Office, Manchester. Born Ardwick, 5 March 1885. Son of William (although early records give his name as John) and Annie Royle, of 25 Albion Street, Brooks Bar. Father and older sister, Eveline, also worked at the Post Office.

Joined the 2nd Volunteer Battalion Manchester Regiment, then enlisted in the 6th Battalion on formation of the Territorial Force in 1908, age 23. Lance corporal from 1908, sergeant from 1912. Signed Army

Form E.624 volunteering for overseas service in early September 1914. Embarked with the 1/1st East Lancs Signals Company for Egypt in September 1914. Served with No. 4 Signals Section in Egypt in 1914–15. Landed at Helles on 6 May. Made sergeant Royal Engineers and granted fourth rate of engineer pay on 30 May. Admitted 1st Field Ambulance then 11th Casualty Clearing Station at W Beach suffering diarrhoea on 11 August 1915. Transferred to a hospital ship the next day (Royle stated in a later medical examination that he had suffered from dysentery and this was probably the cause of his being evacuated sick from Gallipoli). Treated at the 21st General Hospital, Alexandria, until 24 November 1915 then transferred to the convalescent depot at Mustapha. Embarked for England (time expired) in March 1916. Called up under the Military Service Act in March 1917 as Sapper 238056 Royal Engineers, with rank of lance corporal in a wireless section. Transferred to Z Reserve 4 March 1919.

Initiated into the Richmond Masonic Lodge no. 1011 in the latter part of 1919, at which time he was 34 years of age, living at 39 Norton Street, Brooks Bar, Manchester, and working as a postal clerk. Married Elizabeth Jones (born 11 February 1888) in 1922. The couple were living at 370 Kings Road, Stretford in 1939. Died Manchester, 1961, age 75.

Karno – Major Lawford

Biography included in the following section.

Mall – Lance Corporal Mallalieu

Sapper 617 John Mallalieu, Royal Engineers (TF), formerly Private 617, 6th Manchesters, later Sergeant 444594, Royal Engineers

Born around 1884. Also named Mallalien on some military records. Enlisted in the 6th Manchesters on 29 May 1908, shortly after its formation as part of the newly formed Territorial Force and is shown in C Company's year booklet for 1911 as being in No. 1 Section and living at 22 Oak Road, Lower Broughton, Salford. A former longstanding member of Volunteer Association (possibly the 2nd Volunteer Bn, Manchester Regt), he was awarded the Territorial Force Efficiency Medal on 1 October 1912.

Signed Army Form E.624 volunteering for overseas service in early September 1914. Embarked with the East Lancashire Division for Egypt in September 1914. Served with No. 4 Signals Section in Egypt in 1914–15 as Sapper 617. Landed at Helles on 6 May and presumably remained there until the 1/1st Signals Company was evacuated (28 December to 3 January 1916).

Awarded the Distinguished Conduct Medal (LG 26 April 1917). His citation reads 'for conspicuous gallantry and devotion to duty. He has performed consistent good work throughout, and has at all times set a fine example of courage and determination.' Mentioned in Despatches (LG 6 July 1917).

Mallalieu's main service records appear not to have survived, however, his entry on the 1914–15 Star Roll confirms he served for the duration of the war. At some time during his service, he was wounded and was discharged due to wounds (King's Regulations para 392 xvia) on 8 March 1919, 'surplus to military requirements (having suffered impairment since entry into the service)' and was entitled to the Silver War Badge (B 341650). His address at this time was 21 Esmond Road, Cheetham Hill, Manchester.

McLoughlin

**Probably Driver 1061 James McLoughlin, Royal Engineers (TF),
later Pioneer 444059, Royal Engineers**

Unfortunately, it appears that McLoughlin's only surviving military records are his Medal Index Card and his entry on the British War Medal and Victory Medal Roll, neither of which give any information as to his service overseas. McLoughlin's relatively low service number does suggest however that he either went out to Egypt with the division in September 1914 or arrived with the draft of reinforcements on November 1914. He presumably landed with No. 4 Section at Helles on 6 May and may well have remained there until the 1/1st Signals Company was evacuated (28 December to 3 January 1916).

Noble

Probably Pioneer 1392 George Richard Noble, Royal Engineers (TF). Formerly Private 1392, Manchester Regiment, later Sapper 3618, Royal Engineers (TF) and Lance Corporal 438775, Royal Engineers

Letterpress printer of Salford, Manchester. Born Pendleton, 19 April 1889. Son of George Noble, lorry driver and porter, and Elizabeth Ann.

Enlisted with 1/8th Bn Lancashire Fusiliers on 4 August 1908. Attended the School of Signalling and received his Signalling Certificate on 28 June 1908. Enlisted with 6th Manchesters on a four-year engagement on 10 April 1911 at age 24.

Signed Army Form E.624 volunteering for overseas service in early September 1914. Attached 1/1st Signal Company on 10 September 1914. Embarked with the East Lancashire Division for Egypt in September 1914. Served with No. 4 Signals Section in Egypt in 1914–15. Landed at Helles on 6 May and was 'remustered' as sapper and granted 4th rate of engineer pay on 26 June 1915. Probably remained at Helles until the 1/1st Signals Company was evacuated (28 December to 3 January 1916).

Disembarked at Alexandria from Mudros on 16 January 1916. Embarked for England on 25 March 1916 and was discharged on 14 April 1916, 'time expired,' having served five years five days. Married Lily Baguley, a cigarette maker of Pendleton, on 8 April 1916 at St John's Wesleyan Methodist, Langworthy Road, Weaste.

Called up under the Military Service Act, going before a medical board in June 1916 at Pendleton Town Hall. Appointed lance corporal, Royal Engineers, regimental number 438775, on 18 November 1916. Embarked Devonport in March 1917 for Basra, Iraq. Joined 14th Divisional Signal Company, 14th (Indian) Division, Mesopotamia Expeditionary Corps, on 10 August 1917. Admitted 23rd British Stationary Hospital, Baghdad, for two weeks in early January 1918. At this time was charged with 'losing by neglect Govt property (i.e.) Jackets Felt Signalling, 1' for which he had to reimburse the army 9 shillings and 6 pence. However, his character reference was recorded as 'a very excellent man.' Contracted malaria in August 1918 and was admitted to the 32nd British General Hospital, Amarah, reported as dangerously ill. He was taken off the dangerously ill list on 15 September, and discharged at Kut in November 1918.

Noble embarked for England from Basra on 27 February 1919 and was transferred to Z Reserve on 1 May 1919. He made a claim for disability, due to headaches which he attributed to malaria, and was examined on 19 May. The claim was rejected with the examining physician, stating Noble was of 'normal appearance, seemed quite fit—no physical sign of any diseases.' At this time, Noble, and wife Lily, were living at 181 Hodge Lane, Seedley, Manchester.

The 1939 census shows Noble as working as a rotary machine winder for a newspaper company and living at 72 Chestnut Drive, Woodheys, Sale, Cheshire, with his wife, his wife's mother, and two children, Lily and Arthur. He was still living at the same address when he died on 10 April 1941, age 51.

Ormy – Sergeant Ormesher

Sergeant 764 Charles Alfred Ormesher, 6th Manchesters, later CQMS 3721, Royal Engineers (TF) and CQMS 444578, Royal Engineers

Shipping clerk. Born Manchester on 2 March 1888. Son of John Edward Brookes, salesman, and Hannah, of Broughton Road, Salford. May have attended Royal Technical Institute, Salford.

Originally enlisted in the 6th Manchesters (his regimental number indicates considerable pre-war service) and later transferred to the Royal Engineers.

Signed Army Form E.624 volunteering for overseas service in early September 1914. Embarked with the East Lancashire Division for Egypt in September 1914. Served with No. 4 Signals Section in Egypt in 1914–15. Landed at Helles on 6 May and may well have remained there until the 1/1st Signals Company was evacuated (28 December to 3 January 1916).

Ormesher's main service records appear not to have survived, however, his entry on the 1914–15 Star Roll confirms he served for the duration of the war. Transferred to the regular RE, and served in the Engineers for the remainder of the war. Disembodied 9 January 1920.

Married Louisa Bayley in early 1920.

The 1939 census shows Ormesher as working as a bank clerk and living at 214 Heywood Road, Prestwich, Lancashire. He was still living at the same address when he died on 17 April 1971, age 83.

Pearson

Probably Driver 1121 Edward Pearson, Royal Engineers (TF), later Driver 440142, Royal Engineers

Carter and horseman of Manchester. Born in Salford 3 May 1890. Son of Edward Pearson, warehouseman, of Birmingham, and Annie Baldwin of Salford. Eldest of four children.

Records of Pearson's enlistment appear not to have survived. However, judging by his service number he probably enlisted a year or two before the outbreak of war.

Signed Army Form E.624 volunteering for overseas service in early September 1914. Embarked for Egypt with the East Lancashire Division in September 1914. Served with No. 4 Signals Section in Egypt in 1914–15. Landed at Helles on 6 May. Admitted to No. 11 Casualty Clearing Station on 3 July 1915 suffering influenza. Transferred to a hospital ship. Re-joined unit from RE details on 21 August 1915. Probably remained at Helles until the 1/1st Signals Company was evacuated (28 December to 3 January 1916).

Served with the 42nd Division in Egypt 1916–17. Arrived in France with the division from Egypt on 4 March 1917. Later served in an RE Cavalry Corps bridging park.

Married Ethel Gate, age 25 years, in the Dock Mission Hall, Salford, on 16 February 1918, during a fortnight's leave.

Taken ill (trench fever, bronchitis) July 1918, evacuated through No. 21 Casualty Clearing Station and No. 2 Canadian General Hospital, admitted to Toxteth Park Hospital, Liverpool, 29 August 1918. Discharged from hospital 31 January 1919, the medical board considering his condition 'fair'. No pension awarded.

In February 1919, Pearson was living at 531 Eccles New Road, Weaste, Manchester. Sometime later he moved to Lancaster and the 1939 census shows him living with Ethel at 59 Cleveleys Avenue, Lancaster, Lancashire.

Had two sons with Ethel, Leslie Edward (born 1920) and Stanley William (born 1923). Both died on active service in WWII: Leslie, RAF pilot with 77 Squadron, Stanley, a gunner with the Royal Artillery. Died in Lancaster in 1957, age 67.

Poole

Private 1112 Arthur Poole, attached 1/1st Signal Company, Royal Engineers (TF), formerly Private 1112, 6th Manchesters

Born Longsight, Manchester, 13 January 1895. Son of Frederick and Margaret Norbury Poole, of 30 Trafford Road, Eccles. Attended Royal Technical Institute, Salford.

Records of Poole's enlistment appear not to have survived. His regimental number, however, indicates he was probably a pre-war territorial.

Signed Army Form E.624 volunteering for overseas service in early September 1914. Embarked for Egypt with the East Lancashire Division in September 1914. Served with No. 4 Signals Section in Egypt in 1914–15. Landed at Helles on 6 May. Killed in action at Gallipoli, 5 July 1915, age 25. Buried Twelve Tree Copse Cemetery, Special Memorial C. 25. Also commemorated on the honour board of St Andrew's Church, Chadwick Road, Eccles.

Ridings, C.W.

Probably Sapper 838 Charles William Ridings, Royal Engineers (TF), formerly Private 838, 6th Manchesters, later Acting 2nd Corporal 165863, Royal Engineers

Clerk/bookkeeper. Born Salford, 11 November 1887. Son of Sidney James Ridings and Mary Alice Travis.

Attended Royal Technical Institute, Salford. Enlisted in the 6th Battalion, Manchester Regiment on a four-year engagement on 12 March 1909, age 21 years. Then a clerk at textile firm S. L. Behrens & Co. Older brother of Sidney Ridings (also No. 4 Section—listed below). Re-engaged for one year with the battalion on 13 February 1913 and again on 20 February 1914.

Embodied as a private in the 6th Manchesters in August 1914, attached to the 1/1st Signal Company. Signed Army Form E.624 volunteering for overseas service in early September 1914. Embarked with the East Lancashire Division for Egypt in September 1914. Served with No. 4 Signals Section in Egypt in 1914–15. Landed at Helles on 6 May.

Wounded in the back by a bullet on 10 August. The incident is recalled in Riley's diary:

'We heard, also, that Ridings at Brigade headquarters had been wounded the day before. Full details were given me later by a disinterested party. It seemed that Nature had called upon him to go a certain distance, just after he finished his duty in the signal office, and he was standing in a low trench when the bullet caught him in the back. Thomas tied him up. Tim came along to see if Ridings would have brandy or whisky. He preferred whisky, and then he was taken away on a stretcher. Noble told me that he had been amused. Riding's parting instructions concerned the disposal of a pair of spurs, of which he was proud, and he asked Ormy to look after them. They found a resting place in the nullah, however, Ridings got through safely.'

Evacuated to Egypt, 11 August 1915, having spent 99 days on the peninsula. Presumably remained in Egypt until 30 January 1916 when he was sent back to England. Discharged, time expired, on 3 March 1916.

Married Dorothy Buckley Seddon on 12 December 1916.

Recalled to service, joined an RE depot from England on 16 December 1916. Served with 6th Divisional Signals Company on the Western Front. Appointed acting lance corporal in August 1917, and acting 2nd corporal in March 1918. Transferred to Z Reserve 3 March 1919.

The 1939 census shows Ridings working as a sales manager for a chemical dyestuffs company, and living with his wife in Parkside Avenue, Salford. Died Poole, Dorset, 17 November 1980, age 92.

Ridings, S.

Probably Pioneer 3271 Sidney Ridings, Royal Engineers (TF), formerly Private 1193, 6th Manchesters, later Private 23319, Royal Warwickshire Regiment

Correspondence clerk (engineering works). Born in Broughton, Salford on 2 October 1893. Son of Sidney James Ridings and Mary Alice Travis of Broughton, Salford. Younger brother of Charles William Ridings (also in No. 4 Section—listed above).

Joined the Territorials in 1910 age 18. Embodied private with 6th Manchesters, 5 August 1914. Signed Army Form E.624 volunteering for overseas service in early September 1914. Transferred to 1/1st East Lancs Signal Company as pioneer on 10 September 1914. Presumably embarked with the East Lancashire Division for Egypt in September 1914. Served with No. 4 Signals Section in Egypt in 1914–15. Landed at Helles on 6 May but it is unclear how long he served there.

Embarked for England from Egypt (time expired) 31 December 1915. Joined 11th Battalion Royal Warwickshire Regiment as Private 23319 on 24 December 1916. Disembodied 8 July 1919, when he gave his address as 2 Douglas Street, Higher Broughton, Salford.

The 1939 census shows him living at 22 Rectory Villas, Kirkmanshulme Lane, Longsight, Manchester and working as a civil servant at the Ministry of Labour. Married Agnes K Humphreys, Ashton, October, 1941. Died 1970, Ashton, age 76.

Unfortunately, many of Sidney's original service records appear to have been lost. Those that are available contain several clerical errors and form an incomplete record of his service. The situation is compounded by him having two Medal Index Cards, one of them giving his parent unit incorrectly as the East Lancs Regt, an error repeated on his 1914–15 Medal Roll (both also state the first served theatre of war as '3' and the entry date as 21 May 1915). His records also show that he disembarked back at Alexandria on 19 or 21 May 1915 but do not indicate if he returned to Gallipoli. The same records show his overseas service as 'Egypt 10/9/14 to 31/12/15.'

Thomas

Probably Private 2391 Richard Thomas, Manchester Regiment, later Pioneer 11367, Royal Engineers (TF) and Pioneer 400528, Royal Engineers

Born 1888. Judging by his service number he probably enlisted around or a little before the outbreak of war.

Arrived in Egypt 2 November 1914 and presumably served with No. 4 Signals Section in Egypt in 1914–15, landed at Helles on 6 May and may well have remained there until the 1/1st Signals Company was evacuated (28 December to 3 January 1916). Discharged 18 March 1919 and granted a pension for his rheumatism. His Army Form S.B.36 gives his discharge address as 50 Coupland Street, Hulme, Manchester.

However, another note on the form dated 15 March 1920 states 'Man resides in Essex.'

Vick

Probably Sapper 798 Ernest Henry Vick, Royal Engineers (TF)

Born 29 May 1890. Son of William Henry Vick and Annie Sinclair Rowlandson of Douglas, Isle of Man. Member of Manchester Students' section of the Institution of Electrical Engineers in 1914. Residence given variously as Hale and Altrincham.

Enlisted East Lancs RE (TF) 21 November 1912. Signed Army Form E.624 volunteering for overseas service in early September 1914. Presumably embarked with the East Lancashire Division for Egypt in September 1914, served with No. 4 Signals Section in Egypt in 1914–15, landed at Helles on 6 May and may well have remained there until the 1/1st Signals Company was evacuated (28 December to 3 January 1916).

Awarded the Distinguished Conduct Medal (LG 21 June 1916) 'for conspicuous gallantry when repairing telephone wires under heavy fire,' at Gallipoli. Also Mentioned in Despatches (LG 13 June 1916).

Discharged as medically unfit on 26 June 1916. Entitled to the Silver War Badge (No. 10963). Married Annie Gertrude O'Mara on 8 October 1917. Freemason, initiated into the Stamford Lodge, Altrincham, 3 February 1919. Member of Institution of Electrical Engineers until at least 1930. Resident of Douglas on the Isle of Man from 1917 until his death on 22 March 1966, age 75.

Tim – Captain Williamson

Captain Charles Harry Williamson, 7th Manchesters (TF), later Royal Flying Corps

Chemist, of Eccles, Manchester. Born Lancashire, September 1887, son of Harry Williamson, chartered accountant, and Mary Elizabeth Blyton.

Commissioned 2nd lieutenant into the 7th Manchesters on 7 February 1911. Promoted to lieutenant on 5 January 1912 and captain on 26 September 1914. Signed Army Form E.624 volunteering for overseas service in early September 1914. Embarked with the East Lancashire Division for Egypt in September 1914. In command of No. 4 Signals

Section in Egypt in 1914–15. Landed at Helles on 6 May and remained in command of No. 4 Section until evacuated sick in September 1915.

Awarded the Military Cross (LG Supplement 26 November 1916) 'for conspicuous gallantry in action. He established and maintained communications under heavy fire with great courage and skill.'

Married Ada Roberta Ambler, age 25, on 1 November 1915 at St Mary the Virgin, Eccles.

Transferred to No. 14 Squadron, Royal Flying Corps, Palestine, as an observer. Killed in a flying accident at Rafah, 27 March 1917, age 29. The engine of his B.E.2e aeroplane stalled shortly after take-off (pilot 2nd Lieutenant Cecil Charles Gibbs also killed). Buried Kantara War Memorial Cemetery, grave reference B. 159, Egypt.

Withington

Probably Sapper 1521 Bernard Withington, Royal Engineers (TF), later Corporal 444115, Royal Engineers

Electrical engineer and draughtsman of Brooklands, Sale. Born Sale, Cheshire, 27 June 1881. Son of Ernest Withington, merchant, and Annie Tysoe.

Enlisted Territorial Force, East Lancashire Royal Engineers, on 1 October 1914 at 33 years of age. Rated 'very good' (highest rank) in test of trade proficiency by an electrical engineer of the Lancashire Dynamo & Motor Co., probably his employer. Joined the 42nd Division in Egypt in early March 1915.

Presumably landed with No.4 Section at Helles on 6 May. Wounded in the right arm or shoulder in June, and evacuated to hospital in Malta, arriving on 12 June. Returned to base depot, Alexandria, on 17 July 1915, and embarked for Gallipoli again on 2 August 1915.

Served with the 42nd Division in Egypt 1916–17. Arrived with the 42nd Division in France on 3 March 1917. Appointed lance corporal 19 June 1917, paid from 1 October 1917, then acting 2nd corporal 23 August 1918, and corporal 31 October 1918. Appears to have served with 42nd Divisional Signal Company for the duration of the war. Transferred to Z Reserve on 9 April 1919. Awarded Meritorious Service Medal on 3 June 1919 in recognition of 'valuable service rendered with the Armies in France and Flanders.'

Seems not to have married. Lived most of his life at the family home Avondale, Whitehall Road, Brooklands, Sale. In 1933 was listed as honorary secretary of the Brooklands Cricket Club. In 1939 was living at Avondale with mother Annie and sister Dorothy and retired but 'manager of company owning office buildings [in the] city.' Died in Southport, 18 March 1979, age 97, leaving an estate valued at £84,294.

* * *

Officers and other ranks mentioned by Riley, together with officers in the chain of command

Lt. Colonel Francis Isaac Bentley, TD
Temporary CO of the 8th Manchesters, 4 June to 16 July 1915

Born in Huddersfield on 14 July 1868. Bentley, described as a merchant on his Masonic membership (East Lancs Centurion Lodge) was commissioned as 2nd lieutenant into the 5th (Ardwick) Volunteer Bn on 7 March 1891. He was promoted to lieutenant on 23 July 1892, to captain on 9 December 1896 and granted the honorary rank of major on 7 April 1906 (substantive 27 April 1912). He retained his rank and seniority on the formation of the Territorial Force on 1 April 1908, when the battalion was renamed as the 8th (Ardwick) Bn Manchester Regiment.

As senior major and 2ic of the battalion he volunteered for overseas service in early September 1914. He served with the 8th Manchesters in Egypt from 25 September 1914 until the battalion embarked for Gallipoli on 2 May 1915, and disembarked with it on V Beach on 6 May 1915. He assumed command of the battalion after Lt. Colonel Heys (see below) was killed on 4 June. Promoted to temporary lieutenant colonel (substantive on 9 September 1916) he remained in command until 16 July 1915 when he handed over to Lt. Colonel D.F. McCarthy-Morrogh, CMG (see below). It is assumed he continued to serve at Helles until the division left on 29 December 1915.

In April 1917 he applied unsuccessfully for a Silver War Badge which would indicate he was no longer fit for active service. He resigned his commission on 30 September 1921 and was appointed Honorary Colonel of the 8th Manchesters on 28 February 1925.

After the war he worked in the family business, Isaac Bentley and Company Ltd., travelling extensively in Europe, Asia, Africa and the Americas. He died at Ashley, Bucklow, Cheshire, on 9 February 1938.

Lt. Colonel Albert Canning, CMG

CO of the 7th Manchesters from 16 July 1915

Born in Ramsbury, Wiltshire, 26 October 1861, Canning served in the ranks of 19th Hussars 1882–88, including Egyptian Expedition 1882–84, Soudan 1884 (battles of Teb and Tamai) and Soudan Expedition 1885 (Suakin), gaining the Bronze Star with three clasps. Commissioned second lieutenant into the South Wales Borderers in April 1888. Promoted to lieutenant on 6 March 1891 and captain on 9 October 1895. He was appointed adjutant of the 5th Bn Leinster Regt on 22 January 1898. Promoted to major on 27 May 1903, he went on to command the 3rd Bn Leinster Regt, and retired on half pay on 5 August 1911. He was recalled from the Reserve of Officers list and appointed as CO to the 7th Manchesters on 16 July 1915. He remained in command of the battalion until the 16 December 1915 when he took over command of the 127th Brigade (having already commanded the brigade temporarily on 21 August to 27 August and again on 17 to 22 September). Lt. Colonel Darlington (see below) refers to Canning's first stint in command of the brigade in a letter:

'Gen. Lawrence has gone again on another job and the Brigade is being taken charge of by an ex-regular, who is senior in the Brigade and who commands —— [7th MR]. He is a very nice old gentleman. General —— [Douglas] is exercising supervision over the whole firing line! so you can see how fatuous the whole position is.

'Our little Willie would rather do that than have what he calls 'a civilian' commanding the brigade.'

Appointed CMG and Mentioned in Despatches for his service at Gallipoli (LG 13 July 1916). He was later promoted to colonel.

Gerald B. Hurst held a high opinion of Canning as recorded in his book *With Manchesters in the East*.

'On the 16 July the command was passed over to Lieutenant-Colonel

A. Canning, a veteran of the Egyptian War of 1882, who had previously commanded the Leinster Regiment in Cork. We could have had no greater confidence in any possible Commanding Officer, and while he acted as Brigadier of the Manchester Territorials his influence was no less inspiring. The record of our later campaign on Gallipoli is closely associated with his name and work.'

He died in Swindon in 1960.

Captain Peter Hubert Creagh DSO

Adjutant, to the 7th Manchesters, and temporary CO from
4 June to 16 July 1915

Born in Marlow, Ireland on 18 August 1882. He attended the Royal Military College in 1902 and was commissioned into the Leicestershire Regt as second lieutenant on 22 October 1902. Promoted to lieutenant on 10 July 1905 and to captain on 13 November 1908, he was appointed adjutant of the 1/7th Manchesters on 12 June 1911. He served with the battalion in Sudan and Egypt and disembarked with it on V Beach on 6 May 1915. He was placed in temporary command of the battalion after the death of Major Staveacre (see below) on 4 June, and remained in command until 16 July 1915. He was evacuated through illness at the end of August. Awarded the DSO and twice Mentioned in Despatches for his service at Gallipoli (LG 5 November 1915 and 28 January 1916).

After recovering he re-joined the 7th Manchesters and remained attached to the battalion until September 1916 when he returned to his parent unit. He served with the Leicester Regt in Egypt and Mesopotamia, was promoted to major on 22 October 1917. He was promoted to lieutenant colonel and appointed CO of the 2nd Bn Leicestershire Regt on 25 July 1929. Again, Mentioned in Despatches on 22 January 1919.

Gerald B. Hurst describes Creagh in his book *With Manchesters in the East*: 'Captain Creagh of the Leicestershire Regiment was a fine Adjutant, whose ability and character were to win him recognition in wider fields.' Later Hurst recounts that when the Brigade was disembarking on V Beach, the battalion's RSM (H.C. Franklin—see below) overheard some Indian muleteers talking in Hindustani. 'Here is another of the regiments of shopkeepers.' One pointed to Creagh and said 'but he is a soldier.'

Lt. Colonel Sir Henry Clayton Darlington, CMG, TD

CO of the 5th Manchesters

Born on 27 June 1877 and educated at Shrewsbury school, he later read law, qualifying as a solicitor in 1904. Enlisted in the 1st Volunteer Bn Manchester Regt on 27 April 1897 and was promoted to lieutenant on 20 July 1898. He volunteered to serve in the South African War, and as a lieutenant commanded the battalion's Active Service Section in the 1st Volunteer Service Company, attached to the 1st Bn Manchester Regiment (of which his father was the CO). He took part in operations in Natal, March to June 1900, the Transvaal east of Pretoria, July to 20 November 1900 (including the actions at Reit Vlei and Belfast) and in the Transvaal again, 30 November 1900 to 1901 and received the Queen's medal with three clasps. He was made honorary lieutenant in the army on 24 June 1902 and promoted to captain on 28 March 1903. He retained his rank and seniority on the formation of the Territorial Force when the battalion was renamed as the 1/5th Bn Manchester Regiment on 1 April 1908.

Promoted to major on 16 September 1913 and in September 1914 volunteered for overseas service. He was made temporary lieutenant colonel and appointed CO of the 5th Manchesters on 14 September 1914 and commanded his battalion in Egypt from 25 September 1914 until embarkation for Gallipoli on 2nd May 1915. He disembarked with the battalion on V Beach on 6 May 1915 and remained in command (also taking temporary command of 127th Brigade from 7 to 30 July) until evacuated sick on 30 September 1915. He was appointed CMG in 1916 and was twice Mentioned in Dispatches, for his service on Gallipoli (LG 5 November 1915 and 13 July 1916).

After recovering he reassumed command the 5th Manchesters, was made substantive lieutenant colonel on 1 August 1917 (with precedence from 1 June 1916). Mentioned in Dispatches again 21 December 1917. He remained in command until 1920. Appointed to command the 127th Brigade and promoted to colonel on 3 May 1920. In 1921 he was appointed a Deputy Lieutenant for Lancashire and CB (Companion of the Bath, Civil Division). In 1925 he was created KCB (Knight Commander of the Bath, Military Division). Author of *Letters from Helles*, a book of frank and revealing letters written to his wife. He died on 25 December 1959.

General Sir Francis John Davies, KCB, KCMG, KCVO, ADC

GOC of VIII Corps from 8 August until the evacuation

Born on 3 July 1864 in the parish of St. George's Hanover Square, London. He was educated at Eton College, and commissioned into the Worcester Militia in 1881. He transferred to the Grenadiers Guards (his father and grandfather's former regiment) as lieutenant on 14 May 1884, becoming the adjutant to the 2nd Bn Grenadier Guards in 1893. Promoted captain on 28 October 1895, he was posted to South Africa in 1897 where he became deputy assistant adjutant general for the Cape of Good Hope, and was promoted to major on 12 July 1899.

After the outbreak of the South African War in October 1899, he served as deputy assistant adjutant general responsible for intelligence at army headquarters in South Africa. Took part in operations in the Orange Free State in April and May 1900 including the actions at Vet River and Zand River. Also in May 1900, took part in operations in the Transvaal including an action near Johannesburg. He was subsequently appointed Acting Commissioner of Police for Johannesburg in 1900, and received a brevet promotion to lieutenant colonel dated 29 November 1900 (substantive 19 April 1901). He was Mentioned in Despatches (LG 16 April 1901) and received the Queen's medal with three clasps.

He returned to the United Kingdom in 1902 and was temporarily employed in the Intelligence Department. He became deputy assistant quartermaster general at the War Office on 7 September 1902 and was appointed assistant director of military operations in 1904. He was the British delegate to the International Conference on Wireless Telegraphy in Berlin in 1906 and appointed assistant quartermaster general for Western Command in 1907. He became the general officer commanding 1 (Guards) Brigade in 1909, made temporary brigadier general on 1 August 1910 and was promoted to major general on 18 May 1911. He was appointed director of staff duties at the War Office in 1913 and in October 1914 was made GOC 8th Division, then fighting on the Western Front in 1914 (in which capacity he led the division at the Battle of Neuve Chapelle and the Battle of Aubers Ridge).

In late July 1915 he was sent to Gallipoli as a permanent replacement for Lt. General Hunter-Weston, taking over command of VIII Corps from Major General Douglas on 8 August. His dismay at the ineffectiveness of the preliminary bombardment for the 6 August advance at Helles was later recalled by Hamilton in his diary:

'Fresh from France he watched the artillery preparation at Helles and (although we had thought it rather grand) says we simply don't know what the word bombardment means. Instead of seeing, as in the Western Theatre, an unbroken wall of flame and smoke rising above enemy trenches about to be stormed, here he saw a sprinkling of shells bursting at intervals of 20 yards or so—a totally different effect. And yet the Turks are as tough as the Germans and take as much hammering!'

Davies brought to Helles valuable experience gained on the Western Front and his contribution to what was a very difficult period (and the greater part) of the campaign has been largely overlooked. He inherited a shattered and demoralised corps, starved of resources and reinforcement. Over the five months of his tenure his ideas and energy were the catalyst for a myriad of tactical and systemic improvements which greatly improved the fighting efficiency of his force, allowing his troops to achieve tactical superiority over the enemy facing them.

Following the evacuation he commanded IX Corps, Egyptian Expeditionary Force for most of 1916, and latter months returned to the UK to become Military Secretary. After the War he was appointed general officer commanding-in-chief for Scottish Command in 1919, retiring in the post in 1923 when he was appointed Lieutenant of the Tower of London.

In addition to the British honours mentioned above, Davies was also Mentioned in Monro's Dispatches (LG 10 April 1916) and awarded the following foreign honours: the French Commander of the Legion of Honour (1916), the Belgian Grand Officer of the Order of the Crown (1917), the Japanese Order of the Sacred Treasure (1918), Grand Officer of the Order of the Crown of Italy (1919), the American Distinguished Service Medal (1919) and the Serbian Order of the White Eagle with Swords.

He died in Pershore, Worcestershire on 18 March 1948.

Major General Sir William Douglas, KCMG, CB, DSO
GOC of the 42nd Division

Born on 13 August 1858 and educated at Bath. Gazetted into the 1st Bn The Royal Scots on 30 January 1878 and was promoted to lieutenant on 25 November 1878, serving as adjutant, 1st Bn Royal Scots from 24 March 1880 to 23 March 1887.

Served in the Bechuanaland Expedition, 1884–85. Promoted to captain on 24 June 1885. Appointed adjutant 3rd Royal Scots (Militia) February 1888 to February 1893, and adjutant 1st Royal Scots, 20 February 1893 to 20 August 1894.

He was promoted to major on 24 July 1895 and attended Staff College 1896-97. He served in South Africa, 1900–02, and took part in operations in the Orange Free State, February to May 1900. During operations in the Transvaal, east of Pretoria, July to 29 November 1900. Took part in the actions at Belfast (26 and 27 August 1900) and Lydenburg (5 to 8 September 1900).

CO to 1st Bn Royal Scots from 24 August 1900, and in command of a column during operations in the Transvaal, November 1900 to November 1901. Promoted to lieutenant colonel on 5 December 1900. Mentioned in Despatches (LG 16 April 1901), received the Queen's medal with three clasps, the King's medal with two clasps, and was created a Companion of the Distinguished Service Order (LG 19 April 1901).

Made brevet colonel 10 February 1904, promoted to colonel on 1 March 1906 and was colonel to the General Staff, 6th Division, and subsequently became (when the title of the appointment was changed) GSO 1st Grade, 8th Division (the 6th Division becoming the 8th Division) Irish Command, from 1st March 1906 to 31 October 1909. Created a CB in 1908.

He commanded the 14th Infantry Brigade from 1 November 1909 to 9 November 1912. Promoted major general on 10 August 1912 and commanded the 42nd Division from May 1913 to 11 March 1917.

Served in Egypt from 10 September 1914 to 5 May 1915 and at Gallipoli from 9 May to 30 December 1915, during which time he was placed in temporary command of VIII Corps on several occasions, the most notable being from 24 July to 8 August (during the last major battle at Helles). Twice Mentioned in Despatches (LG 21 September 1915 and November 1915) and created KCMG in November 1915.

Later served in Sinai, 1916–17, during the battle of Romani and the capture of El Arish, and commanded the Desert Column from 23 October 1916 to 8 December 1916. Twice Mentioned in Despatches (LG December 1916 and July 1917) and awarded the *Croix de Guerre* with Palm (LG 21 May 1917).

Left the division on 11 March 1917 to give evidence in the Dardanelles Inquiry, he later commanded the Western Reserve Centre until retiring on 19 August 1918. He died in 1920.

Known almost universally as 'Little Willie' he was despised by practically all the officers and men in his division. Douglas's ADC, Captain Harold Cawley MP wrote of Douglas in a letter to his father in September:

'My own general is disliked by all his troops, particularly by his officers. He has a third-rate brain, no capacity to grasp the lie of the land and originality or ingenuity. He has been to the trenches three times since he landed, hurried visits on which he saw nothing and he hardly ever goes to an observation point with his field glasses. The result is that he does not understand the lie of the land on his own front. When there is an attack, he works out the details and leaves nothing to the Brigadiers and commanding officers who know the ground. The result last time [August Battle] was that the best Manchester Battalions were sent to an impossible place which every colonel and adjutant regarded as only to be taken after some other commanding trenches had been cleared ...'

The other ranks were no less scathing. An unnamed NCO told Chaplain Kenneth Best that 'there are only two ways of General D[ouglas] getting killed—by lyddite on top of [his dugout] direct hit, or by a bullet from one of his own men.'

Notorious for his abrasive nature and for micro managing his subordinates and local operations (while having little understanding of the ground or firing-line conditions). However, despite Douglas's outward appearance of a brusque, unemotional commander, he was not without feelings and was greatly affected by the losses the division suffered in June and August. Hamilton recalled Douglas as a 'melancholy man before whose eyes stands constantly the tragic melting away without replacement of the most beautiful of the Divisions of Northern England.'

RSM 4234 Harry Carter T. Franklin, (later Lieutenant) MC

RSM of the 7th Manchesters

Born on 16 August 1874 in Stockport, Cheshire. Franklin enlisted as a regular in the Manchester Regiment in May 1893, later serving in India and probably saw active service there and also in South Africa. In 1905 he was stationed with the 2nd Bn Manchester Regiment at Fort George on Guernsey and was a Freemason in the local Mariners Lodge.

He was attached to the 1/7th Manchesters prior to outbreak of war, and served with the battalion in Sudan and Egypt and disembarked with it on V Beach on 6 May 1915. Franklin was with Major Staveacre (see below) when he was killed on 4 June 1915 as they were both carrying ammunition to the firing-line. On being shot in the back, Staveacre said to Franklin: 'Never mind me. Carry on, sergeant major,' and died at once. He was commissioned in the field on 10 July 1915, having served in the ranks for over 22 years and remained with the 7th Manchesters. He took over as adjutant from Captain Creagh in August 1915. He was awarded the Military Cross (LG 3 June 1916) and Mentioned in Despatches (LG 13 July 1916) for his service at Gallipoli. Promoted to lieutenant on 2 July 1916.

After Gallipoli it appears Franklin was transferred back to one of the regular battalions. He survived the war and died in Ampthill, Bedfordshire in February 1932.

Brigadier General Herbert Cokayne Frith, CB

GOC of the 125th Brigade

Born on 12 July 1861 in Gainsborough, Lincolnshire. Commissioned into the Argyle and Bute Artillery (Militia) in 1881, he joined the 2nd Bn Somersetshire Light Infantry as a lieutenant on 28 January 1882, and was promoted to captain on 23 September 1887. He was employed with the Egyptian Army from 23 Sept 1885 to 4 October 1895, serving in the Frontier Field Force in Soudan, 1885–86 and was at the Action of Giniss, and being awarded the Bronze (Khedive) Star. In 1889 he took part in the Action of Toski (Soudan) and was awarded the clasp and also

4th Class Medjidie. Posted to the Indian Army as station staff officer class 1 (Punjab district) on 28 July 1897 until 28 July 1902. Promoted to major on 27 January 1900. Listed as a qualified interpreter in Arabic in October 1902, he was also fluent in Turkish, French, Persian, Urdu and Pushtu. Promoted to lieutenant colonel 27 November 1909 and took over command of the 1st Bn Somerset Light Infantry. He was promoted to colonel on 2 June 1913 and relinquished command of his battalion on 27 November 1913, to take command of the Lancashire Fusiliers (125th) Brigade. Listed as temporary brigadier general 5 August 1914.

He commanded the brigade in Egypt and arrived with it at Helles on 5 May 1915 and continued to command throughout the campaign. He was made temporary major general on 30 December 1915 to 20 January 1916. Awarded the CB in 1916 and was twice Mentioned in Despatches for his service on Gallipoli (LG 5 November 1915 and 13 July 1916).

He commanded the 125th Brigade in Egypt in 1916–17 and moved with it to France in March 1917. He returned to England on 23 June 1917 to take up command of the Home Service Brigade, an event commemorated in the divisional history:

'General Frith was the last of the General Officers who had served with the Division from the outbreak of war. For three years he had commanded the Lancashire Fusilier Brigade, which had become much attached to him, for he was quick to recognize and give credit for good work, and he possessed a remarkable memory for faces, invariably knowing each officer by name from first meeting.'

Frith was awarded the Order of St. Stanislas, 2nd Class with Swords and retired on 1 November 1918. He died on 5 March 1942.

Lt. Colonel Harry Edward Gresham, TD

CO of the 7th Manchesters until 27 May

Born in Chorlton, Manchester in early 1865. Commissioned into the 4th Volunteer Bn Manchester Regt as second lieutenant on 3 October 1890. Promoted to lieutenant on 28 March 1894, to captain on 24 April 1895 and was appointed as instructor of musketry on 12 July 1901. He retained his rank and seniority on the formation of the Territorial Force when the battalion was renamed as the 1/7th Bn Manchester Regiment on 1 April 1908. Awarded the Territorial Decoration on 24 March 1911.

Promoted temporary lieutenant colonel on 14 May 1912, when he took command of the 7th Manchesters.

He volunteered for overseas service in early September 1914 and commanded his battalion in Sudan and Egypt from 25 September 1914 until embarkation for Gallipoli on 2nd May 1915. He disembarked with the Manchester Brigade on V Beach on 6 May 1915 and continued to command his battalion until 27 May when he was invalided back to England, handing over command to Major Staveacre (see below). He relinquished his commission on 2 June 1916 on account of ill health (with permission to retain his rank and uniform) and retired from the TF on 29 July 1921. He was described by Gerald B. Hurst in his book *With Manchesters in the East*:

'Lieutenant-Colonel H. E. Gresham, who had commanded since 1912, was an ideal C.O.—a Territorial of long service and sound judgement, a fine shot and in civilian life a distinguished engineer.'

He died in Bournemouth, Hampshire on 29 November 1933 (with an estate valued at £359,980, the equivalent of £26,000,000 in 2021 terms).

Sgt 1126 (later Captain) James (Joseph) Cox Harrop

C Company, 9th Manchesters

Born in Ashton under Lyne on 11 January 1891 and christened as Joseph Cox Harrop. His father died when he was eight years old and he spent most of his early life living in his paternal grandmother's baker's shop in Old Street Ashton. There are no records of his enlistment in the 1/9th Manchesters but judging by his rank and number he would have joined at least five or six years before war broke out. He volunteered for overseas service in early September 1914 and sailed with the battalion for Egypt on 10 September 1914. Harrop and Riley met in Egypt when the former was part of a guard party (made up by 9th Manchesters) at the Abu Zabal Marconi signal station, which was about 14 miles north-east of Cairo and reputed to be the largest Marconi station in the world.

He landed with the battalion at V Beach with his battalion on 9 May 1915 and is thought to have served through most of the campaign. Although the 9th Manchesters did not take part in the advance on 4 June, the battalion made two small attacks later that month and Harrop was involved in both actions. The first was on 7 June against

Turkish trenches G10 and G11 and again on 18 June against the Turkish held portions of H11 and H11a.

He was promoted to colour sergeant some time before his discharge on 10 December 1915 (either due to sickness or as a 'Time Expired' man—on completion of his service). He re-enlisted in 1916–17 and served as a colour sergeant in the 2nd Manchesters (No. 41447) until commissioned as 2nd lieutenant into the 12 Bn Manchester Regt on 30 May 1917. He was promoted to temporary captain on 28 May 1918 (until 27 June 1918) while commanding a trench mortar battery in France and to temporary lieutenant on 30 November 1918. Harrop continued to command a trench mortar battery until 13 February 1919. He is believed to have died in Colchester in 1953.

Lt. Colonel (temp. Brig. Gen.) Thomas Walter Brand Viscount Hampden, GCVO, KCB, CMG, KStJ, JP

GOC of the 126th Brigade

Born in London on 29 January 1869, the son of Henry Robert Brand 2nd Viscount Hampden and Susan Henrietta Cavendish. Educated at Eton and Trinity College Cambridge. Commissioned as 2nd lieutenant into the Royal Scots, Lothian Regt (Militia) on 11 April 1888. Transferred to the 10th Hussars on 8 June 1889 and promoted to lieutenant on 10 June 1891. Adjutant to the 10th Hussars from 30 May 1894 to 29 May 1898 and promoted to captain on 16 February 1898. Appointed ADC to the Governor and Commander in Chief, New South Wales (his father) from 9 July 1898 to 15 December 1898—described on his record as 'Special Extra Regimental Employment' ...

He married Lady Katherine Mary Montagu-Douglas-Scott on 29 April 1899. The ceremony was held at Westminster Abbey with the Archbishop of Canterbury officiating. Guests included the Prince of Wales, the Duke of Cambridge and the Marquis of Salisbury.

Adjutant to the Cavalry Brigade from 9 January 1899 until 8 October 1899. Made brevet major on 29 November 1900 (substantive 14 January 1903). Brigade major of the Cavalry Brigade in South Africa from 22 May to 23 July 1901. Adjutant to the Imperial Yeomanry from 24 July 1901. Mentioned in Dispatches (LG 16 April 1901) and received the Queen's Medal with six clasps.

He went onto the Reserve of Officers list on 14 December 1904. Assistant Private Secretary to the First Lord of the Admiralty in 1905–06 (unpaid). He became the Third Viscount of Hampden on the death of his father on 22 November 1906.

He was promoted to lieutenant colonel in 1/1st Bn the Hertfordshire Regt on 12 February 1913. The battalion, with Hampden in command, joined the Expeditionary Force in France on 6 November 1914 and served in the trenches during the closing stages of the First Battle of Ypres. In January 1915 he handed command of the battalion to Lt. Colonel Croft. Made temporary brigadier general on 5 July 1915, he arrived at Helles and assumed command of 126th Brigade on 13 July 1915. He relinquished command temporarily on 1 November 1915 when he went to England for two months leave. He returned on 20 December and again assumed command of the brigade, but left six days later on 26 December to take command the 6th Mounted Brigade. Seven times Mentioned in Despatches (mostly for staff work).

Lt. Colonel William George Heys, TD

CO of the 8th Manchesters

Born in Peckham, Surrey, around 1867. By 1871 he and his parents were living in Gorton, Manchester. As a young man Heys was employed as a Consulting Engineer's Assistant in his father's firm William E Heys and Son, Patent Agents and Consulting Engineers. Commissioned into the 5th Volunteer Bn Manchester Regt (Ardwick) 23 August 1890, he was promoted to lieutenant on 4 July 1891. He became a Freemason and was initiated into the East Lancashire Centurion Lodge on 4 November 1895 (like several other officers in the local Volunteer battalions). He was promoted to captain on 17 June 1896 and given the temporary rank of captain in the army on 20 March 1901.

He served in the South African War, commanding the 2nd (K Company) and 3rd Volunteer Active Service Company, attached to the 1st Manchesters from April 1901 to April 1902, and took part in all the treks whilst the 1st Manchesters formed part of Colonel Park's column, as well as carrying out garrison duties in at Lydenburg. He contracted enteric fever in April and was invalided home on 5 June 1902. He received the Queen's medal with three clasps.

Made honorary captain in the army on 20 November 1902, honorary major on 19 November 1904 and major on 22 January 1908. He retained his rank and seniority on the formation of the Territorial Force when the battalion was renamed as the 1/7th Bn Manchester Regiment on 1 April 1908. Awarded the Territorial Decoration on 24 March 1911. He was gazetted lieutenant colonel and appointed to command the Ardwick Battalion, now renamed 1/8th Bn Manchester Regt, on 7 March 1914.

He volunteered for overseas service in early September 1914 and commanded his battalion in Egypt from 25 September 1914 until embarkation for Gallipoli on 2nd May 1915. He disembarked with the Manchester Brigade on V Beach on 6 May 1915 and continued to command his battalion until his death on 4 June. At the beginning of the battle Heys was in the 8th Manchesters Battalion HQ just behind Wigan Road but was called to 127th Brigade HQ shortly after noon to take command of the brigade from Brigadier General Lee (see below) who had been badly wounded in the preliminary bombardment. He arrived at brigade HQ at 12.25 p.m. and was in turn relieved by Lord Rochdale (see below) at 3.30 p.m. after learning his battalion had lost all but one of its officers. He set off with Captain Talbot (attached 1st Lancs Fus.) and an orderly, to rendezvous with Major Bentley (see above) in the 8th Manchesters HQ (then in the first objective line, G11). As the party neared G11 it came under shrapnel fire which killed all three men. Heys was temporarily buried in the parados of G11 but was later reburied in Lancashire Landing Cemetery. Mentioned in Dispatches (LG 5 November 1915). An enthusiastic and dedicated soldier who on his appointment to command the 8th Manchesters practically gave up his business to devote his time to the battalion.

Major Carlos Joseph Hickie, CMG

Brigade Major of the 126th Brigade

Born in Dublin on 10 December 1872. Educated in Oscott College, Birmingham, and Beaumont College, Oxford, and at the Royal Military College Sandhurst. He was commissioned into the Gloucestershire Regt as 2nd lieutenant on 21 October 1893 and promoted to lieutenant on 12 January 1898. Served in the South African War 1899–1902, including the actions of Rietfontein, Lombard's Kop and the defence of Ladysmith (slightly wounded at Rietfontein, 24 October 1899). Received the Queen's medal with four clasps and the King's medal with two clasps. Promoted to captain in the King's Own Yorkshire Light Infantry 22 March 1902 and to major in the Royal Fusiliers in 1912.

He was appointed brigade major to the East Lancs (126th) Brigade on 5 August 1914 and served with the brigade in Egypt and at Gallipoli. Attached to 127th Brigade HQ on 2 June for the duration of the Third Battle of Krithia and was slightly wounded in the head around 2 p.m. on 4 June. He returned to the 126th Brigade but had to be admitted to hospital on 25 June to have his wound treated, later leaving the peninsula for treatment.

In January 1916 he was placed in command of the 14th Bn Hampshire Regt then serving on the Western Front. Appointed to command a brigade in August 1916 and commanded the 115th, 224th and 7th Infantry Brigades successively. Temporary brigadier general August 1916 to 1919. Appointed CMG in 1919 and Mentioned in Despatches (LG 4 January 1917 and 5 July 1919). He died at Slevoyre, Tullyglass, County Tipperary, Ireland in December 1959.

Captain (later Brevet Lt. Col.) Philip Vaughan Holberton
Adjutant of the 6th Manchesters

Born in Twickenham, Middlesex, on 24 May 1879. He was educated at Shrewsbury School and the Royal Military College Sandhurst (January 1900 and passing out on 29 January 1901. As the best cadet in his class, he won the Sword of Honour which was presented to him by Queen Victoria. Commissioned 2nd lieutenant on 8 January 1901 into the 2nd Bn Manchester Regt, which was at the time in South Africa. He joined the battalion in the Harrismith area of South Africa in mid-June 1901. In August he was assigned to the new Mounted Infantry Company and was involved in fighting on 12 November when his company encountered a group of 400 Boers near Schalkie in the Orange Free State. He was slightly wounded in the action being hit by a bullet just over his heart, with his equipment stopping most of the force. Promoted to lieutenant on 27 November 1901, and received the Queen's medal with five clasps.

He returned to Aldershot with his battalion on 27 September 1902. Served as adjutant to the battalion from 1 December 1903 until 30 November 1906. Posted to the West African Regt in Sierra Leone on 12 January 1907 and remained with that regiment until 3 July 1910. He re-joined the 2nd Manchesters, then at Mullingar, County Westmeath, Ireland, during July 1910. Appointed adjutant to the 1/6th Manchesters on 4 November 1911 and promoted to captain on 1 December 1911.

He served with the 6th Manchesters in Egypt and arrived with the battalion on V Beach on 6 May 1915. On 3 August he led a small party of men to remove a Turkish traverse in a communication trench running up the north-west side of the Vineyard, in order to improve the field of fire from the 6th Manchester's barricade. A bombing party successfully kept the Turks back while the digging party completed its work. He took part in the August fighting and moved with the battalion to the left subsection on 19 August, when the 42nd Division relieved the 29th Division. On 12 October he took over command of the battalion from Lt. Colonel Pilkington who was evacuated to hospital, but was himself evacuated from the peninsula on 20 October suffering from jaundice. Twice Mentioned in Dispatches for his service on Gallipoli (LG 5 November 1915 and 28 January 1916).

He was promoted to brevet major on 8 November 1915 (substantive 8 January 1916). He re-joined the division in Egypt in 1916 and served as brigade major to the 126th Brigade from the 5 April to 19 October 1916. Placed in command of the 1/5th Lancashire Fusiliers on 19 October 1916. He moved with his battalion to France in March 1917 and was promoted to brevet lieutenant colonel on 3 June 1917. On 21 March 1918 the German Army launched its Spring Offensive (*Kaiserschlacht*) and the 1/5th Lancs Fusiliers were sent to defend the village of Gomiecourt. Around 2 a.m. on 26 March Holberton was walking through the position encouraging his men when he shot through the head and killed instantly. He was buried close to where he fell. When the area was recaptured in September 1918 his grave was identified, and on 18 September, almost 40 officers and many men from the 1/5th Lancs Fus. and the 6th Manchesters attended his reburial service. He is now buried in Achiet-Le-Grand Communal Cemetery Extension grave IV.F.8. He was awarded the Serbian Order of the White Eagle (with Swords) 4th Class and was Mentioned in Despatches a further three times.

Lt. General Aylmer Gould Hunter-Weston, KCB, DSO

GOC 29th Division, March 1915 to 24 May 1915. GOC VIII Corps from 24 May to 20 July 1915

Known alternately as 'Hunter-Bunter' or the 'Butcher of Helles'. Much has been written about this controversial general and some have questioned why Hunter-Weston, a Royal Engineer (who had never commanded a division in the field) should have been placed in command of an infantry division, let alone one given such a demanding task. Given the reluctance among the 'Westerners' to lose good men from the Western theatre, it's possible that he was the best that Kitchener was prepared to spare at the time. General William Marshall (see above) offers his own explanation in his memoir, *Memories of Four Fronts*:

'To our great regret General Shaw left us. He was succeeded in command by General Hunter-Weston; presumably because Hunter-Weston was a fluent French scholar and we were to act in close concert with the French during this adventure.'

Promoted beyond his abilities, having risen from the rank of temporary brigadier general to temporary lieutenant general in 16 months. His tactical naivety and insistence on carrying out his main attacks in broad daylight, always with inadequate artillery support, cost the lives of many.

Marshall, who rarely criticised his contemporaries was shocked at Hunter-Weston's callous attitude towards casualties and recalled Hunter-Weston's reaction to the losses suffered by the Manchester Brigade in a night advance:

'"There you are! You see the thing has been done with no casualties." I gently murmured "Fifty," to which he retorted: "Well! That's nothing, it would have been worth doing if you had had five hundred."'

Hunter-Weston was evacuated suffering from 'heat stroke' on 20 July 1915 and never returned to the peninsula. Served later as an army corps commander in France from March 1916 until May 1919. Promoted lieutenant general (LG 1 January 1919).

An undoubtedly courageous man, described by Hamilton as a 'slashing man of action,' the majority of Hunter-Weston's contemporaries however, held a different opinion. Major General Egerton, GOC of the 52nd Division, had many run-ins with Hunter-Weston both on his attitude towards casualties, and his tendency to micromanage his subordinates. Egerton later described the orders issued by Hunter-Weston for the 12 July battle as 'absurdly voluminous orders, in fact they were silly and ludicrous. Anyone who doubts this assertion can turn them up and see—just the sort of rubbish that the "Scientific Corps" would issue. The Div'l Commander had simply to adopt them word for word.'

Field Marshal Haig was even more damning, describing Hunter-Weston as 'a rank amateur.'

Major Henry Lewkenor Knight, CMG, DSO

Brigade Major of the 127th Brigade

Born at Foyhill near Litchfield, Staffordshire on 24 March 1874. Attended the Royal Military College Sandhurst in 1894. Commissioned as 2nd lieutenant into the Royal Irish Fusiliers on 10 October 1894 and promoted to lieutenant on 3 May 1898. Appointed acting adjutant to the 2nd Bn Royal Irish Fusiliers on August 1895 to August 1899. Served with his regiment as captain (substantive captain 1 May 1902) in South Africa 1899–1900 and on staff duties with the Mounted Infantry until invalided on 15 December 1900. Mentioned in Despatches (LG 10 September 1901) and received the Queen's medal with five clasps.

Appointed adjutant to the 1st Volunteer (City of Dundee) Bn Royal Highlanders on 17 May 1901 to 15 August 1904. Appointed adjutant to the 4th Bn Royal Irish Fusiliers on 19 May 1905. Seconded to the General Staff on 16 April 1912. Promoted to major on 21 January 1914, and appointed as brigade major to Manchester (127th) Brigade on 5 August 1914.

He served with the brigade in Egypt, landed at V Beach on 6 May 1915 and continued as its brigade major until being temporarily attached to the 125th Brigade from 20–25 December 1915. Made temporary lieutenant colonel on 20 December 1915. He served in the Salonika Campaign as GSO 1 to the 10th Division from 30 December 1915 to 15 June 1917, as brigade commander, 80th Infantry Brigade from 16 June to 24 August 1917 and on the staff of XVI Army Corps as brigadier general from 25 August 1917 to 24 February 1919.

Made brevet lieutenant colonel on 3 June 1916 (substantive 14 March 1917) and temporary brigadier general on 16 June 1917. He was awarded the DSO in the King's Birthday Honours List in 1917, appointed CMG in 1918–19, awarded the Order of the Redeemer 3rd Class, the Greek Military Cross, the Greek Medal for Military Merit, 2nd Class and was five times Mentioned in Despatches.

He was described by Gerald B. Hurst in his book *With Manchesters in the East* as 'a tower of strength on Gallipoli.'

Brevet colonel on 3 June 1919 (substantive 4 August 1921). He retired on half pay as an honourary brigadier general on 17 May 1929. He died at Le Court, Liss, Petersfield, Hampshire on 28 March 1945.

Major Arthur Niven Lawford

OC, 1/1st Signals Company, 42nd (East Lancs.) Division.
Later Lt. Colonel and CRE 42nd Division

Mechanical engineer of Manchester. Born 22 November 1884, Oswestry, Shropshire. Son of William Robinson Lawford, an estate agent, and Isabella Harriet Douglas Niven. Educated Colet House, Rhyl, and Cheltenham College. Technical education Victoria University, Manchester, with four years apprenticeship at British Westinghouse Co., Trafford Park. Member of the Old Cheltonian Lodge (no. 3223) from 1911. Married Vera Margaret Hawson in 1913.

Commissioned second lieutenant into the 3rd Lancashire Royal Engineers (Volunteers), on 21 February 1903. Promoted to lieutenant on 21 May 1904. On formation of the Territorial Force on 1 April 1908, appointed to 1/1st East Lancashire Field Company, East Lancashire Divisional Engineers. Promoted to captain on 4 May 1912.

Commanded the 1/1st East Lancashire Divisional Signals Company at its mobilisation on 5 August 1914, when he was promoted to major. Signed Army Form E.624 volunteering for overseas service in early September 1914. Embarked with the East Lancashire Division for Egypt in September 1914. Commanded the company in Egypt in 1914–15. Landed at Helles on 6 May and presumably remained there until he succumbed to sickness 22 September 1915, and was evacuated. (Command of the company was taken temporarily by 2nd Lieut. A. Roberts, then, from 10 October, by Captain R.W. Dammers, Sherwood Foresters.)

Mentioned in Despatches (LG 1 December 1916). Promoted lieutenant colonel on 3 March 1917 (with precedence as of 20 November 1916). Awarded Belgian *Croix de Guerre* (LG 15 April 1918).

Possibly served as CRE to the 42nd Division in late 1918 or early 1919. Granted the rank of captain in the regular army and transferred to the Royal Engineers, 5 October 1921. Attached Royal Air Force in Iraq as staff officer, from 1 April 1922. Qualified for GSM with Iraq clasp. Awarded the Territorial Decoration (LG 4 July 1922).

Granted the rank of major in the regular army 18 April 1931 (lieutenant colonel TF). Placed on the Retired List (with pay) 22 November 1934. Granted the rank of lieutenant colonel 22 November 1934. Died Sussex, 29 March 1950, age 65.

Brigadier General Hon. Herbert Alexander Lawrence, KCMG

GOC of the 127th Brigade from 21 June 1915

Born on 8 August 1861 at Southgate, London. He was the fourth son of Sir John Laird Mair Lawrence, later first Baron Lawrence (1811–79), British imperial statesman and Viceroy of India, 1864–9, and his wife, Harriette Katherine (1820–1917), daughter of the Reverend Richard Hamilton of Donegal. He was educated at Harrow School and the Royal Military College Sandhurst. On 10 May 1882, commissioned into 17th Lancers, then serving in India. Appointed adjutant on 13 May 1890 to 12 May 1894. He returned to England with his regiment in 1891 and was promoted to captain on 2 February 1892. He attended Staff College at Camberley and served as a staff captain (intel.) at Army HQ from 1 September 1897 to 23 May 1898. Appointed deputy assistant adjutant general (intel.) at Army HQ on 24 May 1898 to 8 October 1899, when he was posted to South Africa to carry out the same role on the Intelligence Staff of Sir John French's cavalry division from 9 October 1899 to 5 February 1901. Promoted major on 22 November 1899 and to brevet lieutenant colonel on 29 November 1900, he acted as DAAG (intel.) and deputy adjutant and quarter master general (intel.) from 6 February 1901 until 7 March 1902. Twice Mentioned in Despatches (LG 4 May 1900 and 8 February 1901) and received the Queen's medal with six clasps and the King's Medal with two clasps. He returned to England with the 17th Lancers in September 1902 and resigned his commission on 13 May 1903 having been overlooked as commanding officer of the 17th Lancers in favour of Douglas Haig, then junior in service. He took up a career in banking and in 1907 became a partner in Glyn, Mills, Currie and Co., the bank in which his father-in-law was a senior partner.

At the outbreak of war, he was recalled from the Reserve of Officers and posted as GSO1 to the 2nd Yeomanry Division. He served with the division in Egypt until June 1915 when he was sent to Gallipoli and took command of the 127th Brigade on 21 June. He was sent to Suvla during August and placed in temporary command of the 53rd (Welsh) Division. He returned to Helles in late August and re-assumed command of the 127th Brigade. Promoted to major general and placed in command of the 52nd Division on 17 September 1915. At the end of the campaign, he was appointed to oversee the embarkations for the evacuation of Helles. Twice Mentioned in Dispatches for his service on Gallipoli (LG 5 November 1915 and 13 July 1916).

He moved with the 52nd Division to Egypt in 1916. Promoted temporary lieutenant general and achieved great success in command during the battle of Romani in early August 1916. After a disagreement regarding the planning of Palestine Campaign, he was sent to command the 71st Home Forces Division in England on 23 October 1916.

On 12 February 1917 he was given command of the 66th (2nd East Lancashire) Territorial Division. The 66th Division fought on the Western Front at Ypres in October 1917. During the winter of 1917–8 Field Marshal Haig's command underwent major change. In January 1918, in a surprising appointment, Lawrence replaced Brigadier General John Charteris as chief intelligence officer. Soon afterwards, at the end of January, he was promoted to the more important post of chief of the general staff, in succession to Sir Launcelot Kiggell. He retained this post throughout 1918. Promoted to lieutenant general on 3 June 1918 and general on 3 June 1919, he retired later that year. In 1925 he was made Honorary Colonel of the 6th Manchesters, a title he held until 1932.

His many honours include Commander of Legion of Honour (1916), 2nd class Serbian order of Karageorge, with Swords (1916), Knight Commander of Bath (1917), *Croix de Guerre*, France (1916), *Croix de Guerre*, Belgium (1918), American Distinguished Service Order (1918),

Grand Cross St Benedict of Aviz (1918), Grand Cross Crown of Romania (1918), Grand Officer Legion of Honour, France (1919), *Grand Cordon* (Crown of Belgium), 1st Class Rising Sun Japan, and Knight Grand Cross (1926). Lawrence was also Mentioned in Despatches a further six times (10 times in all).

After the war he returned to Glyn Mills and Co. as managing partner and under his leadership it became Britain's largest private bank. In 1934 Lawrence was appointed chairman. He died on 17 January 1943 at Woodcock, Little Berkhamsted, Hertfordshire.

Brigadier General Noel Lee, VD
GOC of the 127th Brigade until 4 June 1915

Born in Altrincham in first quarter of 1868, third son of Sir Joseph Lee. He was educated at Eton College before going into the family textile business Tootal Broadhurst Lee and Co.

Having been prevented from joining the regulars by his father he joined 6th Lancashire Rifle Volunteers (2nd Volunteer Bn Manchester Regt from 1888) and was commissioned as 2nd lieutenant on 25 December 1886. Promoted to captain on 1 February 1890. Like many of his fellow officers he was a Freemason, being initiated into the Social Lodge, Manchester on 17 October 1899. Promoted to major in May 1901 (substantive 2nd February 1902), to honorary lieutenant colonel and appointed CO of the 2nd Volunteer Bn Manchester Regt on 17 May 1906. He was awarded the Volunteer Officers Decoration (VD) in June 1906 and made honorary colonel in 1907. He retained his rank and seniority on the formation of the Territorial Force when the battalion was renamed as the 1/6th Bn Manchester Regiment on 1 April 1908. He was a member of the Territorial Force Advisory council and the East Lancashire TF Association. In September 1911 Lee was appointed commander the Manchester Brigade (the first territorial officer to be given command of a brigade) and relinquished command of the 6th Manchesters. He was made substantive colonel on 10 March 1914 and temporary brigadier general around the time the 42nd Division was mobilised in early August 1914.

He commanded the Manchester Brigade during its time in Egypt and Cyprus, and at Gallipoli from its landing on 6 May 1915 until he was seriously wounded in the preliminary bombardment for the Third Battle of Krithia on 4 June. He was evacuated on 4–5 June and arrived at Malta around 10–11 June. At first his condition seemed to improve but he suffered a haemorrhage and died on 22 June 1915 at the Blue Sisters Hospital in St Julians.

Lee was widely acknowledged as one of the division's brightest and best commanders. When Brigadier General William Marshall (see below) was sent by Hunter-Weston to 'tutor' Lee in late May 1915, he found him to be 'a really good Brigadier—and very much liked and trusted by his officers and men.' Lee's divisional commander Major General Douglas (see above) wrote of him:

'He is a very great loss to the Brigade, he has done splendidly—the most gallant, hardworking, thorough leader that I had, and I don't know how I shall replace him. I am sure that I shall not be able to find his equal.'

Lee was buried in the Pieta Military Cemetery in Malta[206] and received a posthumous Mention in Despatches (LG 5 November 1915) for his service at Gallipoli.

Lt. Colonel Donald Florence MacCarthy-Morrogh, CMG
CO of the 8th Manchesters from 16 July 1915

Born in Killarney, Kerry on 7 October 1869, and educated at Stonyhurst College. He was commissioned as 2nd lieutenant into the 3rd Bn (Militia) Munster Fusiliers on 4 March 1896. Promoted to lieutenant on 3 February 1897 and captain (in the Militia) on 5 June 1899. Attached as lieutenant to the 2nd Nigerian Regt, West African Frontier Force on 6 May 1899, promoted to captain on 9 June 1899, he remained with the force until 1909. Received the Ashanti Medal and clasp, the Munshi and Kaduna Expeditions Medal and clasp and Bornu Expedition Medal and clasp. He was transferred to the 4 Bn Royal Munster Fusiliers on 2 August 1908 and promoted to major on 3 September 1909.

He assumed command of the 8th Manchesters on 16 July 1915, and remained throughout the rest of the campaign. After losing his adjutant,

---

206 Riley visited Lee's grave in Malta, and took a photograph. A print was among the items he took to a meeting of the 6th Manchesters' Old Members Association in 1932.

Capt. Peter Murphy on 13 October (see below), MacCarthy-Morrogh made most of the entries in the battalion diary, often using it to vent his frustration with higher command, the lack of resources (building material in particular) and the poor quality of the later reinforcements his battalion received. He was Mentioned in Despatches (LG 13 July 1916) and made CMG on 2 June 1916. Substantive lieutenant colonel 26 July 1917. He resigned his commission on 10 September 1921. He died on 15 May 1932 in Skibbereen, Cork.

Brigadier General (later Lt. General) Sir William Raine Marshall, GCMG, KCB, KCSI, CB

GOC of the 87th Brigade and temp GOC of the 42nd Division from 24 July to 8 August 1915

Born on 29 October 1865 in Stranton near Hartlepool, County Durham. He was educated at Repton School and at the Royal Military College Sandhurst. He was commissioned as lieutenant into the 1st Bn Sherwood Foresters (Derbyshire Regt) on 30 January 1886. Posted to the 2nd Bn in India in March 1890. He returned home in May 1892 and was promoted captain on 23 September 1893. He returned to India at the end of May 1894 and served in the frontier campaigns of Malakand and Tirah in 1897–98 and was present at the storming of the Dargai Heights and the capture of the Sampagha and Arhanga Passes, earning the Indian Frontier Medal of 1895 with two clasps.

He returned to the UK in October 1898, and was posted to Malta in October 1899, to organise and command a school for Mounted Infantry (MI). In May 1900 he was sent to South Africa to command a company of MI, and in January 1901 he was given command of a battalion of MI (promoted brevet major on 9 July 1901). In December 1901 he was placed in command of a Mounted Column (of several thousand men) which he continued to lead until end of hostilities on 31 May 1902. He was slightly wounded in the campaign, twice Mentioned in Despatches (LG 9 July and 10 September 1901) and received the Queen's medal with three clasps and the King's medal with two clasps.

Promoted to brevet lieutenant colonel on 26 June 1902, he returned with his regiment to the UK in October 1902, and for the next eight years served as a company commander. Made substantive major on 7 December 1904 and brevet colonel on 26 June 1908.

In January 1911 he was appointed Assistant Commandant to the School of Mounted Infantry at Longmoor, returning to his regiment in September of that year. After serving for two years as 2ic the 1st Bn Sherwood Foresters he was promoted to substantive lieutenant colonel on 11 February 1912 and given command of the battalion. At the end of 1912 Marshall was sent with 1st Bn Sherwood Foresters to India, to serve as coastal and internal defence troops in the Bombay area. Shortly after the outbreak of war Marshall and his battalion were recalled to England arriving on 2 October 1914, later joining the 8th Division at Hursley Park (then under the command of Major General Francis Davies— see above). The 8th Division reached France on 5 November and Marshall remained in command of the battalion until recalled to England in February 1915 having been appointed to command the 87th Brigade of the 29th Division, then earmarked for operations at the Dardanelles. Mentioned in Dispatches (LG 17 February 1915) for his work in France.

He joined the 87th Brigade in Rugby and with it embarked at Avonmouth 18–22 March 1915. After disembarking at Alexandria to reload and organise stores, and at Mudros en route to Helles, he landed at X Beach shortly after the Royal Fusiliers on 25 April. On 27 April he assumed temporary command of the 29th Division. Major General Hunter-Weston reassumed command on the following day but Marshall was charged with pressing the attack of the division in what became known as the First Battle of Krithia. He commanded the 87th Brigade during the Second Battle of Krithia and was sent to the 127th Brigade on 25 May to 3 June 1915, in order to 'tutor' Brig. General Noel Lee (see above) which he considered 'a most unpleasant duty,' as he did not feel he had the necessary experience. In fact, he found Lee to be 'a really good Brigadier and very much liked and trusted by his officers and men.'

On 3 June, Marshall returned to his brigade which, although forming the 29th Division's reserve for the Third Battle of Krithia, would soon be fully engaged in the battle. In the middle of June, Marshall was promoted to major general but continued to command the 87th Brigade which took part in the Action of Gully Ravine from 28 June to 5 July.

On 24 July, Marshall was placed in temporary command of the 42nd Division (General Douglas having taken temporary command of VIII Corps after Hunter-Weston's health had broken down). On 8 August, General Davies took command of VIII Corps and Marshall went back to his brigade only to be appointed GOC the 29th Division on 15 August (after General de Lisle's departure to Suvla to temporarily command IX Corps). Marshall and the 29th Division followed de Lisle to Suvla on 19 August. On 23 August, General Byng arrived at Suvla and took command of IX Corps, de Lisle re-assumed command of the 29th Division and Marshall was placed in permanent command of the 53rd (Welsh) Division until it was evacuated in mid-December, Marshall being held back to assist in the main evacuation of Suvla on 19 December 1915. He was Mentioned in Dispatches three times for his service on Gallipoli (LG 5 August 1915, 5 November 1915 and 13 July 1916).

After Gallipoli Marshall he was posted to Salonika to command the 27th Division. In early September 1916 he was appointed to command III (Indian) Army Corps on the Mesopotamian front and was promoted to temporary lieutenant general. He participated in the capture of Kut-al-Amara in February 1917, and in the capture of Baghdad the following month. On General Sir Frederick Maude's death, Marshall succeeded his Commander in Chief as GOC the Mesopotamia Expeditionary Force and in this capacity accepted the surrender of the Ottoman army at Mosul on 30 October 1918, with the signing of the Armistice of Mudros.

His post war career took him back to India to command the Southern Army which he did until 1923, before retiring the following year, later writing his memoir *Memories of Four Fronts*. A modest, methodical and highly capable soldier, Marshall's self-confessed lack of military ambition had seen him sidelined for the greater part of his career. But when given the opportunity to command, he quickly showed his true worth and went, in the space of six years, from commanding a company of a hundred men, to an Army with a ration strength of nearly half a million. Marshall was rewarded with numerous British honours: KCB, KCSI, GCMG, together with the White Eagle of Serbia, 2nd Class with Swords, the French Legion of Honour and the Chinese order of Wen-hu, and was Mentioned in Dispatches a further three times (nine times in all). He died in France on 1 June 1939.

A/RSM 3757 (later Captain and Adjutant) Peter Murphy
RSM and later adjutant to the 8th Manchesters

Born on 6 August 1874, Murphy enlisted in the Manchester Regiment as a regular soldier in December 1892. Served in the South African War, 1899 to 1902, taking part in the Defence of Ladysmith and Operations in Orange River Colony, including the action at Belfast. Received the Queen's Medal with two clasps.

He rose to the rank of colour sergeant and at some time before the outbreak of war was attached to the 1/8th (Ardwick) Bn Manchester Regiment as acting regimental sergeant major. He sailed with the battalion in September 1914 to Egypt, disembarking at Alexandria on 25 September 1914. Murphy served with the battalion in Egypt (and possibly Cyprus) until 4 May when the battalion embarked for Gallipoli, landing with the 8th Manchesters at V Beach on 6 May 1915. He was commissioned 2nd lieutenant in the field on 2 July 1915 and made temporary captain on 8 August 1915. He served as temporary adjutant from late August until he was invalided off the peninsula on 13 October 1915, and was Mentioned in Despatches (LG 5 November 1915) for his service on Gallipoli.

He re-joined the 8th Manchesters in Egypt in 1916 and resumed his role as the adjutant on 22 April. He was promoted to substantive lieutenant on 1 July 1916 and was still serving as temporary captain and adjutant in October 1917. Sometime after this date he changed his name by deed poll to Peter Smith and his later records either show either names or just his new name. He was awarded the Silver War Badge (B.13923—in the name of Smith) on 16 November 1918 and was at that time living at 187 Queens Road, Cheetham, Manchester. He died on 11 November 1922 (his widow's address is shown on his Medal Index Card as 153 Welsh Road, Nantwich, Cheshire).

Major (later Lt. Col.) Richard Bottomley Nowell, TD
Second in Command and temporary CO of the 9th Manchesters

Born in Ashton-under-Lyne on 7 September 1880, the son of a surgeon. He was commissioned into the 3rd Volunteer Battalion, the Manchester

Regt on 21 February 1903 and was promoted to captain on 10 June 1905. He retained his rank and seniority on the formation of the Territorial Force when the battalion was renamed as the 1/9th Bn Manchester Regiment on 1 April 1908.

He volunteered for overseas service in early September 1914. He served with the 9th Manchesters in Egypt from 25 September 1914 until the battalion embarked for Gallipoli on 5 May 1915, and disembarked with the 9th Manchesters Transport Section at V Beach on 9 May 1915. He temporarily took command of the battalion on 22 May to 24 May 1915 (after the CO, Lt. Colonel Wade had been wounded) and again from 8 June to 16 July 1915 (promoted temporary lieutenant colonel on 9 July 1915). He was wounded on 7 August while commanding the left half of the battalion (in support of the 127th Brigade) but later re-joined the battalion and left with it on 29 December 1915. Nowell remained with the 9th Manchesters as its second in command, serving at first in Egypt and from March 1917 on the Western Front until posted to the reserve battalion in April 1918. He survived the war and was awarded the Italian Order of the Crown (Officer). He died in Brazil on 22 February 1959.

Lt. Colonel C.R. Pilkington, CMG

CO of the 6th Manchesters

Born into a wealthy mining family in the Haydock area of Lancashire, he was commissioned as 2nd lieutenant in the 2nd Volunteer Bn the Manchester Regiment on 12 July 1899.

He served in the South African War, 1900–1, as a lieutenant with the 77th Imperial Yeomanry. After taking part in the relief of Mafeking, was present during operations in the Transvaal, May and June in 1900, in the Transvaal, east of Pretoria, July and August 1900, in Orange River Colony, September to 29 November 1900 and again on 30 November to January 1901. Received the Queen's medal with four clasps.

He was promoted to captain on 16 February 1901 and made honorary lieutenant in the Army on 19 August 1901. He retained his rank and seniority on the formation of the Territorial Force when the battalion was renamed as the 1/6th Bn Manchester Regiment on 1 April 1908 and was promoted to major on 24 July 1908

In August 1914, as second in command of the 6th Manchesters, he volunteered for overseas service. He served with the battalion in Egypt from the 29 September 1914 until embarkation for Gallipoli on 2nd May 1915, when he took over command of the battalion. He disembarked with the Manchester Brigade on V Beach on 6 May 1915, was made temporary lieutenant colonel on 1 June 1915 and on 7 August temporarily took command of the 8th Manchesters when the two battalions combined for the attack on the 7th. He continued to command the 6th Manchesters until he was evacuated due to sickness on 12 October 1915. He was awarded the CMG (LG 8 November 1915) and was Mentioned in Dispatches (LG 5 November 1915) for his service on Gallipoli. He later re-joined the battalion in Egypt in 1916 and served with it throughout the rest of the war.

Brigadier General Donald Guy Prendergast, CMG

GOC of the 126th Brigade until 13 July 1915

Born in Jhansi, India on 11 September 1861. Educated at Wellington School and fluent in Urdu, Hindustani, Arabic and French. Commissioned as 2nd lieutenant into the Royal Denbigh and Merioneth Regt (Militia). Promoted to lieutenant and transferred into the Prince of Wales's Volunteers (South Lancashire Regt) on 5 December 1883, and promoted to captain on 22 January 1890. He served with the 10th Soudanese Bn in the Dongola Expeditionary Force under Kitchener in 1896, including the engagement at Firket and the operations at Hafir. Mentioned in Despatches (LG 3 November 1896) and received the Khedive's Medal with two clasps. Promoted to major on 28 February 1900. Served in the South African War 1900–2 with the Johannesburg Mounted Rifles, took part in operations in the Transvaal, February 1901 to March 1902, in Orange River Colony, March to May 1902, and on the Zululand Frontier of Natal, September and October 1901. Received the Queen's medal with four clasps and the King's medal with two clasps.

Promoted to lieutenant colonel on 27 March 1910, substantive colonel on 2 June 1913, he retired on half pay on 27 March 1914. Recalled on 20 July 1914, made temporary brigadier general on 5 August 1914 and appointed GOC the East Lancashire (126th) Brigade. Commanded the brigade in Egypt and disembarked with it at V Beach on 9 May 1915.

He left the peninsula on 21 May to have dental treatment in Alexandria, and resumed command 21 June. After a serious altercation with Major General Douglas over Douglas's criticism of the 126th Brigade, which Prendergast felt unjustified, he resigned his command on 13 July 1915, and left the peninsula shortly afterwards. Chaplain Kenneth Best summarises the event in his diary:

'General Prendergast goes to Little W and they have high words. E. Lancs Brigade not given fair chance—given dirty job when exhausted: all censure, no praise. Gained no kudos for work done in conjunction with Regulars there. As good as other Brigades. Little W said they were useless—so General P. has been gazetted out.'

Prendergast continued to serve as a brigade commander until 1 September 1916 when he was moved to HQ Staff. He retired on half pay on 11 September 1918 and was awarded the CMG on 1 January 1919. He died at Westminster, London on 21 April 1938.

Lt. Colonel Lord Rochdale (George Kemp)

CO of the 6th Lancs Fusiliers until 29 September 1915

Born in Rochdale on 9 June 1866, he was educated at Mill Hill and Shrewsbury schools, Balliol College, Oxford, and finally at Trinity College, Cambridge. On leaving university he entered the family business of Kelsall and Kemp (flannel manufacturers) and pursued an interest in politics. Commissioned as 2nd lieutenant in to the Duke of Lancaster's Yeomanry on 3 October 1888 and promoted to captain on 18 July 1891. As the Unionist Party candidate, he was elected MP for Heywood in the 1895 election and retained his seat in the autumn 1900 election (while serving in South Africa 1900–1902).

Served in the South African War with the Duke of Lancaster's Own Yeomanry, promoted to major on 20 September 1901. He was placed in command of the 32nd Bn Imperial Yeomanry on 13 January 1902 and promoted to lieutenant colonel (temporary rank in the army) on 22 January 1902. Twice Mentioned in Despatches (LG 8 February and September 1901) and received the Queen's medal with two clasps.

He resigned his commission on 22 January 1904 to devote himself to the family business. He was knighted in the King's Birthday Honours list in 1909. In 1910 was again elected MP, this time as Liberal candidate for

North West Manchester, but resigned his seat in 1912 due to his objections to certain Liberal Party policies. He was made Lord Rochdale in the King's Birthday Honours list in 1913 for his services to politics. With the launch of the Territorial Army, Lord Rochdale became chairman of the East Lancashire Territorial Association and on 13 December 1909 took over command of the 1/6th Lancashire Fusiliers. At the outbreak of war, Lord Rochdale, by now 48, volunteered for overseas service and went to Egypt as the CO of the 1/6th Lancashire Fusiliers.

He landed with his battalion at Helles on 5 May 1915, the day prior to the Second Battle of Krithia. The following day he led his battalion in an attack on Gully Spur, displaying great personal courage as he encouraged his inexperienced troops. As one on the division's most experienced commanding officers he was chosen to be temp. GOC of the 126th Bde, from 21 May to 3 June, and temp. GOC of the 127th Bde from 4 June (taking over from Lt. Colonel Heys who had himself taken temporary command of the brigade when Brig. General Lee was wounded) to 21 June 1915.

He was a vociferous critic of the way the campaign was being conducted, and using his House of Lords privilege (and against the advice of his superiors) he left Helles for England in early July. On 26 July he met with the Prime Minister, Herbert Henry Asquith, the 1st Lord of the Admiralty, Arthur Balfour, and the Secretary of State for the Colonies (and leader of the opposition) Andrew Bonar Law and submitted a detailed, and highly critical report, fully aware of the damage he was doing to his career. He returned to Gallipoli in early August and was again placed in temporary command of the 127th Brigade from 19 to 26 August. Rochdale was evacuated from the peninsula on 29 September suffering from para-typhoid and phlebitis. He never again commanded on active service and after recovering went onto the Reserve of Officers list.

Despite Rochdale's significant contributions in the campaign, and the many instances of personal bravery, these remained unrecognised, no doubt as a consequence of his actions in July, and it shows a shocking vindictiveness within the award process that he did not even receive a Mention in Despatches. He died in Lingholm near Keswick, Cumberland, on 24 March 1945.

Captain (later Lt. Col.) John Malcolm Brodie Sanders MC
Adjutant of the 5th Manchesters

Born in Remington, Warwick on 13 December 1886. Commissioned as 2nd lieutenant into the Leinster Regt on 29 August 1906, promoted to lieutenant on 23 December 1907. He was employed with the West African Frontier Force from 2 March 1910 to 13 November 1912. Promoted to captain on 12 November 1913 and appointed adjutant of the 1/5th Manchesters on 1 January 1913.

He served with the battalion in Egypt and disembarked with it on V Beach on 6 May 1915. He was wounded in the fighting of 6–7 August, evacuated on 18 August 1915. For his service on Gallipoli, he was awarded the Military Cross (LG 2 February 1916) and Mentioned in Dispatches (LG 28 January 1916). Saunders later served as DAAG, No. 3 Section on the Suez Canal Defences from 10 July until 20 October 1916 and afterwards was attached to the 4th Bn KOSBs. He commanded the battalion from 21 October 1916 to 10 May 1917 and again from 8 June to 18 September 1917. Promoted to temporary lieutenant colonel on 22 January 1919 (substantive on 18 November 1922). He was appointed Unofficial Member of the Legislative Council of the Nyasaland Protectorate on 9 May 1929 and on 8 August 1946 he was released from the Reserve of Officers list.

Major James Herbert Staveacre
CO of the 7th Manchesters from 27th May to being KIA on 4 June 1915

Born in Stockport in September 1872. He was already a member of the 4th Volunteer Bn Manchester Regiment when he volunteered to serve in the South African War, 1901–2, signing a Short Service Attestation (for one year or the duration of the war) on 12 January 1900, to serve in the ranks with the Imperial Yeomanry (as Private 1894). He took part in the operations in Cape Colony and Orange River Colony, 1900–1 and received the Queen's medal with three clasps.

Commissioned as 2nd lieutenant into the 4th Volunteer Bn Manchester Regt. Promoted to lieutenant on 25 October 1905, to captain on 3 March 1906 and appointed Instructor of Musketry. He retained his rank and seniority on the formation of the Territorial Force when the battalion was renamed as the 1/7th Bn Manchester Regiment on 1 April 1908. Promoted to major on 3 August 1912.

In September 1914 he volunteered for overseas service and served with his battalion in Sudan, Egypt and later at Gallipoli, arriving on V Beach with the Manchester Brigade on 6 May 1915. He was killed on 4 June while organising the resupply of ammunition to the firing-line. On being shot in the back, Staveacre said to RSM Franklin (see above) 'Never mind me. Carry on, sergeant major', and died at once. Staveacre was buried in Redoubt Cemetery and received a posthumous Mention in Dispatches (LG 5 November 1915). Gerald B. Hurst wrote of him in his book *With Manchesters in the East*:

'In Major Staveacre, the junior Major, we had an incomparable enthusiast, with a zest for every kind of sport, a happy gift of managing men and an almost professional aptitude for arms which had been enriched by his experience in the Boer War.'

Major (later Lt. Col.) Claude Swanwick Worthington DSO and Bar, TD

CO of the 6th Manchesters from 24 October 1915

Born on 7 October 1877 at Alderley Edge, Cheshire. Educated at Sedbergh School and Manchester University where he read law. A keen sportsman, he played rugby in the first XV for Manchester Rugby club, cricket for Alderley Edge and Lancashire, and was a 'fearless climber' and an enthusiastic walker.

Worthington was commissioned into the 2nd Volunteer Bn the Manchester Regt in March 1900. Promoted to captain on 7 February 1906. He retained his rank and seniority on the formation of the Territorial Force when the battalion was renamed as the 1/6th Bn Manchester Regiment on 1 April 1908.

He was promoted to major on 25 February 1914 and in September 1914 he volunteered for overseas service and served with his battalion in Egypt and later at Gallipoli, arriving on V Beach with the Manchester Brigade on 6 May 1915. He was medically evacuated on 31 August and returned to Helles on 24 October when he took command of the battalion (Lt. Colonel Pilkington having been evacuated 12 days earlier).

He remained in command for the rest of the campaign. He was awarded the DSO and was also twice Mentioned in Dispatches (LG 5 November 1915 and 28 January 1916) for his service at Helles.

He continued to command to battalion on its return to Egypt until Colonel Pilkington re-joined in July 1916, after which Worthington reverted to second in command. He later served on the Western Front and in October 1917 was wounded by shrapnel while commanding the 8th Bn Duke of Wellington's Regiment. He went on to command the 5th Bn Dorset Regt, winning a bar to his DSO (awarded posthumously) on 27 September 1918. He was fatally wounded while searching for wounded men in broad daylight. He died of wounds on 14 October 1918 and is buried in the Mont Huon Military Cemetery, Le Treport, France.

Order of Battle & Field State 42nd (East Lancashire) Division 2–5 May 1915

Showing all units that embarked for Gallipoli

Details of personnel and appointments are taken from the 42nd Division War Diary—Appendix 37—Order of Battle 29 May 1915, with the exception of the CO of the 1/9th Manchesters, Lieutenant Colonel D.H. Wade, who had been wounded and evacuated by this date.

Divisional Headquarters

GOC, Major General William Douglas, CB, DSO

Captain H.T. Cawley, MP, ADC

Lieutenant J.W Fry, ADC

Lieutenant Colonel A.W. Tufnell, GSO 1

Lieutenant Colonel F.A. Earle, GSO 2

Captain S.H. Kershaw, GSO 3

Colonel E.S. Herbert, AA & QMG

Captain R.S. Allen, DAA & QMG

Major R.J. Slaughter, DAQMG

Colonel J. Bentley-Mann, ADMS

Captain C.M. Drew, DADMS

Captain Briercliffe, Sanitary Officer

Lieutenant Colonel T. Marriott, ADVS

Captain J. Magill, VO

Major O.R.E. Milman, DADOS

Captain T.B. Forwood, APM

Divisional Signal Company

Major A.W. Lawford

Divisional Artillery

Due to the lack of space for artillery at Helles, only the 5th Lancs Battery and two guns of the 6th Lancs Battery were landed, all other batteries and guns being returned to Egypt.

1/1st East Lancs Brigade RFA
    4th Lancs Battery
    5th Lancs Battery (grouped with 29th Div. Artillery)
        Major J.C. Browning
    6th Lancs Battery
    1st Ammunition Column
    2nd Ammunition Column
1/3rd East Lancs Brigade RFA
    18th Lancs Battery
    19th Lancs Battery
    20th Lancs Battery
    3rd Ammunition Column

Divisional Engineers

Lieutenant Colonel S.L. Tenant, CRE

    1/1st East Lancs Field Company
    Major J.H. Mousley
    1/2nd East Lancs Field Company
    Major L.F. Wells

The main recruiting centre for each of the division's infantry battalions is shown in brackets.

125th (Lancashire Fusiliers) Infantry Brigade

Brigadier General H.C. Frith, CB
Brevet Major A.J. Allardyce, Brigade Major
Captain J.C. Kenyon, Staff Captain

1/5th Bn Lancashire Fusiliers (Bury)
Lieutenant Colonel J. Isherwood, VD
1/6th Bn Lancashire Fusiliers (Rochdale)
Lieutenant Colonel Lord Rochdale
1/7th Bn Lancashire Fusiliers (Salford)
Lieutenant Colonel A.F. Maclure, TD
1/8th Bn Lancashire Fusiliers (Salford)
Lieutenant Colonel J.A. Fallows, TD

126th (East Lancashire) Infantry Brigade

Brigadier General D.G. Prendergast, CMG
Major C.J. Hickie, Brigade Major
Captain T.C. Robinson, Staff Captain

1/4th Bn East Lancs Regt (Blackburn)
Lieutenant Colonel F.D. Robinson, VD
1/5th Bn East Lancs Regt (Burnley)
Lieutenant Colonel W.E. Sharples, TD
1/9th Bn Manchester Regt (Ashton under Lyne)
Lieutenant Colonel D.H. Wade
1/10th Bn Manchester Regt (Oldham)
Lieutenant Colonel J.B. Rye, VD

127th (Manchester) Infantry Brigade

Brigadier General Noel Lee, VD
Major H.L. Knight, Brigade Major
Captain T.C. Nevill, Staff Captain

> 1/5th Bn Manchester Regt (Wigan)
> > Lieutenant Colonel H.C Darlington
> 1/6th Bn Manchester Regt (Stretford—Manchester)
> > Major C.R. Pilkington
> 1/7th Bn Manchester Regt (Manchester city centre)
> > Lieutenant Colonel H.E Gresham, TD
> 1/8th Bn Manchester Regt (Ardwick—Manchester)
> > Lieutenant Colonel W.G. Heys, TD

East Lancs Divisional Train ASC

Due to lack of space at Helles only No. 2 Company was allowed to land with the division. The other three companies were then sent back to Egypt.

No. 1 (Headquarters) Company
No. 2 (Lancs Fusiliers) Company
> Major A. England
No. 3 (East Lancs) Company
No. 4 (Manchester) Company

Divisional Royal Army Medical Corps

Although the 1/1st and the 1/3rd field ambulances both landed with the division, only C Section and part of B Section of the 1/2nd Field Ambulance landed at Helles on 10 May, with the remainder landing on 17 June 1915.

1/1st Field Ambulance
> Lieutenant Colonel H.G. Parker
1/2nd Field Ambulance
1/3rd Field Ambulance
> Lieutenant Colonel W.M. Steinthal

Summary of arms on embarkation for Gallipoli

	Officers	Other ranks	Guns	MGs
Headquarters & Signal Company	25	249		
Artillery	57	1,257	24	
Engineers	15	394		
Infantry	386	10,830		24
ASC	24	313		
RAMC	30	644		
Total	537	13,687	24	24

Summary of arms for 15 September 1915

	Officers	Other ranks	Guns	MGs
Headquarters & Signal Company	19	218		
Artillery	23	294	18	
Engineers	21	341		
Infantry	160	5,302		24
ASC	10	126		
RAMC	24	481		
Total	257	6,762	18	24

The loss in the division's field strength is particularly significant given the figures above include infantry reinforcements of approximately 100 officers and 3,500 other ranks. The 18th Battery RFA and the 1/2nd West Lancashire Field Company RE had also joined the division in the interim period.

APPENDIX VI

Station call signs

Battalion, brigade and divisional headquarters were connected by signal offices. To communicate, signallers employed field telephones that could transmit and receive both Morse code and voice. Flags, lamps, lights and heliographs were used for visual signalling. The station call signs below are derived from Alec Riley's text. The call signs were changed, according to Riley, on or about 7 July 1915. Officially, the territorial divisions and infantry brigades were designated with a numerical prefix from 25 May 1915. Where known, the station is listed.

Call sign	Station	Dates
AG	8th Manchesters	6 May – 7 July
BK		
BKA		
BS	7th Manchesters	6 May – 7 July
BY		
GN	Divisional HQ	6 May – 7 July
MC	Manchester Brigade HQ	6 May – 7 July
MRE	5th Manchesters	From 7 July
MRE	6th Manchesters	From 7 July

MRG	7th Manchesters	From 7 July
MRH	8th Manchesters	From 7 July
MV	Central Visual Station (in Redoubt Line)	
OM		
QEL	East Lancashire Brigade HQ	
QG		
QLF	Lancashire Fusiliers Brigade HQ	
RC		
SR	6th Manchesters	6 May – 7 July
TN		
WG	5th Manchesters	6 May – 7 July
YDB	42nd Division HQ	From 7 July
ZLE	125th (Lancs Fusiliers) Brigade HQ	From 7 July
ZLF	126th (East Lancs) Brigade HQ	From 7 July
ZLG	127th (Manchester) Brigade HQ	From 7 July

Additional notes, and a description of the Dardanelles and the peninsula

These notes appear at the end of the Riley's handwritten diary.
The disparate collection comprises two army documents that he copied
by hand, a list of rations that show how the 6th Manchesters were
reduced in numbers between embarkation and late June,
and a general description of the history and geography of the peninsula.

Copy: VIII Army Corps Order – Special

Gallipoli Peninsula
6/8/15

The attack today is the first stage of operations which will it is hoped, at last carry us onto the position for which all ranks have so hardly fought since the landing three and a half months ago.

Other forces, besides our own, are attacking at the same time and will prevent the enemy sending reinforcements to help the Turks in front of us.

The fine shooting of our ships and heavy batteries during the last few days has seriously damaged several of the enemy's batteries and caused the removal of others.

The French Corps is once more assisting our attacks with their artillery and they are themselves taking part in the advance which is to take place during the next few days.

The Major-General Commanding does not need to say more to the men of the 8th Corps, but merely wishes to impress on them that the attacks of which today's is the first are the most important yet undertaken, and that on the manner in which they are carried out and the determination with which the ground captured is held and extended, depends the future progress of the whole of this campaign.

It is now the beginning of a fresh year of war, and it is hoped that the advance of the 8th Corps will be the turning point, and the capture of KRITHIA and ACHI BABA the first steps towards the final victory of ourselves and our allies over all our enemies

H. Street.
Brigadier-General, G.S.,
VIII Army Corps.

Copy: AAG Intelligence Staff,
Surrender of Turkish Troops

In view of the importance of securing Turkish prisoners, both Military and civilians, for the purposes of the Intelligence Staff, it is desirable that, whenever possible, the surrender of such persons should be accepted.

Experience in other fields of the war against Turkey has shown that many Turkish soldiers are serving under compulsion and are anxious to give themselves up at the first opportunity. From these men information of great military value has often been obtained. Consequently, where such a course does not expose our men to any danger, facilities should be given for as many surrenders as possible.

Turkish soldiers as a rule manifest their desire to surrender by holding their rifle butt upwards and by waving clothes or rags of any colour. An actual white flag should be regarded with the utmost suspicion as a Turkish soldier is unlikely to possess anything of that colour.

The following phrases, to be shouted to those apparently desirous of giving themselves up, will assist our officers and men to accept a BONA FIDE surrender without exposing themselves to any unnecessary danger.

In no case should our troops leave their positions or cover for the purpose of receiving prisoners of this type.

Surrender	Tesslim ol (singular) Tesslim Olunuz
You will be well treated	Sizé Eyi Bakilajak
Throw down your arms	Sillahlareneze Brak
Throw down your rifles	Tufeyini Ashaya
Throw down your sword and revolver	Kelech ve Revolver Ashaya Koi
Hold up your hands	Elerinize Yukari Koi

Higher than that	Daha Yukari
Advance slowly	Yawash Gel (in plural) Geliniz
One by one	Bir Bir Halt Dour
Walk to left	Sola Yuru
Walk to right	Sagha Yuru
Attention	Asker Hazer ol March Marsh
Come over this way	Bou Tarafa Ghel

Printing Section
Med. Exped. Force
GHQ

Specimen lists of rations and issues
from QMS Warburton's FS correspondence book, 1/6th Manchester Regiment, MEF

To show decrease in this battalion up to end of June.

1. Rations

20,360	lbs	Flour	on board (*Derfflinger*)
		No bacon	
25	gals	Lime juice	No. 1 Hold
124	gals	Rum	No. 1 Hold
60	gross	Matches	No. 1 Hold

Landing rations

13,832	lbs	Biscuits	
3,458	lbs	Ham	
13,832	lbs	Meat	
2,594	lbs	(33) cases Cheese	No. 1 Hold
450	lbs	Tea	No. 1 Hold
2,594	lbs	Sugar	No. 1 Hold
3,548	lbs	Jam	No. 6 Hold
433	lbs	Salt	No. 1 Hold
25	lbs	Pepper	No. 1 Hold

29	lbs	Mustard	No. 1 Hold
1,729	lbs	Dried Veg	No. 6 Hold?
12	gals	Lime juice	No. 1 Hold
62	gals	Rum	No. 1 Hold
247	lbs	Tobacco	No. 1 Hold
3,592		Matches	No. 1 Hold
60		Candles (lbs?)	No. 1 Hold
2,652		Iron Rations	No. 6 Hold
2,610	lbs	Ham	No. 1 Hold
		Biscuits	No. 1 Hold

Issue 4 May 1915

Cheeses	5th Manchesters	6
	6th Manchesters	6
	Signal service	1

	Bully beef	Jam (lbs)
Brigade Staff (Challinor)	3	2
NZ ASC – 2 men	2	1
5th Manchesters	816	324
Signal service	22	5
A Company (6th Manchesters)	219	45
B Company	189	38

C Company	214	45
D Company	230	48 (+ 3 for ASC)
Australians	96	20
	1791	**531**

2. Strength on board: 822 NCOs and men (6th Manchesters)

(Issued to) signal service:
14 oz Cigarettes. 8 oz Tobacco. 24 boxes Matches.

3. One day's shore rations issued 6 May 1915

Signal service 'don't require any' (Sergeant Royle).

4. Iron rations (1/6 Battalion Manchester Regiment), Cairo, 2 May 1915

A Coy	237	
B Coy	212	(13 retd.)
C Coy	235	
D Coy	232	and 4 for officers

5. 3 June 1915

Officers and Men	703
Natives	3
Horses	11
Mules	9

A Coy	4	officers	161	men	
B Coy	6		127		
C Coy	5		159		
D Coy	4		161		
Headquarters	4		16		
S. Bearers			14		
Transport			22		
Natives			3		
Beach			3		
Base			4		
	25		**670**		**= 695**

6. Stores

Bread, jam, tea, lime juice, pepper, biscuits, bacon, sugar, rum, tobacco, cheese, fresh meat, dried veg., salt, matches, mustard, candles, preserved meat, M & V, chloride of lime, toilet paper, eggs, soap, Maconochies

7. Iron rations

36	Deficient
17	Issued 21/6/15
19	No. 2 Company

8. Issue of rum, 21 June 1915

62	A	10⅓ gills
68	B	11⅓
68	C	11⅓
51	D	8½
50	MG?	8⅓
299		

Tea	A	5
	B	5
	C	6
	D	4
	MG?	4

9. Battalion strength, 25 June 1915: 360

10. Battalion strength on Sergeant Webb's figures, 30 June 1915

A Coy	68
B Coy	52
C Coy	58
D Coy	57
M. Gun	52
Headquarters	15
RAMC	6
Transport	19
Base	7
	334

The Dardanelles, and the Gallipoli Peninsula

The following notes deal with the natural features, peculiarities, and antiquities of the above; and although they relate, chiefly, to the Cape Helles area of the peninsula, they include other details likely to interest those who know the place. The notes have been compiled from several authorities, ancient and modern, and from my own personal observations during and after the campaign. Names given to certain points and localities during the campaign of 1915–16 have been used. They have become more or less permanent as far as English maps are concerned. Beaches, nullahs, and large natural features are quite easily identifiable on the actual country; but in the cases of such names as 'firing-line,' 'redoubt,' 'Eski Line,' etc, identification is not always easy. I have made a few references to such places, as landmarks only.

The notes are confined to descriptions of the country altogether apart from the war; but natural features had, of course, considerable effects on the operations. The notes may interest those who have read books dealing with the campaign at Helles, particularly as it is difficult to find any commented accounts of the place. I have taken them from a number of sources, isolated notes, paragraphs, and quotations, from published books.

I give a list of the chief references:

> *Macedonia, Thrace and Illyria* – S. Casson (Oxford University Press).
> *Troja* – Schliemann pp.254, 262.
> 'Dardanelles.' Lt. Col. English, in the Geological Society's quarterly journal. Vol. 60, pp.2–3. 1904.
> Articles in the *Encyclopaedia Britannica*.
> Herodotus (translated) – IX 116, 120, VI 140, VII 22.
> Pausanias (translated) – I 34, III 4, 5.

Homer (translated) – *Iliad*, II 700, 702.

Thucydides (translated) – VII 102, 107.

Xenophon (translated) – *Hellenica*, XI 1–20.

The Official History of the Gallipoli Campaign.

Wordsworth: 'Protesilaus.'

Byron: No other writer or poet has given better descriptions of the Near East which apply so faithfully to Gallipoli, although not necessarily written with special reference to it.

Local names

The meanings of certain local names will be found helpful.

Achi Baba (Altchi Tepe)	Lime, chalk, white hill. Through wrong naming on the first maps issued to the troops, it kept, and still keeps to 'Achi Baba'.
Ari Burnu	Cape of bees (Anzac)
Bagh	Vineyard
Burnu	Cape
Çanak Kala, Chanak	Pottery Fort (Turkish for 'Dardanelles')
Bahr	Sea
Chift	Farm
Dagh	Mountain
Dere	Valley
Eski	Old
Gaba Tepe	Rough Hill
Hissar	Castle
Helles (Hellespont)	In antiquity was Cape Mastousia (Μαστουσία – Strabo)
Iskele	Pier
Kale (Kalah)	Fortress
Kenpru (Kupru)	Bridge
Kilisse	Church
Kapu	Gate

Kemer	Aqueduct
Kevi	Cliff
Kalid Bahr	Key of the Sea
Kirte	Krithia
Kiryn	Well
Kum	Sand (?)
Lala	?
Liman	Bay, harbour
Mezarlik	Cemetery
Sari Bair	The yellow ridge
Su	River (water)
Settülbahur	Gate of the Sea (Sedd-el-Bahr)
Tarla	Field
Tekki	Shrine
Tepe	Hill
Yol	Road
Yolji	Traveller

Map distances

Cape Helles (Lighthouse)	to Achi Baba	$5\frac{1}{2}$ miles
	to Tekki Burnu	$\frac{7}{8}$ miles
	to Old Castle	$\frac{11}{16}$ miles
	to Kum Kale	$2\frac{3}{4}$ miles
	to Kilid Bahr	13 miles
Tekki Burnu	to X Beach	1 mile
	to Gully Beach	$1\frac{7}{8}$ mile
	to Y Beach and Gurkha Bluff	$3\frac{1}{4}$ miles
Pink Farm	to Gully Farm	$\frac{13}{16}$ miles
	to Gully Beach	$\frac{7}{16}$ miles
	to Clapham Junction	$\frac{5}{8}$ miles
	to Krithia	$2\frac{1}{2}$ miles

Krithia	to Achi Baba (summit)	$1\frac{1}{2}$	miles
	to Fusilier Bluff	$1\frac{1}{4}$	miles
	to Vineyard	1	miles
Sedd-el-Bahr Castle	to Eski Hissarlik Point	$1\frac{1}{2}$	miles
Eski Hissarlik Pt	to Kereves Dere	$1\frac{1}{4}$	miles
Kereves Dere	to Gully Beach	$2\frac{1}{4}$	miles
X Beach	to Morto Bay	$1\frac{1}{2}$	miles
Y Beach	to Fusilier Bluff	$\frac{3}{4}$	miles
Gurkha Bluff (top) and over Bruce's, Essex, Border and Trolley Ravine	to Fusilier Bluff	$\frac{5}{8}$	miles
Clapham Junction	to Eski Line	$\frac{1}{4}$	miles
	to Redoubt	$\frac{11}{16}$	miles
Redoubt	to Vineyard (K Rd)	$\frac{1}{4}$	miles
Great Gully, from Beach	to fork, NW of Krithia	$2\frac{3}{4}$	miles
Kilid Bahr	to Chanak	1,400	yards
	to Maidos	3	miles
	to Gaba Tepe	5	miles

The interest in these map references is that they mean very little on the actual country. A simple mile can include a climb up a steep ravine, a descent into Great Gully, a climb up the far side and then several hundred yards of thick scrub with innumerable trenches to cross. It can take a considerable time to walk one mile at Helles.

The Aegean Sea

Takes its name from Aegean, the son of Uranus (heaven) by Gaea (earth) who, in mythology and by many writers, is represented as a marine god, living in the sea bearing his name. The islands of Tenedos, Lemnos, Imbros and Samothrace are the chief places of interest near the Dardanelles on the Mediterranean side. On Lemnos, Hephaestus is said to have fallen when hurled from Olympus. The volcanic nature of the island accounts for the location there of the workshop of Hephaestus.

The Argonauts found it inhabited only by women who had killed their husbands. Conquered by a Persian general of Darius, it was delivered by Miltiades who made it subject to Athens. The deep harbour of Mudros became famous in 1915. Imbros, as a resting-place, and Imbros and Samothrace, seen as silhouettes against the red sunset skies, from the peninsula, were also famed in 1915.

* * *

'Of the past great traffic through the Dardanelles in Antiquity, only a fraction rounded Cape Helles, making for the northern shores. The majority of towns and settlements were then, as now, on the southern limestone; for the colonists sought the shelter of the deep ravines from the prevailing north and north-west winds. Fields and crops were mostly on the red loams of the north.'

* * *

The Dardanelles

Is the name of the long winding channel dividing Europe and Asia. Its flanks are each the off-shoots of a continent. It gives access from the Aegean to the Sea of Marmora (Propontis), Istanbul, the Bosphorus and the Black Sea (Euxine).

Like the Bosphorus, it is the old bed of a submerged river. Originally, both were gorges into which the sea had access. The full length of the Dardanelles is 47 miles and the narrow portion, from Gallipoli town to the Aegean, is 33 miles. The passage is 7,000 yards at its widest; and at one point, the Narrows, it is only 1,400 yards. In the Great War, control of the Narrows was essential for both sides. The Turks and Germans had it and kept it, in spite of several narrow escapes. Two famous military passages, across the Straits, were made in ancient times—both by bridges of boats. One was in 480 BC when Xerxes crossed from Asia to Europe, and the other was in 334 BC when Alexander crossed from Europe to Asia.

In early days the Straits were not vigorously defended; but in the 17th century, with improving ordnance, the forts of Kum Kale on the Asiatic side and Sedd-el-Bahr (1658) on the European side, both at the entrance to the Waterway, were built. They are 4,000 yards apart and were known as the New Castles of Asia and Europe. Further up, at the Narrows, are two more forts, the Trefoil or 'Ace of Spades' fort at Kilid Bahr, and the Sultanieh Kale (Sultan's Fort), the latter on the Asiatic and the former on the European sides.

In antiquity, the Dardanelles was known as the Hellespont, or Sea of Helles—Hellespontus. In mythology, Helle was the daughter of Athamas and Nephele, a king and queen in Thessaly, and the sister of Phrixus. Athamas grew tired of Nephele and took another wife. When Phrixus was about to be sacrificed Nephele rescued him and Helle and the three rode away and through the air, on the Ram with the Golden Fleece, the gift of Hermes, making for Colchis. Between Sigeum and the Chersonesus, Helle fell off the Ram and into the sea, and was drowned. The water was, therefore, called Hellespontus, the Sea of Helle.

The site of Abydos is near Nagara Point (Asia Minor) and the site of Sestos is near Ak Bash, Kilia Liman. In another legend, Leander swam each night from Abydos to Sestos, crossing the Hellespont to see his girl Hero, a priestess of Aphrodite, until, at last, he did it once too often, and was drowned in a storm, and his body was washed to the rocks on the European side. Hero threw herself down from a tower. The Hellespont has been swum several times, notably by Lord Byron, by officers of the British Navy and by others.

There was a time when the Trojans tried to tax the Greek ships passing through the Straits to and from the Euxine and to make their crews unload cargos on the Trojan shore, carry them overload to the Propontis and re-ship them. In revolt against this, the Greeks fought, and the Trojan War, 1194–1184 BC, decided the question as to who should control the Greek shipping, in their favour. The sixth city of Troy was destroyed. In those days control of the Dardanelles was important. Nearly 3,000 years later, the British and French fought the Turks that Russia might be helped, and shipping have free and unrestricted passage to and from the Black Sea and the Mediterranean.

The realm of Priam, king of Troy, falls away from the slopes of Mount Ida to the sea, and three miles from the coast a barren mound marks the site of Troy. Near the promontories of Sigeum and Rhoteum, are mounds marking the traditional graves of the Heroes. The Asiatic side has low, wooded hills, and a green landscape in spring. Near Erenkeui there is a high limestone bastion, over which rises the coast-road, of the type found on the opposite shore.

Vast traffic through the Hellespont encouraged settlement along its shores and famous towns were Troy, Dardanus, Abydos, Lamsachus, Madytos, Koila, Elaeus, and Sestos. A large necropolis, of late date, has been found at the head of Kilia Liman (Koila), and at Madytos (Maidos) ruins of the old town have been found. The ruins of Sestos are on the flattened summit of a steep bluff, 300 feet high.

Lamsachus, whose ruins are under a poor Turkish village, is opposite Gallipoli town. It was the birthplace of several famous men and its wine was popular. It was besieged by Miltiades, Tyrant of the Chersonesus and hero of Marathon. Miltiades II controlled both ends of the Straits by holding a position at the Propontis opening and another at Elaeus on the Chersonesus.

Elaeus stood on the promontory forming the north-east extremity of Morto Bay on the Gallipoli Peninsula. Its approximate site may be said to be marked by the point known as Zimmerman's Farm. This place was known as Eski Hissarlik (Old Castle), and the promontory is now called Eski Hissarlik Point. There was an old Turkish fort here, abandoned in 1871. Like the present French cemetery and memorial, which is near the site of Elaeus, it commanded a view of the entrance to the Straits, and was an important place in Hellenic times. Colonised by Athens, it was held by Miltiades II, who used the harbour—Morto Bay. Its period was late 6th century BC, also the 5th and 4th centuries BC. It was occupied by the Persians before 480 BC, prominent in the struggle for the Hellespont in the Peloponnesian War and had other adventures. In 360 BC, when Kotys held the rest of the Chersonesus, it was the only bit retained by the Athenians. It played a part in the war between Constantine and Licinius, and was repeopled by Justinian. The harbour has a depth of seven to eight fathoms. This, Kilia Liman and Sestos Bay, were stopping places for vessels, whose crews traded and paid taxes, thereby supporting the local people. (Kilia Liman is probably the best harbour in the Straits. The bay is deep and good, and has a shelving beach and wide foreshore, backed by an extensive plain.) A supposed suburb of Elaeus was Krithote, which may have been of ancient origin. Bronze coins have been found, inscribed Κριθουσιων, or abbreviations, and the Chersonesus symbol, the ear of corn. It is interesting to compare this with modern Turkish coins of small value. Ptolemy mentions a Κριθεα. It was a ruin in Strabo's time. It is supposed that Krithia as it was, and as its ruins are, (on the open limestone plateau of Achi Baba, near the north shore of the peninsula) marks the site of ancient Krithote.

The Gallipoli Peninsula, forming the northern side of the Dardanelles, is the Thracian Chersonese of Antiquity. The name means the peninsula of Thrace. Its old name was Chersŏnēsus Thracia (Ch = K). Chersonesus means 'land island,' peninsula (Χερσος—dry, and νῆσος—island). Thracia, the land west of Istanbul, runs in a south-west direction into the peninsula, which extends for 50 miles between the Gulf of Saros and the Aegean, and the Dardanelles. In the 5th century BC, Miltiades defended it, by building a wall across it at Bulair, against the plundering raids of the Thracians.

It is convenient, at this point, to mention the tumulus on Morto Plain. It is one and three-eighth miles from Cape Helles, three quarters of a mile from Morto Bay, and seven-eighths of a mile from X Beach, and between the site of Elaeus and Sedd-el-Bahr, roughly. The tumulus is known, or was known, as Kara Agatch Tepe, 'the hill planted with black trees.' It is of great antiquity, and fragments of pottery, similar to those of the first settlement of Hissarlik (Troy), across the Straits, have been found there. Schliemann, in 1884, gives the height as 10 metres, and the probable circumference at the base—126 yards. The surroundings then were gardens and the earth was full of bits of pottery. The tumulus has been much cultivated and was much higher than it is now, originally. In 1884, the west, south and east sides were terraced for cultivation, and planted with vines, almonds and pomegranates. Schliemann's illustration shows fragments of terrace-walls. The top and the north slope were sown with barley. When I saw it last, it was a rough weedy mound with two wide cross-cuttings through it made by excavators.[207]

207 These trenches, 10 metres deep, were dug by archaeologist Robert Demangel, under the auspices of the French army of occupation, between 1921 and 1923.

In antiquity the tumulus was the tomb of Protesilaus (or *Protesilaon*, tomb or sanctuary). Protesilaus, in Greek legend, was the son of Iphiclus and husband to Laodamia. He commanded the Greek contingent from Phylace in Thessaly, at the siege of Troy, and was the first to jump on Trojan soil, from the boats, although he knew it meant instant death— at the hands of Hector. Laodamia loved Protesilaus dearly, and when she heard of his death, she begged the gods to allow her to speak to him for three hours and her request was granted. He was led back to the upper world, and when he died a second time Laodamia died with him. Another legend tells that during a halt on the peninsula of Pallene, Aethilla (carried off by Protesilaus, who had survived the siege of Ilium) and other captive women set fire to the boats. Protesilaus, unable to continue his voyage, built the city of Scione. The sanctuary had a famous oracle, and legends of trees growing on it are given by Philostratus and hinted at by Homer. Famous also in Hellenic times, it was later embroidered by much romance. Here, Alexander paid his devotions before crossing to Ilium and the Tomb of Achilles. There is a story that nymphs planted elm-trees round the grave. These grew well, until they were high enough to command a view of Ilium across the Hellespont, and then withered away, while fresh branches sprang from the roots. Schliemann, in *Troja*, tells us that in Philostratus there is a dialogue between a vine-dresser and a Phoenician captain, in which the vine-dresser speaks of the elm-trees, planted by the nymphs round the tomb of Protesilaus, of which he says the branches turned towards Troy blossomed earlier, but also shed their leaves quickly and withered before their time. Also, if the elms grew so high that they could see Troy, they withered away, but put forth fresh shoots from below. Some fragments remain of a tragedy by Euripides about Protesilaus. Wordsworth used the story as a poem-subject. The oracle had declared that victory should be the lot of the side from which should fall the first victim of the war, and Wordsworth represents Protesilaus, or his brief return to earth, as relating to Laodamia the story of his fate:

The wished for wind was given; I then revolved
The oracle, upon the silent sea;
An' if no worthier led the way, resolved
That of a thousand vessels mine should be
The foremost prow impressing to the strand,—
Mine the first blood that tinged the Trojan sand ...

... upon the side
Of Hellespont (such faith was entertained)
A knot of spiry trees for ages grew
From out the tomb of him for whom she died;
And ever when such stature they had gained
That Ilium's walls were subject to their view,
The trees' tall summits withered at the sight,
A constant interchange of growth and blight.

* * *

The Gallipoli Peninsula

Is, in itself, of small value, but it has political and strategic importance
from its position as the north side of the Dardanelles. It has high
ground commanding the Narrows, and it must be remembered that the
Dardanelles separates two continents, and acts as a main water channel
between seas and races.

The 1915–16 campaign was located in areas quite different from each
other. At Suvla the hills are low and rounded and there is much fairly
flat country. At Anzac the rough barren hills rising sharply from the
shores are mostly of loamy clay, yellow and glaring; and they are ribbed
and ravined by the winter rains into grotesque forms. They have thick
scrub on the tops. Helles has cliffs on the Aegean side, hollowing and
sloping gently from them to the Dardanelles and at Cape Helles there is
a ridge with higher points.

Achi Baba

Achi Baba is 218 metres high (usually marked as 600 feet), and it's the
culminating point of the Helles area. It is a great mass, with off-shoots

spurs and ravines and not merely a long terraced ridge, as it looks to be from Helles. Except for a few smaller ones, about half a mile in length on the Aegean side, most of the spurs run north-east or south-west towards Helles, two arms diverge from the middle terrace, in front of the hump, at right angles, a short arm going west and a larger one going south. There is a farm on the western arm. In the angle runs a small nullah tributary to Kirte Dere or Krithia Nullah. Beyond the crest other spurs and ravines lead north and south towards the Aegean and the Dardanelles. Map measurements of Achi Baba are: Area of flat top ⅜ × ¼ miles (length to north-east); second plateau 2¾ miles × 3 miles at longest part, but much indented; third and lowest plateau, 5 × 4 miles (extreme left north-west to south-east), much indented.

On cold clear days the views from the top are good, but not by any means striking, Helles looks flat. Beyond Achi Baba is the Kilid Bahr plateau, over Soghan Dere, on the Dardanelles side. On the Aegean side is Sari Tepe, a large mass of high ground—the Anzac background and objective. The top of Achi Baba is rough and scrubby and has many young trees. The terraces are similar, and the same applies to the ravines.

The peninsula

The peninsula is rolling, hilly and unfertile, with steep hills and deep valleys. It is deeply cleft and torn. On the coasts high cliffs and slopes fall abruptly to the shore. There is a lot of low scrub, a few woods in the hollows, cypress near Morto Bay, olive trees isolated or in groups and other trees grow here and there. Water is scarce, the cultivation in patches and the people are few. Cultivation is more extensive on Morto plain. Rain waters are carried off by brooks and temporary rivers which increase or decrease in volume with equal speed. There are deep valleys in the limestone country and into them the waters have carried a clayey sub-soil. Level places have been formed, and where the valleys approach the coast there are small coastal flats, 200–300 yards wide. In the south there are several sandy bays and beaches and these were used for the landings in 1915. The country is beautiful for a few weeks in spring when the landscape is coloured by wildflowers and Achi Baba and other hills are green; but, in the summer sun the flowers fade and the landscape is brown and tawny.

Geologically, the peninsula consists largely of freshwater deposits, sandstones, clays etc. The spoon-shaped tip is due to a dip in the stratified bands of calcareous sandstone which tilt inwards and downwards from sides to centre. This tilting is clearly shown in photographs of the Aegean cliffs near X Beach and in those of Kereves Dere and the Dardanelles cliffs. The yellow calcareous sands and sandstones of the cliffs in the Krithia and Anzac areas (Miocene beds) take curious forms, due to their disintegration in dry hot summers, followed by torrential winter rains, which act rapidly washing the loosened earth down. Their appearance is grotesque—yellow ribs and smaller gutters. There is little vegetation on these cliffs and not enough to hold the water to prevent disintegration.

Weather

The peninsula is bracing in winter and spring and relaxing in summer, when the heat is great. The formation of the country is such that, the sun reaches every fold of the land, except in early morning and late evening. There is little rain from May to October as a rule. Anzac is malarial but cooler than Helles. North winds are healthy. South winds from Egypt etc., are depressing, and bring sand flies and mosquitoes. In December and February there are snow blizzards; in March, northerly gales, cold winds and much rain; in April and May there is lightning and destructive tropical storms; in August, there are south winds, dust and grit storms, followed by sub-tropical rain at times, in the latter part of the year. From autumn to December the country recovers some of its beauty. In spring, early morning mists hang about the hills and high ground. The place is depressing when the sun is not shining. I like to think of Gallipoli as it is in spring, a pleasant green countryside, dotted with olive trees and coloured by wildflowers; where birds sing, the sky is blue, and the sun not too hot. And, also, to remember the landscape seen from high ground near Krithia, looking over park-like country to the blue Aegean and the Dardanelles.

Population

Only a few hundred people live on the peninsula, mostly at Sedd-el-Bahr and on a few lonely farms. They are very poor. They graze sheep and cattle, grow wheat, maize, a little cotton, a few olive groves, and do a little fishing. The soil of Helles produces poor harvests. Before 1914–15 the Helles people were mostly Greeks, thrown out of their own country by the Greek government. Sedd-el-Bahr is a street of poor one-storeyed houses, and a few others outside and below. Two cafes are its social centres. There is a naval signal station on the cliffs above Morto, and a new Cape Helles lighthouse, which flashes round its long white beam at night. The old fort has been patched up.

Fauna and flora

Animal life, birds, insects etc. include fox, hare, jackal, boar, stoats, wild-cat etc; owls, partridges, thrushes, yellow finches, robins, nightingales (particularly in Soghan Dere). Centipedes, scorpions, spiders, fire-flies, glow-worms, sand-flies, cicadas, praying-mantillas (summer), frogs, lizards, green lizards (summer), tortoises, snakes of many varieties and colours. One variety of spider has a web, which, when stretched from bush to bush, is strong enough to be felt through clothing.

Trees and flowers include dwarf oak (with small shiny leaves, rather like those of holly), crab apple, olives, cypress (near Sedd-el-Bahr), pines, firethorn, Valonia oak, stone-oak (low and scrubby, used for tanning). There are small straggling groups of trees, many olive and other trees, isolated, a few patches of olive cultivation and pines on stony uplands which are stunted. The Vineyard flourishes but is untended. Coarse grass, grows high in summer, thistles growing to four and six feet high, rosemary, tamarisk, brambles and fig-trees (both grow well in old trenches and sheltered places). In autumn there is much heather. There are poppies, yellow rock-rose, red pea, blue toad-flax, red pheasant's eye, yellow clover, thyme, pink and red campions, scarlet and blue pimpernels, blue anchusia, violets, mallow, yellow lotus, pink milk-wort, irises, dandelions, anemones, giant and small daisies. The small white flowers of the water-crocus look pretty on a stream surface.

Krithia

Krithia, which from Helles appears to be a line of ruined houses, is as broad as it is long. A rectangular group of ruins, with a smaller rectangular group on the east side. The stones are grey or light coloured. It has numerous lanes and alleys, and the only wide lane leaves the main road halfway through the village, emerging into open country on the west. In places, where the fallen stones are hidden by growth, Krithia is dangerous and careful watch has to be kept for deep wells. Parts of the walls are still 10 or more feet high.

Roads

Roads are (or were) bad, and little better than tracks. In places they cross stream beds by primitive bridges often of rotten material. I have seen thick planks and corrugated iron used. If it was not for the IWGC roads at Helles would not exist except as tracks.

Spurs

Four long spurs divide the last few miles of Helles. They have water-courses between them. They had no particular names during the campaign, but are now known as:

1. Gully Spur. High tapering ground between the Aegean and Great Gully. It is the narrowest spur and varies in width from a quarter mile to less than 100 yards. Mostly bare, except for low scrubby bushes. South of Y Ravine it is still more bare.

2. Fir-Tree Spur, between Gully Ravine and Kirte Dere. Intersected by a series of tiny transverse nullahs running into Kirte Dere. On it were several straggling fir-copses. Poor and stunted trees grow on it now.

3. Krithia Spur, between Kirte and Kanli Dere, is half a mile at its broadest; more open and less broken than No. 2. Had a few firs growing in the loamy, sandy ground. Along its east side and close to Kanli Dere, runs the straight Krithia Road.

4. Kereves Spur, on the Dardanelles side. Curving south, it is the highest and most irregular of the spurs.

The ravines

Zighin Dere (Great Gully) runs from the north shore at Gully Beach. It has deep and confusing tributary gullies running into it, with rugged light earth banks, and bluffs 50 or more feet high, with scrub and trees whenever they can get a hold. At the far end, the ravine shallows and widens until it ends in high and open country.

Kirte Dere (Krithia Nullah) starts in open country, near Krithia. Two small nullahs approach until they meet near the east side of the Vineyard, and from this point the main nullah continues to Morto plain, joined here and there by other small branches.

The two upper nullahs are known as East and West Krithia nullahs. At the 'Y', the ground between the fork is rough and its sides steep in places. In the centre the 'V' is convex. From a position on the west side of the main nullah, south of and looking towards the 'V', the left slope is gradual at first, and then becomes slightly convex. The east cliff of East Krithia Nullah is very broken and 12 to 15 feet high. To right of the observer the scrubby-topped cliff edge drops from 25 feet at observer's point to 15 feet where East Krithia Nullah bends to the right. Here the two sides are 50 feet apart. Both sides are overlooked and commanded by the ground in front and on the opposite sides.

West Krithia Nullah: From a point a short distance above the 'V' and on the left side, the foreground curves slightly to the nullah edge. Beyond, to the front, it falls, rises again, and then comes a slight and narrow depression, backed by a seven-foot rise. To right of this, on the nullah edge, is a short ravine 20 feet deep, with a waterfall. Further right comes a steep slope. In the left central distance, an easy slope commands the ground from which this observation was made.

East Krithia Nullah: From a point a similar distance above the fork (to that in West Krithia Nullah), an almost flat grassy stretch ends at a cliff 20 to 30 feet high. To the front it falls to a shallow nullah where the stream ends as a waterfall. Ahead, East Krithia Nullah becomes shallower. To right is a concave cliff, with an overhanging and rocky edge. This point is commanded by ground in front and to the right.

Kanli Dere (Achi Baba Nullah), at a point roughly in line with those taken in East and West Krithia Nullah: To north, this becomes more difficult country. It has sides 12 to 15 feet high, narrows, bends sharp left, and then widens. It then bends right, to a place where the sides are 30 to 40 feet high. In the near right foreground is a short wide branch, 12 feet wide at the bottom and shallowing as it ascends the slope. Beyond, there is first a sharp drop and then a more gradual slope to the nullah bed.

Kanli and Kirte Deres are more or less similar, but Kirte Dere (Krithia Nullah) is the more varied of the two. It has small waterfalls, where the stream-bed stratum is broken and the water drops to lower levels, usually with pools below the falls. (There is a well-known fall near Redoubt and the duplicate firing lines.) The Dere is mostly shallow, with sides of light or tawny earth, occasionally rocky, on which coarse and thick weedy vegetation grows. The stream is shallow in summer, and a deep and dangerous torrent after the rains. It has a few deep pools. There are frogs and tortoises and patches of stagnant scum in summer, where mosquitoes breed. Krithia Nullah was a great highway in 1915, and its sides contained innumerable shelters and dumps. There are a few low falls in Kanli Dere, also.

Kereves Dere is a large and wide ravine, running from Achi Baba to the Dardanelles.

Geology

Geological details vary considerably. A line drawn from Gallipoli town to the north coast near Krithia, roughly divides the hard rocky lining of the Dardanelles channel, and the soft crumbling soil of the north coast.

The northern shores mostly show soft contours, have red and light loams, shallow beaches, crumbling cliffs. They are more productive and more traversable laterally than the south shore.

The south shores, by the Dardanelles waters, have long, abrupt and nearly vertical cliffs, with rare landing places. The hard limestone of these cliffs is arranged in such rigidly horizontal lines as to be mistaken, where exposed, for walls or fortifications, when seen from a distance, and particularly between the bastion of Kilid Bahr and Eski Hissarlik Point, where long stretches of cliff descend to the water without perceptible beaches (excepting Kereves Dere). The same strata can be seen clearly along the west side of Soghan Dere, from the Kilid Bahr–Krithia Road. At Kilia the limestone sinks to a low level, and a valley crosses the peninsula, almost at right angles, between Kilia Liman and Gaba Tepe. This, and one further north, are the only places where wheeled traffic can cross from coast to coast of the peninsula. The limestone plateau, to the north, extends, flat and unbroken, open and unproductive, from Krithia to Cape Helles. (To the east, it is uneven and irregular.) It is cut by deep sheltered valleys, which run from the watersheds of Achi Baba and Sari Bair to the Dardanelles, on the side north of Krithia. The tilting of the calcareous cliffs, on each side of the Helles end, inwards and downwards slightly, give a hollowed effect to this area. Morto Bay is a great bite out of the rim of this concavity. Contrast between the loam of the north half and the limestone of the south half, has influenced human activities and habitations. But accessibility to the main course of water traffic has also been a deciding factor in settlements, as well as local advantages or otherwise, of soils.

Beaches

Morto Bay, curving and sandy, is broken by the outlets of Kanli and Kirte Deres. Beyond Morto Bay is a line of rising and steep cliff, with Sedd-el-Bahr village on the top. A steep path leads down to the Camber, and a small jetty.

The cliff descends to the site of the fort; continuing north-west and west, is the curve of V Beach, 300 yards by 10 yards (average) of sand, bordered in places by a five feet bank. V Beach is at the foot of a natural theatre, rising by gentle slopes to a height of 100 feet. From the point where the shore bends west and slightly south, there is a steep, cliffy and stratified slope, at the top of whose inland end is the ruined Fort No. 1, with its wrecked guns, which commands the beach below.

At the seaward end of the cliff is Cape Helles and its lighthouse, whence a precipitous cliff extends north-west to Tekke Burnu. To the immediate south of this, is a break, opened out by a small gully. At the foot is a strip of deep and powdery dry sand, 350 yards by 15 to 40 yards. In the centre are sand dunes, held by coarse grass. On either side of the sandy strip the cliffs are not high but are almost precipitous. This is W Beach, or Lancashire Landing.

From Tekke Burnu, where the coast bends north-east, there is a very steep cliff, with a recess in it—Bakery Beach.

About 1 mile north of Tekke Burnu, we come to X Beach, a narrow strip of sand about 200 yards long, at the foot of a crumbling but grassy cliff 100 feet high. The road down from the cliffs runs down the face.

The steep cliff continues until it is broken first by Little Gully, and then by the great opening to Zighin Dere, Great Gully or Gully Ravine.

All this coastline is of calcareous sandstone, with little and low scrub. The cliff line is thrown back south of Gully Beach where the ground is rough and broken; continuing again, with the sharp and rising point of Gully Spur, west of the entrance to Great Gully, steep, scrubby and about 150 feet high to Y Beach. Two small breaks in the cliff, caused by winter water courses, give access to the top from Y Beach.

North of Y Beach an immense mass of light earth, with much scrub wherever it can find a hold, and a few small levels, is Gurkha Bluff. From Y Beach to north, there is a marked change in the character of the cliffs, for now they are broken and scrub-covered.

North of Gurkha Bluff are ridges and ravines, alternating. Then comes Fusilier Bluff. This is not a striking feature; but on it was the extreme left of the British line in 1915, sloping down the bluff to the shore.

Most of the details of flora and fauna were supplied by the IWGC Area Superintendent, T. Millington Esq., Chanak.

ABBREVIATIONS AND ACRONYMS

2ic	Second in command
AA & QMG	Assistant Adjutant and Quartermaster General
A/	Acting or Assistant
AAA	End of sentence in signalled message
AAG	Assistant Adjutant General
ADC	Aide-de-camp
ADMS	Assistant Director of Medical Services
ADVS	Assistant Director Veterinary Services
AF	Army Form
APM	Assistant Provost Marshal
ASC	Army Service Corps
Bde	Brigade
Bn	Battalion
CB	Companion of the Order of the Bath
CMG	Companion of the Order of St Michael and St George
CO	Commanding Officer
Coy	Company
CQMS	Company Quartermaster Sergeant
CRE	Commander Royal Engineers
CSM	Company Sergeant Major
CT	Communication trench

DA	Divisional Artillery
DA & QMG	Deputy Adjutant and Quartermaster General
DAA & QMG	Deputy Assistant Adjutant and Quartermaster General
DADMS	Deputy Assistant Director Medical Services
DADOS	Deputy Assistant Director Ordnance Services
DAQMG	Deputy Assistant Quartermaster General
DCM	Distinguished Conduct Medal
DIV	Division
DSO	Distinguished Service Order
FS	Field Service
GCMG	Knight Grand Cross of the Order of St Michael and St George
GCVO	Knight Grand Cross of the Royal Victorian Order
GHQ	General Headquarters
GOC	General Officer Commanding
GSO	General Staff Officer
HMS	His Majesty's Ship
HQ	Headquarters
IWGC	Imperial War Graves Commission
Ks	Kitchener's men
KCB	Knight Commander of the Order of the Bath
KCMG	Knight Commander of the Order of St Michael and St George
KCSI	Knight Commander of the Order of the Star of India
KCVO	Knight Commander of the Royal Victorian Order
KIA	Killed in Action
KStJ	Knight of Justice or Grace of the Order of Saint John
LF	Lancashire Fusiliers

LG	*London Gazette*
MC	Military Cross
MEF	Mediterranean Expeditionary Force
MG	Machine Gun
MGC	Machine Gun Corps
MM	Military Medal
MO	Medical Officer
MP	Military Policeman
NCO	Non-Commissioned Officer
OC	Officer Commanding
OHMS	On His Majesty's Service
PBI	Poor Bloody Infantry
QM	Quartermaster
QMS	Quartermaster Sergeant
RAMC	Royal Army Medical Corps
RE	Royal Engineers
Regt	Regiment
RFA	Royal Field Artillery
RND	Royal Naval Division
RFA	Royal Field Artillery
RSM	Regimental Sergeant Major
SAA	Small Arms Ammunition
SMLE	Short Magazine Lee-Enfield
TBD	Torpedo Boat Destroyer
TD	Territorial Decoration
TF	Territorial Force
VC	Victoria Cross
VD	Volunteer Officers' Decoration
VO	Veterinary Officer
WO	Warrant Officer

BIBLIOGRAPHY

Archival sources

Imperial War Museum, 'Private Papers of A Riley', Documents.14130

—, battlefield relics, EPH 6758–84, EPH 6786–99, EPH 6808–18, EPH 6820–25, EPH 6828–41, EPH 6849, EPH 6856, EPH 6858, EPH 6860–62, EPH 6864–77, EPH 6891, EPH 6913

—, photographs, Q 81419–62

Liddell Hart Military Archives, King's College London, HAMILTON, Gen Sir Ian Standish Monteith (1853–1947), GB0099 KCLMA Hamilton, 14/7/6, 15/5/17

Published sources

'The Silent Nullahs of Gallipoli', *Twenty Years After: The Battlefields of 1914–18, Then and Now*, 1936–38, pp. 1224–1235

A History of the East Lancashire Royal Engineers / Compiled by Members of the Corps (London: Country Life, 1921)

Aspinall-Oglander, C.F., and Archibald F. Becke, eds., *Military Operations, Gallipoli*, History of the Great War Based on Official Documents / by Direction of the Historical Section, Committee on Imperial Defence (London: William Heinemann, 1929–1932)

Behrend, Arthur, *Make Me a Soldier: A Platoon Commander in Gallipoli* (London: Eyre & Spottiswoode, 1961)

Best, Kenneth, and Gavin Roynon, *A Chaplain at Gallipoli: The Great War Diaries of Kenneth Best* (London: Simon & Schuster, 2011)

Bigwood, George, *The Lancashire Fighting Territorials (in Gallipoli)* (London: 'Country Life' & George Newnes, 1916)

Bonner, Robert, *Volunteer Infantry of Ashton-under-Lyne: Including the Biography of William Thomas Forshaw VC* (Knutsford, Cheshire: Fleur de Lys Publishers, 2005)

Bonner, Robert (ed.), *Great Gable to Gallipoli – The Diary of Lieutenant Colonel Claude S Worthington DSO, 5 October 1914 – 25 September 1916. 6th Battalion The Manchester Regiment* (Knutsford, Cheshire: Fleur de Lys Publishers, 2004)

Campbell, Captain G.L., *The Manchesters* (London: Picture Advertising Co. Ltd, 1916)

Cherry, Niall, *I Shall Not Find His Equal: The Life of Brigadier-General Noel Lee, The Manchester Regiment* (Knutsford, Cheshire: Fleur de Lys Publishing, 2001)

Darlington, Henry, *Letters from Helles* (London: Longmans, Green and Co., 1936)

Gibbon, Frederick P., *The 42nd (East Lancashire) Division: 1914-1918* (London: Country Life, 1920)

Hamilton, General Sir Ian, *Gallipoli Diary* (London: E. Arnold, 1920)

Hartley, John, *6th Battalion, the Manchester Regiment in the Great War: Not a Rotter in the Lot* (Barnsley: Pen & Sword Military, 2010)

Hurst, Gerald B., *With Manchesters in the East* (Manchester: The University Press, 1918)

Purdy, Martin, and Ian Dawson, *The Gallipoli Oak* (Ramsbottom, Lancashire: Moonraker Publishing, 2013)

Watkins, Charles, *Lost Endeavour* (Eldenbridge, Kent: Promotion House, 1970)

ACKNOWLEDGEMENTS

Mike and Bern thank friends and family for their help in producing this book. Bill Sellars in Eceabat gave invaluable editorial advice, and assistance with fact checking. Mike's sister Norma Wallworth in Woodley researched Alec Riley's family history. R.W. Filla in Glebe set high standards for map-making. The Bolton family and Ross J. Bastiaan kindly permitted us to reproduce photographs from their archive and collection. We benefited greatly from the support and knowledge of two eminent Gallipoli historians. Stephen Chambers shared from his extensive collection a better print of the signaller that features on the front cover. He also found the 1938 newspaper article by Riley that is included as Appendix III. Peter Hart was generous with his contacts and experience. We've also learnt from other students of the campaign, in particular Jim Grundy, Emre Özmen and Michael D. Robson. Last but definitely not least, Mike and Bern would like to thank their respective spouses: Viv for her assistance with the introduction and biographies and Cheryl for creating the logo and artwork for the book's cover, and both for their continued toleration of two Gallipoli campaign obsessives.

INDEX

Robinson, Lieut. Geoffrey Nicolas 46, 82
Rochdale, Lt. Col. Lord 66, 81–82,
    293–294
Romanos Well 55, 58, 61, 72, 84, 120, 136
Rose, Sgt W. 138, 141
Ross, Maj. Edward Harry 140
Royle, Sgt Graham 5, 9, 14, 15, 25, 79,
    80, 82, 95, 106, 109, 112–113, 123,
    124, 125, 126, 129, 155, 253–254,
    313
rum 47, 80, 82, 95, 107, 109, 124, 162,
    193, 311, 312, 314, 315
  rum-jars 206, 208, 212
Rylands, Capt. Reginald Victor 49–50,
    56, 57

S

Samothrace 159, 209, 221, 232, 320–321
Sanders, Capt. John Malcolm Brodie
    152, 155, 295
Sanderson, CQMS Alexander 122
sausage (observation balloon).
    See aeroplanes
Savatard, Capt. Thomas Warner 56
S Beach ii, 20
Sedd-el-Bahr 23, 111, 163–166, 203, 226,
    322, 328–329, 333
Senior, L/Cpl James Kneale 67
Shell Bivouac 158
Shrapnel Point 172, 209
Shrapnel Valley 20, 26, 39, 40, 48–49,
    54, 120
signal offices 44, 62, 118–119, 128, 134,
    144–145, 175, 177, 191
  BK 83, 85
  BKA 83
  BS 107
  BY 79
  GN 80, 82–83, 159, 167
  MV 107
  QEL 93
  QG 159
  QLF 93
  RC 93–94
  TN 101
  visual stations 131, 177, 181
  YDB 167, 185
  ZLG 109, 114–115, 131–132, 181–182

Skew Bridge ii, 20, 40, 44, 45, 86,
    222–223, 224, 225, 229
Smith, Pte 5
Smyth 50
snipers 22, 26, 27, 29, 33, 34, 35, 36, 37,
    39, 56, 137, 140–141, 153, 154–155,
    164, 211–212, 218
Sorton, Sgt Ernest 69
Standring, Capt. Dudley Hethorn 56
Stanton, Cpl 148
Stanton, Sgt John Matthew 41, 42, 43,
    50, 57, 59, 62, 68, 78, 102, 103,
    104–105, 106, 108, 109, 123, 135,
    139, 140, 141, 152, 153, 182
station calls 79, 108, 305–306. *See
    also* signal offices
Staveacre, Maj. James Herbert 44, 56, 63,
    64, 295–296
Stephenson, Maj. H.M. 32
Stirling, Sgt 69, 178
St. Leger Davies, Capt. Oswyn 81
Straddling 188
Stretch, of the 6th Manchesters 58
Stretford Road 61, 72, 76, 84
Stringer 50, 57, 170, 177, 182
sunsets 55, 67, 99, 141, 159, 169, 178, 179,
    217, 225, 321
Suvla 148, 213, 220, 326
Syers, Capt. Thomas Scott 153

T

Talbot, Capt. Ainslie Douglas 277
Tayleforth, Sgt William 58
Teare, Sgt Thomas Arthur 67
telephones 13, 32, 34, 37, 45, 48, 50, 51,
    57, 58, 73, 75, 91, 99, 105–106, 108,
    118–119, 128, 133, 134–135, 146,
    169, 175. *See also* signal offices
  buzzers 99, 146, 148
  earth pins 34, 114
  lines, laying and repairing 33, 34, 36,
    37, 38–39, 44–45, 45, 48–49, 55,
    65, 69, 79, 85, 99, 103, 105, 114,
    128, 131, 142, 176–177, 191
  Stevenson telephones 156–157
territorials, compared to regulars 51, 97
Thomas, Pte Richard 5, 8, 83, 85, 91, 94,
    95, 103, 109, 131, 154, 177, 178,
    261–262

Figure 47. 'Top of Achi Baba. 1 p.m. June 4, 1930.' (Alec Riley, *Twenty Years After*)

9 780645 235906